ISBN 978-1-5278-6808-3
PIBN 10888963

1 MONTH OF
FREE
READING

at
www.ForgottenBooks.com

By purchasing this book you are eligible for one month membership to ForgottenBooks.com, giving you unlimited access to our entire collection of over 1,000,000 titles via our web site and mobile apps.

To claim your free month visit:
www.forgottenbooks.com/free888963

English
Français
Deutsche
Italiano
Español
Português

www.forgottenbooks.com

Mythology Photography **Fiction**
Fishing Christianity **Art** Cooking
Essays Buddhism Freemasonry
Medicine **Biology** Music **Ancient
Egypt** Evolution Carpentry Physics
Dance Geology **Mathematics** Fitness
Shakespeare **Folklore** Yoga Marketing
Confidence Immortality Biographies
Poetry **Psychology** Witchcraft
Electronics Chemistry History **Law**
Accounting **Philosophy** Anthropology
Alchemy Drama Quantum Mechanics
Atheism Sexual Health **Ancient History**
Entrepreneurship Languages Sport
Paleontology Needlework Islam
Metaphysics Investment Archaeology
Parenting Statistics Criminology
Motivational

Cheetham, Captain Edward, R. N.

Clavel, Captain John, R. N.

Clephane, Andrew, Esq.

Clerke, Richard, Esq. Bognor

Cockburn, Vice-admiral Sir George, Bart. G.C.B.

Cockburn, Sir James, Bart.

Cochrane, Admiral the Hon. Sir Alexander

Cochrane, Captain Sir Thomas

Cochrane, the Hon. Basil

Cochrane, Captain N. D., R. N.

Cochrane, Captain Charles James

Coffin, Admiral Sir Isaac, Bart.

Cole, Captain Sir Christopher, K.C.B.

Collingwood, G. L. Newnham, Esq.

Colpoys, Vice-admiral Edward Griffiths

Cooke, Christopher, Esq.

Crawley, Vice-admiral Edmund

Crandell, Mr. William

Crispin, Captain Benjamin, R. N.

Crosbie, Lieutenant Richard (H. M.'s revenue cruiser Hawke)

Cunningham, Commissioner, Chatham Dock-yard

Dacres, Captain James R., R. N.

Darch, Thomas, Esq., Admiralty

Davies, Lieutenant Louis, R. N.

Davies, Captain Richard P. R.N.

De Starck, Captain Mauritius, R. N.

Derby, the Earl of

Devon, Captain T. B., R. N.

Dick, Captain John, R. N.

Dickinson, Captain, R. N.

Dickinson, Lieutenant D. S., R. N.

Digby, Rear-admiral Henry, C.B.

Digby, Captain George, R. N.

Disney, John, Esq., the Hatch, Essex

Donaldson, Mr. William
Douglas, Vice-admiral John Erskine
Douglas, Captain Peter J., R. N.
Downman, Captain Hugh, R. N.
Dunbar, Captain Sir James, Bart. R. N.
Duncan, — Esq. Bath
Dunn, James, Esq.
Dyer, Thomas, Esq., Admiralty

East India Company, the Hon. the, 40 copies
Edwards, Admiral Sampson
Elliot, the Hon. George, R. N.
Ellis, Mr.
Enderby, Samuel, Esq.
Esdaile, Sir James, Bart.
Exeter, the Marquis of
Exmouth, Viscount

Falcon, Captain Gordon, R. N.
Fane, Captain, R. N.
Farquhar, Captain Arthur, R. N.
Fellowes, Captain J.
Ferrers, Rev. Edmund
Finlayson, John, Esq., Treasury
Fisher, Captain Peter, R. N.
Fitzgerald, Captain Robert L.
Fitz Roy, Lord William, C.B.
Foote, Robert, Esq. Charlton, Kent
Franklyn, Mr. John, Master of the Royal Sovereign yacht
Fry, Alexander Mackay, Esq.

Gabel, the Rev. Dr., Winchester
Garth, Captain Thomas, R. N.
Giffard, Rear-admiral John
Good and Clerke, Messrs.
Goodenough, Thomas, Esq.

Gordon, the Duke of
Gordon, Captain Henry
Gore, Lieutenant-colonel, Coldstream Guards
Grampus, Hospital ship
Grant, Mr. A. W.
Grant, Captain Sir Richard
Grenville, the Right Hon. Thomas
Green, Joseph, Esq. Island of Jamaica
Griffiths, Captain Anselm J.
Gunnell, Samuel Richard, Esq.

Halford, Mr. James
Hall, Captain Robert
Hallowell, Vice-admiral Sir Benj., K.C.B.
Hammond, Captain Graham E., C.B.
Hargood, Vice-admiral Sir William, K.C.B.
Harnage, Captain George, R. N.
Harrison, Lieutenant, R. N.
Harrison, Mr.
Harvey, Rear-admiral Thomas, C.B.
Harvey, Captain Edward
Harvey, H. H., Esq.
Hatley, Captain John, R. N.
Hatt, Mr.
Hawkes, Mr. Thomas
Hay, Captain John B., R. N.
Hay, Colonel, Treasurer of Chatham garrison
Hay, Captain James, R. N.
Hickey, Captain Frederick, R. N.
Hill, Captain John, R. N.
Hill, Captain Henry, R. N.
Hillyer, Captain James, R. N.
Hinxman, John, Esq., Great Russel Street
Holmes, Captain William
Hornby, Captain Phipps, C.B., R. N.
Hornby, the Rev. J. J.

Hoste, Captain Sir William, Bart. K.C.B.
Hotham, Rear-admiral, Sir Henry, K.C.B.
Hotham, Rear-admiral Sir William, K.C.B.
Hunter, William, Esq., Grosvenor Street
Huntingdon, Captain, the Earl of

Inglis, D.D. Esq.
Irby, Captain the Hon. Frederick P., R.N.

Jackson, Mr. John
Jameson, Captain James, E. I. C.
Jones, Captain Richard, R. N.
Jones, James, Esq.

Kaye, Charles, Esq. Dyer's Buildings, Holborn
Keats, Vice-admiral Sir R. G., G.C.B.
Keith, Viscount
Kerr, Captain Alexander R., R. N. C.B.
Kennett, Mrs., Whitehall Place
Kent, John, Esq. •
King, Vice-admiral Sir Richard
King, Captain, R. N
Knight, Edward, Esq. Junior
Knighton, Sir William, Bart. M.D.
Knight, Mrs. E. C.

Lack, Thomas, Esq.
Lacon, Sir E. K.
Leake, Lieutenant John M.
Lee, John Theophilus, Esq.
Library, Chatham Garrison
Library, Royal Marine, Woolwich
Ludlow, Thomas H., Esq., New York
Lynam, the Rev. Robert

M'Douall, Lieutenant-colonel Robert

M'Kinlay, Captain George
M'Murdo, Lieutenant George L. A.
Maitland, Rear-admiral John
Malcolm, Vice-admiral Sir Pulteney, K.C.B.
Maling, Captain Thomas James, R. N.
Manvers, Captain, the Earl of
Marjoribanks, Edward, Esq.
Marryat, Captain Frederick
Marshall, Captain John Willoughby
Marshall, Lieutenant John
Martin, Vice-admiral Sir Thomas B., K.C.B.
Martin, Captain Thomas
Mason, Captain Henry B.
Master, Captain James
Matson, Captain Henry
Matthews, Captain Michael
Mayne, Colonel, Park Street
Melville, Viscount, 2 copies
Middleton, Sir William, Bart.
Moorsom, Vice-admiral Sir Robert, K.C.B.
Money, Colonel James Kyrle, Horn House, Herefordshire
Morgan, Rev. Dr.
Morris, Admiral Sir James Nichol
Moss, Robert Lee, Esq.
Mulgrave, the Earl of
Mundy, Captain George, C.B.
Murray, Lady

Nagle, Admiral Sir Edward, K.C.B.
Navy, the Commissioners for victualling the, 2 copies
Navy, the Commissioners, 2 copies
Neale, Vice-admiral Sir Harry, Bart.
Neave, Sir Thomas, Bart.
Nepean, the Rev. Evan, 2 copies
Northesk, Admiral, the Earl of, 2 copies
Northumberland, the Duke of

O'Connor, Captain Richard I. L., R. N.
O'Connor, Captain Richard, R. N.
Ogle, Rear-admiral Sir Charles, Bart.
Oliver, Rear-admiral Robert Dudley
Owen, Captain Sir Edward W. C. R., K.C.B.
Owen, Captain Charles C., R. N.

Packwood, Captain Joseph, R. N.
Page, Rear-admiral Benjamin W.
Palmerston, Viscount
Parker, Captain William, C.B. R. N.
Parkinson, Captain, R. N.
Parry, Captain William Henry Webly, R. N.
Parry, Lieutenant Edward I.
Pembroke, the Earl of
Penrose, the Rev. Dr.
Phelips, Lieutenant Thomas, R. N.
Phillimore, Captain Sir John, R. N.
Phipps, the Hon. General
Phipps, the Hon. Augustus
Pigot, Captain Hugh
Pilford, Captain John, C.B. R. N.
Pitt, Lieutenant Edward W., R. N.
Pole, Admiral Sir Charles M., Bart., G.C.B., 2 copies
Porter, Mrs.
Prevost, Sir George, Bart.
Prevost, Captain James, R. N.
Pryme, Mrs. Elizabeth, 27, Bridge Street, Blackfriars
    Road
Purvis, Admiral John Child
Putnam, James, Esq.

Ramage, Captain William
Rathbone, Captain Wilson, C.B.
Ray, G. A., Esq.
Renton, Colonel

Rice, Walter, Esq.

Ricketts, Captain Tristram R.

Rigmaiden, Lieutenant James

Rolles, Rear-admiral Robert

Rous, John, Esq.

Rowley, Rear-admiral Sir Josias, Bart. K.C.B.

Russell, Vice-admiral Thomas M.

Ryley, Richard, Esq., Admiralty

Ryley, John, Esq., High Elms

Ryves, Captain George F.

Saumarez, Admiral Sir James, Bart., G.C.B.

Saumarez, Captain Richard

Sawyer, Vice-admiral Sir Herbert, K.C.B.

Sayer, Captain George A., C.B.

Selsey, Captain Lord Viscount, R. N.

Shaw, Captain Isaac, R. N.

Sheffield, Lady, Wimpole Street

Sheffield, Lady, Portman Street

Sheffield, Sir Robert, Bart.

Sheffield, the Rev. Charles

Shepheard, Captain Lewis

Simpson, Captain John, R. N.

Smith, Lieutenant-colonel Sir Charles F.

Smith, Henley, Esq.

Smollet, Captain, R. N.

Somerville, the Hon. Captain, R. N.

Sotheby, Admiral

Sotheron, Vice-admiral F.

Spencer, the Earl of

Spurling, Mr. Stephen

St. Vincent, the Earl of, 6 copies

Stiles, Captain John

Stirling, Captain James

Stopford, Vice-admiral the Hon. Sir Robert, K.C.B.

Stopford, Captain the Hon. Edward

Weeks, Captain John
Wellesley, the Marquis of
West, Lieutenant William Wade, R. N.
Westphfal, Captain E. H.
Whish, Henry France, Esq.
Whittaker, Captain
Wickey, Admiral John
Willes, Captain George W.
Williams, Captain Robert
Williams, the Rev. David
Willoughby, Captain J. N.
Winburn, Esq., Chancery Lane
Windthorpe, Rear-admiral
Wise, Captain W. F., C.B.
Woolmore, Captain
Wormeley, Captain Ralph R.
Woodhead, John, Esq.

Yorke, Vice-admiral Sir Joseph, Bart. K.C.B.
Yorke, the Right Hon. Charles, 3 copies
Young, Captain William
Young, Captain Thomas

French general, and the friend of Napoleon; with it was sent an elegant sword, the gift of the new King of Sweden. The above document was dated Stockholm, 25th of October.

Another, couched in still stronger terms, was addressed to the Admiral, by a nobleman holding a high confidential situation at the same court, but whose name we are not at liberty to reveal. He says—

At length rejoice, my dear Admiral, you have been the guardian angel of my country; you have been, by your wise, your premeditated and loyal conduct, the first cause of the plans which have been formed against the demon of the continent. He was on the point of succeeding; folly and want of confidence in some, have made them doubt the success of the good cause; you have shared my anxiety; but now all is over. Two couriers have arrived this night from the head-quarters of the Emperor, and the Prince Royal. War was declared on the 17th of July: Austria is with us. Thus, if Providence has not decided something against all probability, Bonaparte will be defeated, humanity may breathe again, and Europe be once more raised up. With Wellingtons, Moreaus, Bernadottes, against him, what hopes! and what reasons to depress our enemies! I shall not fail to communicate to you the first news of any importance; for once more I must tell you, that you are the first cause that Russia has dared to make war against France: *had you fired one shot when we declared war against England,* all had been ended, and Europe had been enslaved. I own to you also my satisfaction, that our august Prince Royal has conducted himself in such a manner as to leave your Excellency no cause to repent of what some people were pleased to call "credulity," but which events have proved to be wisdom.

In the preface to the first volume of this Work, we have shewn how much it is in the power of a naval officer to serve his country, by the cultivation of his mind, and by adding, to his nautical

skill, political knowledge and foresight: the proposition is, we think, clearly established and illus-
trated in the conduct of Sir James Saumarez. We
shall not venture to estimate the advantages which
his country, and Europe in general, derived from
his generous magnanimity, while commanding in
the Baltic. At this fortunate juncture, the eyes
of Europe, and of Russia in particular, began to
be opened to the real policy of Napoleon. The
Emperor Alexander saw to what the vast extension
of power would reduce the kingdoms of the continent; for although the ostensible motives of France
were a maritime peace, and the humiliation of the
British flag, no one could doubt, that continental
empire was the secret object of the Adventurer
who had placed himself on the throne of the Capets. Fortunately for the happiness of mankind,
the Emperor Alexander listened to the voice of
reason, the British ministers induced his Majesty to sign a peace with Great Britain at Orebo,
on the 18th of July, 1812; and on the 11th of
August, the London Gazette revoked the order of
reprisals against Russia, which had been in force
since December, 1807. These great events revived
the drooping hopes of those who began to consider
the power of Napoleon as too firmly fixed ever to
be shaken.

The Spaniards, notwithstanding the liberal assistance which they had received from England,
would probably have been reduced to submit
to the government of a Bonaparte, had not this

formidable enemy risen up in the North. The destruction of the French army in Russia was an interposition of Providence not less miraculous than that of the blasphemous Senacherib. From the moment the peace was signed with England, the affairs of France went rapidly into confusion: to the double project of invading Spain and Russia, Napoleon owed his downfall. The British navy surrounding the coasts of Europe, from the Naze of Norway (including the Baltic) to the straits of the Dardanelles, was ready at every point to afford its assistance to the brave, and its protection to the feeble, struggling to throw off the chains of despotic power. The French having crossed the Vistula, had advanced into the Russian provinces, where the armies of that patient and enduring people awaited them with calm determination to meet death in the performance of their sacred obligations. On the side of France, it was a war of plunder: Russia and her allies sought only peace and security. Sir James Saumarez had stationed Rear-admiral Thomas Byam Martin at Riga, to co-operate with the Russian army under Prince Bagration; a division of gun-boats, commanded by Captain Stewart, was placed in advance on the river of Riga. Davoust, the French general, was in the neighbourhood, with a strong body of cavalry, which the Russian General attacked with energy, and defeated: this was the advance of the French army. Nine regiments were cut to pieces; one thousand men, and fifty staff officers, made prisoners. The difficulties which the enemy endeavoured to interpose between the junction of the first and second Russian armies, were by this victory entirely removed; and they were united to prepare for their swarms of enemies that fate, which, sooner or later, awaits every desolating conqueror. Rear-admiral Martin, being at Riga, on the 27th of July acquainted Sir James Saumarez with the junction of these two armies, the greater one being under the command of General Barclay de Tolli. The Emperor Alexander reached Smolensko, to stimulate by his presence the energies of his people. A peace between Russia and the Porte was concluded at the same time, and the armies on the Danube now turned from the Turks to oppose the French.

The British and Russian gun-boats under Captain Stewart, of the British navy, became highly important in the defence of Riga, and effectually prevented the enemy crossing the river at the falls above the town, where they made the attempt, and were driven back. Count Witgenstein defeated General Oudinot, on the 31st of July, and took three thousand prisoners, compelling him to cross the Duna. General Von Essen, the governor of Riga, bore testimony to the services of the British officers, who broke down the only bridge (that of Kalnazeen) over which the enemy could retreat. Captain John Brenton, who commanded the gun-boats at this attack, was honoured by his Imperial Majesty with the order of St. Vlodimir.

In the month of July, Captain G. G. Lennock, having succeeded to the command of the Rosario, chased and drove on shore a division of the flotilla, off the mouth of the Scheldt. Three sail of brigs, to avoid capture, ran aground, and the sea broke over them; four others he compelled to anchor in the breakers, but from their position he was unable to make farther impression.

Captain James P. Stewart, in the Dictator, of sixty-four guns, with Captain Roubillard, of the Podargus, of eighteen guns; Captain Henry Weir, of the Calypso, of eighteen guns; and Lieutenant England, in the Flamer gun-brig, attacked a Danish squadron lying in the harbour of Mardoe, in the Sleeve, with complete success, and came off with great honour.

The Dictator ran into the channel at seven in the evening, engaging the enemy, who was flying from him under a press of sail. At half past nine, after running twelve miles, through a channel so narrow in some places as scarcely to admit the studdingsail-booms being run out, the Dictator's bow was laid upon the rocks, with her broadside bearing on the enemy, who were at that moment within hail, at an anchor, with springs on their cables. The Calypso having in the passage up taken the ground, the Dictator had passed her; but Captain Weir having extricated his vessel, prevented the heavy gun-boats raking the Dictator, which would have done great damage, as that ship could not bring her broadside to bear on them.

The enemy's squadron was posted close to the small creek of Lymgoe, supported by a division of gun-boats. Their force consisted of a large frigate

called the Nyarden, of fifty guns, a brig called the
Laaland, another called the Samsoe, and a third
called the Kiel; but the fire of a two-decked ship
was too heavy for the frigate, which, in half an
hour, was a wreck and on fire; her main-deck was
beaten in. The brigs surrendered, the gun-boats
were either sunk or disabled, and the frigate burnt
to the water's edge.

The Dictator was again unexpectedly attacked
by a strong body of gun-boats, which had retreated
from the action, and either from shame or necessity
had returned to their duty; but they were silenced
by Captain Weir, in the Calypso.

In the mean time, the Podargus and the Flamer,
both lying aground, were warmly engaged with
the batteries and gun-boats; but were soon got
afloat. The Dictator and Calypso coming down
the channel with the prizes, were once more attacked by a fresh set of gun-boats, whose fire
came from behind some rocks, on which the Dictator could not get a gun to bear; at the same
time, the prizes grounded, and having many
wounded men on board, humanity forbade their
being destroyed. Leaving them therefore to their
fate, the British squadron came down the harbour,
having completed as gallant an exploit as any on
record. The Danes acknowledge to have lost
between two and three hundred men; the British
had nine killed, and twenty-six wounded. The
Nyarden mounted long twenty-four pounders on
her main-deck; and had three hundred and twenty
men. The Laaland mounted twenty guns, long

eighteen pounders, and had one hundred and twenty men: she was taken but abandoned. The Samsoe, which had eighteen guns, long eighteen pounders, and one hundred and twenty-five men, escaped.

The Lords of the Admiralty were so much pleased with the conduct of Captain Stewart and his associates, that they granted a very liberal promotion. Captains Weir and Roubillard were posted: the first lieutenant of the Dictator, and Lieutenant England, of the Flamer, were promoted to the rank of commanders. Captain Stewart, who was only acting in the Dictator, was confirmed post; in the following year appointed to the Amphion, of thirty-two guns; and subsequently made a companion of the Bath.

Lieutenant Thomas Jones (the second), with eighteen men in the boats of the Briseis, sloop of war, took out of Pillau roads the Urania, an English merchant-vessel, which had been captured. She was richly laden, and the enemy were removing her cargo. Mr. Jones boarded her at midnight, and drove the enemy from her decks, cut her cable, and brought her out with a schuyt which was lashed alongside. Our loss was one man killed, and three wounded.

Lieutenant William Henry Dixon, of the Britomart, accompanied by the Lieutenants Malone of the Osprey, and Romney of the Leveret, each in a boat from his respective sloop, pursued a lugger privateer, which they saw in the N.W. from Heligoland, eight or nine leagues distant. This enter-

prise seems among others which have been related
in the present year, to partake of a romantic
bravery, either unknown, or very uncommon, in
former wars. The continuation of the calm favoured the approach of the boats; and when it is
considered how perfectly the enemy was prepared,
and how exhausted the Englishmen must have
been after rowing such a distance, we can scarcely
believe it possible that they could have had the
temerity to approach; they did, however, and
boarded her; and after a very animated struggle
of twenty minutes, at the point of their sabres,
carried her. She was called L'Eole, pierced for
fourteen guns, mounting only six, and having a
complement of thirty-one officers and men.

The 14th division of the famous flotilla, consisting of twelve large brigs and one lugger, came
out of Boulogne, and was standing to the westward,
when discovered by Captain Harvey in the Rosario, who chased it. The enemy prepared to
attack, and lay him on board. Captain Harvey
stood on until he could call the Griffon to his
assistance, and having gained the attention of
Captain Trollope, whom he felt certain would give
him proper support, he made all sail in chase of
the enemy, and fell upon their rear, just as they
were entering the port of Dieppe. The French line
received this attack, and returned the fire, while
the Rosario played round them like a yacht at
Spithead, till finding himself secure of his object,
and being quite far enough to windward, he ran

regret, lest it should chance to revive the sorrows of those who may have been deeply interested in the fall of the gallant but unfortunate officer.

Lieutenant Richard Stewart Gamage, first of the Griffon, sloop of war, while carrying on the duty of the ship in the Downs, in the absence of his captain, received a complaint against the sergeant of marines, for improper conduct. The man was called up, and being ordered by the Lieutenant to walk the quarter-deck with a musket on his shoulder, he refused, and threw it down with an air of defiance and contempt, which so inflamed the anger of young Gamage, that he drew his sword, which he had previously gone down to his cabin to procure, and after repeated warnings, ran the unfortunate man through the body, who almost instantly expired. A court-martial was assembled for the trial of the lieutenant : he was found guilty of murder, sentenced to be hanged at the yard-arm, and was executed on board the Griffon, on the 23d of November. The fate of this young officer, whose character was in every other respect unimpeachable, ought to make a deep impression on the minds of our naval youth, who till that time laboured under the mistaken notion that they had a right to take away the life of a fellow-creature at their own pleasure, for any supposed act of disobedience, when it was in their power at the time to appeal to the laws of their country. As this case bears some resemblance to that of Lord Camelford and Lieutenant Peterson, related in the

second volume of this work, we cannot but think
that the sentence of 'honourable acquittal' pronounced on his Lordship, had the worst effect in
misleading the mind of Mr. Gamage, and, we believe, that of many others. Admiral Young, who
commanded the North Sea fleet, made a forci-
ble and feeling address to the officers and ships'
companies then present. The young man was so
sensible of the enormity of his crime, that his mind
was incapable of receiving consolation, and had
his life been spared, he would have lived in un-
abating sorrow and remorse: he died like a Christian and a hero. It is but justice to the court-
martial which tried him, to say, that he was most
strongly recommended to mercy; and no individual
case so deeply occupied the royal bosom, or the
attention of the council. Perhaps it was feared that
the pardoning of this offence might lead the lower
orders to suppose that justice was not duly admi-
nistered. It would have been some alleviation to
the sorrows of the unfortunate young man, and his
surviving relatives, if he could have been shot like
Byng, on the quarter-deck of his ship, instead of
being hanged like the most infamous and hardened
of felons. Deeply as we deplore the death of Lieutenant Gamage, it produced the best effects on the
discipline of the service.

(See the affecting account of his trial and execution, Naval Chronicle, 1812 and 13.)

The Laurel, of thirty-eight guns, a beautiful frigate, which was found on the stocks at Flushing, and

brought away in 1809, was lost in Quiberon bay,
in February, 1812. She was commanded by Captain S. C. Rowley, who was at that time quite a
stranger on the coast, and was coming through the
Teigneuse passage, with the Rota and Rhin frigates,
commanded by Captains Somerville and Malcolm.
Captain Rowley, when the ship struck on the rock
called the Govivas, hailed the Rhin, and saved her
from the same fate; the Laurel was got off, but made
so much water, that they were forced to run her on
shore on a reef called Les Péres. The moment this
was perceived, the battery on the peninsula opened
a heavy fire from great guns and mortars: every
shot struck her, while the ship was beating to pieces
on the rocks, and the people, with scarcely a hope
of escaping to the shore, were exposed at once to
the perils of the sea, and the cruel fire of the enemy.
A flag of truce was hoisted, the colours hauled down,
and not a shot returned, but still the fire of the enemy continued; the wind increased, and the quarterdeck of the ship was under water; nor did these
monsters cease from their purpose, until the boats
of the Laurel, with a part of the men, reached the
shore, and craved a suspension. The fire was then
discontinued for a short time; but the officer who
commanded, refused to allow the boats to return for
the remainder of the crew. The boats of the Colossus, Rhin, and Rota, approaching the wreck, the fire
of the enemy began again, and continued till every
man was taken off, and conveyed to the ships. Cap-

tain Rowley and his officers were the last on board;
they were all honourably acquitted.

Sir Charles Cotton, admiral of the blue, and commander-in-chief of the Channel fleet, died at Plymouth, on the 23d of February, 1812; he was succeeded in his command by Lord Viscount Keith.

One of the first duties of an officer, is to acquire a
complete knowledge of the coast on which he is
employed; without this attainment, his valour or
skill as a seaman can only be partially useful, while
his ignorance may be often fatal. In acquaint-
ance with the French coast, no officer was perhaps
ever more perfect than Captain (now Sir Henry)
Hotham, who, in 1812, commanded the Northumberland, of seventy-four guns, and was ordered by
Rear-admiral Sir Harry Neale to cruise off the Pen-
marks, for the purpose of intercepting a squadron of
French frigates expected to arrive in the port of
L'Orient.

On the 22d of May, Captain Hotham was ten
miles to the southward of the Isle of Groix, the
Growler gun-brig, Lieutenant John Weeks, in company, when two, frigates and a brig were seen in
the N. W. crowding every sail to get into L'Orient.
Captain Hotham's first intention and wish was, by
weathering Groix, to prevent the enemy entering the
channel between that island and the main land; but
finding this impracticable, and being perfectly master of the ground, he dexterously ran round the south-
east point of the island, fetched to windward of the

harbour of Port L'Orient, and continued working in
the channel, exposed alternately to the fire from the
main land or the island, as he tacked towards the
one or the other.

. The French Commodore, as he approached his
port, found himself in great difficulty; a fast sailing
seventy-four gun ship to leeward forbade his entrance,
and if he hauled his wind, he would most probably
be overtaken before night. The only alternative
was to make a bold push between his enemy and
Point Talieu, and to endeavour to gain the protection of the port and batteries of L'Orient: this he
gallantly and judiciously determined to do, but failed
in consequence of the superior local knowledge of
the officer who opposed him. The wind was at
W.N.W. blowing very fresh. At forty-nine minutes
past two, P.M. the enemy bore up in a close line
a-head, and under every sail they could carry. Captain Hotham, with his ship under an easy commanding sail, perfectly prepared for action, and ready to lay
the enemy on board, placed the Northumberland close
to the Pointe de Pierre Laye, with her head to the
shore, and the main-topsail shivering. The French
Commodore hauled so close round the point, that
Captain Hotham did not think it practicable, with a
ship drawing twenty-four feet water, to approach
nearer the shore; he therefore bore up, and ran parallel to them, at the distance of about four hundred
yards, engaging them, and three strong batteries, for
the space of twenty minutes.

By steering close to the dry rock called Le Graul,

Captain Hotham prevented the enemy passing outside of it, and within there was not sufficient water for them to run.   Here the utmost nicety of pilotage was required, for in addition to the difficulty of a navigation with which Captain Hotham, and Mr. H. Stewart, the master of the Northumberland, could only be acquainted by the French charts, the smoke which rolled in dense clouds a-head of the ship, concealed every object from them: here the slightest deviation or fault of the pilot or helmsman might have been fatal to the ship, and never perhaps was an instance of more correct pilotage shewn.   The Northumberland was steered within her own length on the south-west side of the rock; and the enemy, instead of hauling outside of the Northumberland, or coming to the wind and separating, chose, with unpardonable ignorance, to attempt a channel in which they ought to have known there was not sufficient depth of water for them to pass.   They all grounded on the rocks, between the Graul and the main land, with every sail set, and in the utmost degree of confusion.

Seeing them thus securely fast upon their own rocks, Captain Hotham hauled off to repair his damages, which, in his sails and rigging, were very considerable, committing the enemy's ships to the operation of the falling tide, which in a short time left them on their beam-ends, with their mast-heads towards the shore.   While shifting his fore-topsail, and turning to windward in the channel, the Growler gun-brig got alongside of the enemy, and opened her fire within a very short distance. At twenty minutes past five, the Northumberland anchored in six and a half fathoms water, Pointe de Pierre Laye bearing N.W. half N., the citadel of Port Louis or L'Orient E. three quarters N., and the Graul Rock N. half E. four hundred yards. In this position, having the enemy's ships fairly exposed, their keels nearly out of the water, the fire of the Northumberland was deliberately kept up within point-blank range, for one hour and a quarter; the main-mast of one of the frigates and the brig fell: the ships' bottoms being pierced with numerous shot, the crews all deserting them, and the headmost frigate being in flames, Captain Hotham deemed his object completely accomplished; he therefore weighed, and removed from the reach of a strong battery, which, during the last part of the action, from the period of his anchoring, had done him more mischief than all the firing from the ships and batteries in the early part of the day. The Growler kept under sail near the enemy; pouring a constant fire from his long eighteen pounders, and prevented the crews returning to their ships. About eight o'clock, the frigate, which was on fire, blew up. At dark, Captain Hotham came to an anchor out of the reach of the batteries, either from the main land or from Groa; Point Talieu bore N.N.W. half W., south-east point of Groix S.S.W. half W., the French vessels N. by E. At ten o'clock, the second frigate appeared to be on fire, and at half past eleven, she was one mass of flame from stem to stern. On seeing this, Captain Hotham weighed, and with the Growler stood to sea.

In the heat of the action, a seaman, who stated himself to be a native of Portugal, swam on board of the Northumberland. He said, he had been taken in a ship called the Harmony, of Lisbon, by the French ships, whose names were the Andromache, Arianne, and Mameluke brig. The frigates mounted forty-four guns, and had four hundred and fifty men each (including prisoners), and the brig eighteen guns, and, one hundred and fifty men; they had sailed from the Loire, on the 9th of January, had cruised ever since in various parts of the Atlantic, and had destroyed thirty-six sail of vessels, of different nations, Americans, Spaniards, Portuguese, and English, taking out the most valuable parts of their cargoes.

The Northumberland had five men killed, fourteen severely wounded, and fourteen slightly. Mr. John Banks, the first lieutenant of the Northumberland; and Mr. John Weeks, the lieutenant of the Growler, were promoted to the rank of commanders, for their distinguished good conduct on this occasion. Of how much value would the local knowledge of Captain Hotham have proved to his country in the memorable year 1795.

A very remarkable volcanic eruption burst out of the sea, in the month of June, 1812, about two miles from the island of St. Michael's, in a N.N.W. direction. It was preceded by several severe shocks of an earthquake. It formed an island six hundred feet in height, where before the water had been four hundred and eighty feet deep. Captain Tillard, of the Sabrina, who was present, and made drawings of it, gave it the name of Sabrina Island. It soon after sank into the sea, leaving only a shoal, dangerous to shipping. The particulars are in the Naval Chronicle, 1812, part i.

Lieutenant Turner, of the Rota frigate, with the boats of that ship, boarded and took a French privateer, called L'Espador, pierced for ten guns, having only three mounted, and manned with forty-five men, of whom seven were killed and four wounded. The Rota had one killed and four wounded.

Lieutenant Josiah Thompson, of the Medusa, with the boats of that ship, boarded, in the harbour of Arcason, the French national store-ship, La Dorade, of fourteen guns, and eighty-six men. The enemy, prepared for the attack, hailed the boats, but the ship was carried with great slaughter: the whole of the crew, except twenty-three, were either taken, killed, or compelled to jump overboard. The Medusa had none killed, and only five wounded. The prize grounded on the ebb tide, coming down the harbour; and after taking out the wounded and prisoners, the victors set fire to her, and she was totally burned: she was very valuably laden.

In the month of June, Sir Home Popham, in the Venerable, of seventy-four guns, assisted the guerillas at Lequito, a town on the north coast of Spain, in possession of the French, whom they drove out, took away their cannon, ammunition, and small arms, destroyed the fort and convent in which they had taken shelter, and came off without the loss of a man, taking the French commandant and two hundred and ninety soldiers prisoners. Sir Home continued to support the cause of the royalists, by joining with them in an attack upon Bilboa, which the French evacuated. The works of Plenica were destroyed by the Captains Malcolm and Bouverie, in the Rhin and Medusa frigates: all the guns on the banks of the river of Bilboa were either spiked or brought away. The castle of Galea was blown up by Captain Bloye, who destroyed eight twenty-four and eighteen pounders. The batteries of Algosta and Begona were destroyed by Lieutenants Groves and O'Riley: these had between them nine eighteen pounders. On the opposite side of the inlet, the batteries of El Campillo, Las Quersas, and Xebilles, mounting eleven twenty-four pounders, were destroyed by the Lieutenants Coleman and Arbuthnot. On the 25th of June, the French advanced with two thousand men, and entered the ruins of Algorsa, whence they were compelled to retire on the approach of our squadron.

Lieutenant Warrand, in the Sea-lark schooner, fought an action in the month of July, off the Start, which, though the vessels engaged were diminutive in force, evinced a degree of courage and seamanship never exceeded. The enemy was a lugger, of sixteen guns, and seventy-five men; the Sea-lark a vessel far inferior; but Lieutenant Warrand, determined that she should not escape, laid her on board between the fore and main-masts, and in this position engaged her for one hour and thirty minutes, with great guns, musketry, and hand-grenades, when the Frenchman caught fire. Mr. Warrand (being

wounded) directed his master to board her, which
he did, and carried her. She was called La Ville
de Caen, had sailed the day before on a cruise, and
in this action had fifteen men killed, the captain and
sixteen wounded. The Sea-lark had seven killed,
and twenty-two wounded; an immense proportion
between two such vessels. Lieutenant Warrand was
promoted to the rank of commander.

As the war of the revolution draws to an end, the
number and importance of the transactions, naval
and military, leave us but little space to notice the
latter; and that merely to keep up the connexion of
events, and to shew how our generals were employed
in the interior of Spain, while our admirals guarded
the coast.

In the last chapter, we left Captain Eyre making
an effort to draw off the attention of the French from
Valencia, in which the unfortunate Blake was shut
up with twenty-six thousand men, by the victorious
Suchet. A bombardment of short duration, but unusual severity, produced a surrender of this important
place, the capital of the kingdom of Valencia.

On the same day, Marshal Victor was defeated
before the little town of Tariffa, by Colonel Skerritt,
and Captain C. F. Smith, of the engineers. The
force employed in this little spot did not exceed one
thousand eight hundred English and Spaniards,
assisted in the two first actions by a very small British squadron under the command of Captain E. S.
Dickson, in the Stately, of sixty-four guns. The
French army consisted of ten thousand men; and

after three different assaults, in which they were
beaten off with great loss, Victor retired from before
the place, leaving behind him his artillery and military stores.

Ciudad Roderigo was taken by storm by the British army under the Earl of Wellington, who received from the grateful Cortez the title of duke of
the city he had won. Badajoz, after a short siege
and bombardment, was likewise taken by the victorious Wellington on the 6th of April. In these two
famous sieges, prodigies of valour were performed
•by our troops ; and completely undeceived the Portuguese and Spaniards, who had been taught by the
French to believe, that the English, though fine looking men, could not face their enemies in the field.
The loss of the British and Portuguese armies, in
killed and wounded, in the storming of Badajoz,
was little short of five thousand men. These two
places falling, rendered the position of Marshal
Soult, before Cadiz, very insecure. A fruitless attempt was made in February to retake Tarragona,
but it failed. The Spaniards appeared to have lost
all their energies, and sense of national honour.
Lord Wellington, with his army, pushed on from
one strong place to another, until, in the month
of August, his Lordship entered Madrid, and King
Joseph fled to Ocana. On the night of the 24th,
the enemy abandoned the siege of Cadiz, and broke
up his camp on the Isla, leaving a very large
quantity of artillery and powder; most of the guns
were rendered useless; but he appeared to have re-

tired with much precipitation. Thus ended the siege of this place by the French; it had lasted two years and a half. Cadiz, indeed, may be said to have been in a state of siege or blockade by land and sea, with very little intermission for fifteen years.

Lord Wellington defeated General Rouget, who had in the mean time advanced to attack Bilboa, before which place lay Sir Home Popham, in the Venerable, of seventy-four guns. Lieutenant-colonel Skerrit took Seville by assault on the 27th of August.

The French, on the coast of Calabria, were defeated and greatly disturbed by a very distinguished young naval officer (Captain Robert Hall), who commanded the British and Neapolitan flotilla, with the rank of brigadier-general in the service of the King of Naples.

The enemy had thrown up works at Pietro Nera, to protect a convoy of fifty sail of armed vessels, which had assembled to transport naval stores to Naples. Captain Hall having consulted with Lord William Bentinck, who commanded the British army in Sicily, his Lordship ordered four companies of the 75th, under the command of Major Stewart, and a body of seamen under Lieutenant Le Hunte. These officers, without waiting for further assistance, ascended the heights, defended by a complete battalion, two troops of cavalry, and two pieces of artillery. Captain Hall at the same time sent a corporal's party of the rocket corps, whose novel and destructive fire threw the enemy into confusion. Our troops charged: the French still resisted, until their colonel-com-

mandant, and most of his officers, were killed or
made prisoners, and the hill covered with their dead.
The Neapolitan flotilla, under Captain Trubert,
opened its fire on the batteries; but they held out
until stormed by Lieutenant Le Hunte with the seamen. By eight o'clock in the morning, the whole of
the vessels were in possession of the assailants; the
timber launched and brought away; one hundred
and fifty of the enemy killed and wounded; one
hundred and sixty-three prisoners, amongst whom
were the colonel of the regiment, three captains, two
captains of cavalry, and one of artillery: two six
pounders were also brought away. The gallant
Major Stewart was killed after the attack had succeeded, when with Captain Hall he was putting off
from the shore. The loss on our side was, with this
exception, very trifling.

In the month of April, Captain Thomas, in the
Undaunted, whom we mentioned in our last chapter,
as having made two successful diversions in Catalonia,
in favour of the Spaniards, was directed by Sir Edward Pellew to blockade the port of Marseilles,
having under his orders the Volontaire and Blossom.
On the 26th of April, off the mouth of the Rhone,
he came suddenly upon a convoy of twenty-six sail
of gun-boats and merchant-vessels, to which he
immediately gave chase in the boats, drove all on
shore but five, which escaped, brought off seven,
burnt twelve, and left two stranded on the beach.
Among the number burnt was a national schooner,
mounting four long eighteen pounders, and having

seventy-five men.. Captain Stewart, of the Blossom, was principally instrumental in the complete success of this enterprise, by running his vessel close into the beach, among shoals and broken water.

While on this station, Captain Thomas rendered a substantial benefit to the British fleet in the Mediterranean. The greatest inconvenience experienced by ships of war, when cruising, is a want of water: provisions for five or six months are easily carried; but water can rarely be replenished, or made to last with a due regard to health, beyond twelve weeks: at the end of that time, if they continue at sea, the men must go to short allowance of this prime necessary, and fill their empty casks with salt water to preserve the ship's trim. In the Mediterranean, the fleet blockading Toulon repaired to Agincourt sound, or even to Malta (when Minorca was not in our possession) for a supply of water; but Captain Thomas brought his ship to an anchor off the mouth of the Rhone, within two miles of the shore, and filled excellent fresh water out of the sea, when the wind was from the land, and the broad and rapid stream came pouring into the Mediterranean. He sent Captain Stewart, of the Blossom, with a bottle of this valuable article to the Commander-in-chief, Sir Edward Pellew, who instantly sent his ships there from Toulon to complete their water, which they did in a very short time. Captain Thomas also found the anchorage very secure, riding out a gale of wind at S.S.E. for two days, without any strain on his cable, the holding ground being soft mud, and the under-tow or outset of the freshes from the river being stronger than the action of the wind and sea together. In future wars this discovery may be of incalculable advantage to our blockading ships. While the Undaunted lay there, nothing could pass along shore without being discovered. We have even been informed by experienced officers, that so soft is the bottom, off the Malora, and so strongly impregnated is the water with mud, when it blows hard from the sea, that the waves will not break, and that a ship lying on shore will receive little or no damage.

Captain Charles Rowley, in the Eagle, captured off Brindisi, the French frigate La Corcyre, of forty-four guns, but mounting only twenty-six eighteen pounders on her main-deck, and having on board one hundred and seventy seamen, and one hundred and thirty soldiers, with a cargo of wheat and military stores: she was bound with another frigate and a brig to Corfu. Her consorts escaped, and got into Brindisi. The frigates under the orders of Captain Rowley were still more successful; and indeed nothing could be more unfortunate than the French marine appear to have been in the Adriatic.

The Alceste, Captain M. Maxwell, the Active, Captain J. A. Gordon, and the Unité, Captain E. H. Chamberlayne, when lying at Lissa, received information of three French frigates being at the south side of the island. On the 29th of December, in the morning, the enemy was seen off the island of Augusta, and boldly formed in line to engage the British frigates. This determination did not last

long, for seeing our ships bearing down upon them
in close line, two of them ran away to the N.W.
under a crowd of sail. The third steering to the
N. E. was pursued by the Unité. The Alceste
brought the nearest ship to action at one o'clock,
but losing her main-topmast, she dropped a-stern.
The Active soon came up and supplied her place,
which compelled the French Commodore to return
to the assistance of his consort. The action lasted
two hours and twenty minutes, when the French
Commodore, taking advantage of the crippled state
of the Alceste, made sail and escaped. The other
frigate surrendered to the Active, after being totally
dismasted, and having five feet water in her hold.
She was called La Pomone, mounted forty-four guns,
had three hundred and twenty-two men, and was
commanded by Captain Rosamel. The other frigate
was called La Pauline, of the same force, and commanded by Monsieur Montford, with a broad pendant. The third frigate was captured the same day,
after a chase of eight hours, by the Unité: she was
called La Persanne, of twenty-eight nine pounders,
and one hundred and ninety-five men. She had on
board as a cargo, one hundred and twenty iron, and
some brass, guns. This squadron was from Corfu,
bound to Trieste. The Alceste had seven men
killed and thirteen wounded; the Active eight killed.
Captain Gordon lost his leg; Lieutenant W. B. Dashwood (now a post-captain) his arm: Lieutenant Haye
and twenty-four men were also wounded.

A French privateer having arrived in the port of

Palamos, with a cargo of provisions for the army, Lieutenant Isaac Shaw, of the Volontaire, went in with the boats of that ship, and brought her out without loss.

In the month of February, 1812, Lieutenant Bartholomew, in the Richmond brig, attacked the French privateer L'Intrepide, of eighteen guns, and one hundred and eighty men, as she lay in a bay near Vera, on the coast of Grenada. When the Richmond had approached within a short distance of the enemy, the Frenchmen set fire to their own vessel, and escaped to the shore. Lieutenant Bartholomew boarded and brought her out (though in flames), but she blew up in spite of all his exertions.

The enemy having possession of Tarragona, it was closely watched by the British squadron under Captain Codrington, while Lacey, the Spanish general, held his troops in readiness to repel the French approaching Reus, and with the Baron d'Eroles, he defeated them with considerable slaughter, taking six hundred prisoners.

The boats of the Sultan, of seventy-four guns, Captain West, under the command of Lieutenants Anderson and Woodcock, boarded and captured off Bastia two French national armed vessels,—one a settee of eight guns and thirty-one men; the other a brig of six guns and fifty-three men. This was a service of remarkable merit.

Lieutenant Rowland Mainwaring, first of the Menelaus, captured, by boarding with the boats of that ship, near the bay of Frejus, the French brig of war St. Joseph, pierced for sixteen guns, but having none mounted. She was moored within pistol-shot of a battery, to which her halsers were made fast, another battery flanked her, and the shore was lined with musketry.

Venice, the great maritime port of the Adriatic sea, had with much difficulty completed the construction of a seventy-four gun ship, called the Rivoli. The departure of this ship from Venice was anxiously watched and expected by Captain John Talbot, in the Victorious, of seventy-four guns; the Weazle brig, of eighteen guns, Captain Andrews, being in company with him. The Victorious arrived off Venice on the 16th of March, 1812, and on the 21st got sight of the Rivoli. She was attended by a large ship, two brigs, and two gunboats, steering towards the port of Rota, in Istria. The Victorious and Weazle gave chase, and at a quarter past four in the morning, the Weazle, being a-head, brought the two brigs to action. At five, the Victorious being within pistol-shot of the Rivoli, a furious action began : soon after, one of the enemy's brigs blew up ; and at daylight, Captain Talbot saw the Weazle in chase of the other, but recalled her, perceiving that she did not gain upon her enemy. The other ship and the gunboats were not in sight, and the contending ships being in seven fathoms water, off the point of Grao, Captain Talbot thought the brig would be of more service near him, in case of either ship getting on shore. Captain Andrews placed his brig within

pistol-shot on the bow of the French ship of the line,
and gave her three broadsides. It was now nearly
calm; the action had lasted four hours; the fire of the
enemy was very faint; and at a quarter before nine,
he hailed to say that he had surrendered. The ship
was immediately boarded and taken possession of
by Lieutenant Peake, first of the Victorious.

It appeared that the French squadron consisted of
the Rivoli, of seventy-four guns, bearing the broad
pendant of Commodore Barré, the commander-in-
chief of the enemy's force in the Adriatic, the Jena
and Mercierre, brigs of eighteen guns, the Mameluke, of ten guns: the other was a transport or merchant-ship. At no period of the action were the two
line-of-battle ships at a greater distance, than half
musket-shot from each other: the firing ceased at
short intervals, until the fog and smoke cleared away.
The Commodore did not surrender until nearly two
hours after his ship had become unmanageable: his
mizenmast fell just before he struck his colours,
when his captain, most of his officers, and four hundred of his men, were killed or wounded. The loss
on board the Victorious was also very great: she
had forty-two men killed, and ninety-nine wounded.
The Rivoli had on board eight hundred and sixty-
two men at the commencement of the action; the
Victorious no more than five hundred and twelve, of
whom sixty were in the sick list. Captain Talbot
received a medal for this action, and subsequently
was made a knight of the Bath; Captain Andrews
was made post, and Lieutenant Peake, of the Vic-

torious, a commander. It is a curious fact, that after the valuation of the Rivoli, no less a sum than £13,000. was deducted from the proceeds for damages done to the ship in action!

In the month of July, Lieutenant Dobbs, of the Leviathan, with the boats of that ship, attacked a French privateer and some merchant-vessels, in the port of Agay : four of the latter were brought out, and the privateer being on shore was set fire to.

Captain Usher, who for his former gallant services had been promoted to the rank of post-captain, was now in the command of the Hyacinth, of twenty guns, on the coast of Spain, and zealously employed in assisting the Guerilla chiefs in an attack upon the town and castle of Almunecar, seven miles to the eastward of Nessa. Having placed his own ship, with the Termagant sloop of war, Captain Hamilton, and the Basilisk gun-brig, within point-blank shot of the castle, he silenced its fire in less than an hour. On the following morning, the enemy began again, but by ten o'clock the British ships had effectually driven them from the castle to the town, where they fortified themselves in the churches and houses. Unwilling to destroy the unfortunate inhabitants, already enduring too much from the violence and cruelty of their oppressors, Captain Usher returned to Nessa for a reinforcement of Guerilla troops, which he obtained from Colonel Febrieri, an officer of the army of Ballasteros. Taking two hundred infantry on board, and directing the cavalry to march through the mountains to the

appointed rendezvous, he returned once more to
Almunecar, but the French, hearing of his movements, fled towards Grenada.

Captain Usher hoisted the British and Spanish
flags in the town, demolished the castle, situated
on a high and rocky peninsula, with a wall thirty
feet high, a ditch on the land side of as many feet
deep, and sixty feet wide; over this-ditch was a
narrow drawbridge, the only entrance to the castle.
The whole of this was destroyed by mines and
explosion, the ditch filled.up as far as the means
would admit, the artillery brought away, and many
German deserters from the French army joined
the British squadron.

Captain Josias Rowley, of the America, of sixty-
four guns, having with him Captain P. Campbell, of
the Leviathan, seventy-four, and Eclair sloop of war,
fell in, on the 9th of May, with a French convoy of
eighteen sail, which took refuge under the batteries
of Languilla. It was immediately decided to attack
them. The batteries were stormed and taken by the
Captains of marines, Rea of the America, and Owen
of the Leviathan. These officers conducted their
men, and executed the service on which they were
sent, with the most perfect exactness. The resistance
of a strong body of French troops, and batteries of
heavy guns, was overcome: the enemy fled to the
woods, whence they kept up a heavy fire on our
people. The Eclair drove them from the beach and
the houses, and the boats boarded and brought out
the vessels, which they found deeply laden, and

made fast to the houses, their sails and rudders being taken on shore; the marines and the seamen were re-embarked. Captain Bellamy, of the Eclair, Lieutenant Richardson, of the America, who commanded the invading party, and the Lieutenants Molesworth, Moodie, Dobbs, and Hambly, all partook in the honour of this attack. Little loss would have been sustained but for one unfortunate shot, which sunk the America's yawl, as the party was landing, by which accident, ten marines and one seaman were drowned.

It would be a proper precaution, when armed men in boats are approaching batteries, if they were to hold their cartouch-boxes and side-arms in their hands. It was probably owing to their being encumbered with them, and unable to disengage themselves readily, that these brave fellows were lost.

Captain J. T. Nicholas, in the Pilot sloop of war, of eighteen guns, attacked and brought off a convoy of ten vessels near Cape Palineure: the boats were commanded by Lieutenant Alexander Campbell. The prizes were laden with oil, from Pezzo, bound to Naples.

In the month of May, the Pilot, in company with the Thames, attacked the port of Sapri, defended by a strong battery and a tower, which mounted two thirty-two pounders, defended by thirty-eight men. After sustaining the fire of our vessels for two hours, it surrendered at discretion, and twenty-eight vessels laden with oil were brought off; some of them, however, must have been very small, since Captain Napier observes that they were launched, although lying one quarter of a mile distant from the sea-shore.

In the month of June, Lieutenant Isaac Shaw, of the Volontaire, with the boats of that ship, boarded, and after a desperate conflict carried, a French felucca privateer, called La Colombe. She had one long gun, and eight swivels, with forty-five men.

On the 27th of June, the Leviathan, having been joined by Captain Tower, in the Curaçoa, of thirty-six guns, Captain Campbell once more attacked the towers of Languillia and Alassio: the Eclair covered the landing. Lieutenant Dobbs, and Captain Owen, with his marines, landed, and took the batteries, spiking the guns, killing two-and-twenty of the French soldiers, among whom were two officers, and making eighteen prisoners, although the force opposed to them was more than four times their number. The enemy's vessels were all so securely made fast to the houses, whence Captain Campbell found it impossible to dislodge the musketry, that he contented himself with destroying eighteen sail of convoy. After spiking the cannon, the party embarked with very little loss.

In September, Captain Charles Rowley, of the Eagle, of seventy-four guns, sent Mr. Cannon, his first lieutenant, with three barges, to watch the coasting trade of the enemy off Cape Maistro, while he proceeded with the Eagle, and anchored off the mouth of the Po; and was soon after joined by his boats, bringing with them two gun-boats, and thirteen vessels laden with oil, each vessel carrying a six

or eight pounder gun. These had all been taken
under circumstances peculiarly marking the national spirit of our brave countrymen. Twenty-
three sail, under convoy of two gun-boats, had
been seen standing towards Goro: as our boats
approached, they drew up in a line of battle, under
a four-gun battery, and the beach lined with armed
people. Lieutenant Cannon, with his little party,
attacked the gun-boats, which had placed themselves in front, carried one, and turned her guns
on the convoy; with the same success, he attacked and carried the second; and then, with his
whole united force, falling on the convoy, captured all but two, which effected their escape.
Unable to man all his prizes, he burned six, and
returned victorious to the Eagle, but not long to
enjoy the honour of his victory. This gallant and
excellent young officer had received in the battle
a mortal wound, of which he died on the 22d of
September. Lieutenant Festing, who had taken
the command of the boats after the fall of his gallant companion, conducted them to final success
with the same intrepidity.

Captain William Hoste, in the Bacchante, was
equally fortunate on the coast of Istria, in the
same month. Lieutenant O'Brien, with the boats
of the frigate, was detached to bring out from
Lerna some vessels which were loading with ship-
timber in that port. On his approach, he discovered that the merchant-vessels were protected by
an armed xebec, and two gun-boats; he however

boarded and took the whole of them. But this gallant exploit was far exceeded on the 18th, when that officer was sent in pursuit of another convoy, between Termite and Vasto, on the coast of Apulia. It was nearly calm, so that the ship could not approach; but Lieutenants O'Brien and Hood rowed in among them. The merchant-vessels ran on shore; and their crews, armed with musketry, took refuge in a thick wood, close to the sterns of the vessels, while their front was protected by eight armed feluccas. The Lieutenants boarded and carried the whole of them, in defiance of the heavy fire of grape and musketry; and the marines, under Lieutenant Haig, landed and drove the enemy out of the wood. Eight gun-boats, carrying each one twelve pounder, and sixteen men, together with eighteen vessels, laden with oil, almonds, and other merchandise, were brought out, without the loss of one Englishman.

The British parliament, upon whose counsels and wisdom, under Divine Providence, depended the liberties of Europe, assembled on the 7th of January. The speech from the throne was delivered by commission, and adverted to our successes in the preceding year in Europe and Asia. The cause of the Peninsula, supported by our armies, under the Earl of Wellington (it observed), held out the fairest hopes of a triumph over the power of France. These hopes, his Royal Highness the Prince Regent confidently expressed, would be supported by every assistance in the power of the legislature to afford. The disputes with the United States of America were mentioned in terms of gloomy anticipation. The address was opposed in the commons by Mr. Whitbread, whose desponding language tended to depress the spirits of the country, and to induce it to abandon the cause, at the moment that our labours were about to be rewarded by the most brilliant victories.

The thanks of parliament were voted to Lord Minto, the governor-general of India, to the Honourable Rear-admiral Stopford, to Lieutenant-general Sir Samuel Achmuty, and to the army and navy employed in that country, for the capture of the islands of Java, France, and Bourbon.

On a subsequent day, Mr. Brougham brought forward a motion relative to the droits of admiralty, which he said (and we believe correctly), amounted in the last twenty-nine years to the enormous sum of £8,000,000, yielding a yearly revenue to the crown of £180,000. This sum had been principally accumulated by detention of neutral vessels, under an apprehension of approaching hostilities with the powers to which they belonged. Mr. Brougham's motion went to dispute the right of the crown to the disposal of this sum; but it was negatived by a very great majority. We should humbly hope, that in future wars, such a fund might be applied to increasing the pay (not the bounties) to seamen; by which means we shall avoid the necessity of coercion, and prevent in a great measure one cause of dispute with America.

The ill-will and mutual distrust between Great Britain and the United States, have been in the gradual progress of this work accounted for, and recorded. The charges laid against us had, at the commencement of the year, swollen to a degree that forbade the hope of peace. These were the detention of her trade, and the impressment of her seamen. The final act of Commodore Rogers, in attacking the Little Belt, plainly shewed, that America was bent on war with England.

In the session of congress which met in November, 1811, Mr. Madison, with a blamable want of candour, or of correct information, imputed to the Captain of the Little Belt the charge of firing the first shot; but as this was intended to flatter the popular feeling, and answered the purpose, we must leave it recorded on the page of history, and submit the cause to the judgment of impartial posterity.

How it happened that Mr. Percival, so well acquainted with the political sentiments of the Americans, their love of France, and their hatred of England, should have disbelieved that they would go to war with us, can only be accounted for by supposing, that he judged too highly of Mr. Madison's understanding; that as he knew America could derive no possible advantage from war, so he concluded, that her ruler would never have recourse to it, for the gratification of his own selfish passions. But, while he doubted, America had decided; and before the declaration of the

President could reach England, Mr. Percival was
no more. That excellent minister, and upright
man, was shot in the lobby of the house of commons, on the 11th of May, 1812, by one John
Bellingham, who was immediately taken, tried,
and executed on the 18th of the same month.

The winter passed away without any thing
worthy of notice. In the spring, the British squadron assembled at Halifax, where it was evident that
war was confidently anticipated by the Admiral.
The Spartan was sent to Quebec, with money to
pay the troops; and her Captain had orders to co-
operate with and assist the governor of the Canadas, Sir George Prevost, in fitting the gun-boats
for the protection of the river, or in any other way
for the good of the service. The Belvidera was off
New York. The Africa, Guerrière, and Shannon,
cruised in the vicinity of Cape Cod. About the 25th
of June, an express reached Sir George Prevost, at
Quebec, announcing a declaration of war on the
part of the United States against Great Britain;
this act was dated the 18th of June. The American
squadron, under the command of Commodore Rogers, was sent out in search of our ships; but it
would seem, with orders " to drive them out of the
waters of the United States," rather than to capture them. About this time, the British naval
officers were accused of supine indifference in the
discharge of their duty, and to every thing but
the ornamenting of their ships: having, by the
victory of Trafalgar, annihilated the navies of Eu-

rope, it was said, they had resigned themselves to all the pride and insolence of invincible conquerors. The Earl of St. Vincent, in a letter to the Author, in 1813, thus expresses himself, " I hear the exercise of the great gun is laid aside, and is succeeded by a foolish frippery and useless ornament." How far this may have been the case in the Mediterranean, or East or West Indies, with ships of the line, we shall not say; but certainly on the coast of North America, it was not so; the ships on that station, being kept constantly in exercise, under the daily expectation of a war, although, at the same time, due care was taken by the Admiral to avoid giving offence to the Americans. This is proved by the following extract from the orders of Vice-admiral Sawyer, given to the Author, as captain of the Spartan, and dated at Bermuda, the 6th of January, 1812 :

In the execution of this service, you are to be particularly careful to give no just cause of offence to the government or subjects of the United States, and to caution the officers who may be sent on board their vessels accordingly. You are not to anchor in any of their ports, but in cases of necessity.

Similar orders were given to the Little Belt, and all the cruisers. It is therefore not at all credible, that a British naval officer, tenacious of character, and impatient of rebuke, would subject himself to the loss of his appointment, by any deviation from so plain a path.

On the 28th of April, 1812, Bonaparte repealed his famous Berlin and Milan decrees, in consequence of which, on the 23d of June, the orders in council, as far as they related to the United States, were repealed in England. On the same day, Commodore Rogers attacked the Belvidera, off Sandy Hook, near New York; an act of precipitation, which Mr. Madison himself and his country had cause to deplore.

The American squadron consisted of the President, of fifty-four guns and four hundred and seventy-six men; the United States, Commodore Decatur, of the same force; the Congress, Captain Smith, of thirty-six guns; the Essex, thirty-two guns, Captain David Porter; also the Hornet and Argus, two very large and well manned sloops of war. Commodore Rogers sailed from New York on the 21st of June, and on the 23d, fell in with the Belvidera, of thirty-six guns, commanded by Captain Richard Byron, unacquainted with the declaration of war, but perfectly prepared for it as a probable event. Captain Byron at first stood towards the strangers; but having ascertained by their inattention to his private signals that they were Americans, greatly superior to him in force, at half-past eleven in the forenoon he tacked, with very light winds, while the Americans kept the breeze; and at twenty minutes past four, the President began to fire her bow guns at the Belvidera. This was the first act of open and undisguised hostility on the part of America. Captain Byron returned the fire from two eighteen pounders out of his cabin windows, and two thirty-two pound

carronades from his stern ports on the quarter-deck.
The President, having the advantage of sailing,
might very soon have been alongside the Belvidera; but the Commodore kept constantly altering
the position of his ship, to bring his guns to bear.
By thus deviating from his course, he dropped
astern, shewing the same indecision as in the affair
of the Little Belt.   This running fight had lasted
from four till near seven o'clock, when another
American frigate came up, and began to fire, but
at so great a distance, as to excite the laughter of
the people on board the Belvidera.   At half-past
ten, Captain Byron hauled up six points, and the
Americans followed him, though not with the spirit
and determination of men bent on the destruction
or capture of their enemy.   At half-past eleven,
P. M., to the astonishment of the British officers,
the President wore, and hove-to!   Thus ended the
first naval action of the second American war, leaving the conduct and character of Commodore Rogers in a worse state than after the affair of the
Little Belt.

It was affirmed, by way of excuse for the Commodore, that one of his chase-guns had burst, and
killed or wounded twenty-two men, besides six
others who met their fate from the shot of the Belvidera.   But admitting this, still the President was
not disabled; and the indelible disgrace sustained
by Commodore Rogers, on this occasion, was a
just retribution for the injury he had done to the
brave Captain Bingham.   The able and gallant

conduct of Captain Byron was beyond all praise; no ship ever shewed a higher state of discipline, loyalty, and thorough command of all the requisites for a ship-of war.　Mr. Sykes, her first lieutenant, was promoted to the rank of commander, as a compliment, not only to his captain and himself, but to the officers and ship's crew, which certainly would not have been done, had there been any want of discipline, observable in the ship.　The loss on board the Belvidera was two killed, and three or four wounded, among whom were the gallant Byron, and Lieutenant Bruce.　The rigging was much damaged; and, shameful to relate, though a new ship, her ring-bolts, and gun-fastenings, gave way at every discharge.

Captain Byron, on his way to Halifax, detained three American vessels, which he carried in with him, but which were released by Admiral Sawyer, who, with becoming prudence and caution, and still unwilling to believe that the Americans meant more than "to drive us out of their waters," sent Captain Thompson, in the Colibri, with a flag of truce, to New York, to demand an explanation. This overture met with the reception which might have been expected, although the Vice-admiral was perfectly justifiable in sending it.　It was his duty to prove, like Sir James Saumarez, in the Baltic, that no precipitation of his, no eagerness for prize-money, had induced him to grasp at the first excuse for beginning hostilities.　On the return of the Colibri, and the embarkation of Mr.

Forster from the United States, there was no longer
a hope of peace; and the Vice-admiral sent out his
cruisers, in every direction, more with a view to
give assistance to the trade of his country, than to
enrich himself by captures from the enemy.

The American privateers swarmed on the coast
of Nova Scotia, in the bay of Fundy, off the Bermudas, the gulf of Florida, Barbadoes, in short,
every track, every creek, by which our commerce
had been in the habit of passing to and from the
mother country. The madness of the American
government, in thus going to war, without a previous embargo of one year at least, was soon very
apparent by the numerous valuable captures made
by the British cruisers.

The American squadron, whose orders it appears
were to intercept the West India convoy, then on
its passage home, and not very far from them,
might have succeeded, had they not been detained
three days in repairing the damages sustained by
the President, from the fire of the Belvidera.

The squadron under Captain Broke having arrived off New York, that active officer gained intelligence of the American Commodore, and stood to
the southward, in the hope of falling in with the
convoy. He saw and chased the Constitution, but
could not come up with her. He however took
many prizes; burned a number of American vessels; and, on the 25th, spoke an English schooner,
which had parted with the Jamaica fleet on the day
preceding, under convoy of the Thetis frigate.

Captain Broke made all sail to join them, which
he was so fortunate as to effect on the 29th, in
lat, 40° 44′ N., and long. 63° 12′ W., accompanying them as far as the lat. of 43°. and long, 52° W.
when any farther apprehension of their being attacked by the Americans might be dismissed. A
heavy gale of wind, and a thick fog, separated the
ships on the banks of Newfoundland; and early in
the month of August, the provisions and water
being nearly expended, the British squadron returned to Halifax.

In the mean time, the Guerrière cruising alone
on the banks of Newfoundland, on the 20th of that
month, fell in with the Constitution, an American
frigate, of the same force as the President, though
inferior as to scantling. The Constitution, when
first seen, was to windward: it was blowing fresh,
with a heavy sea running. The Guerrière was on
a wind, on the starboard tack. As the enemy appeared determined to fight, Captain Dacres shortened sail to his topsails, foresail, jib, and driver,
and threw his main-topsail to the mast. The Constitution also hove-to, hauled up her courses, took
a reef in her topsails, and handed her topgallant-
sails. Captain Dacres filled, and stood under the
same sail, upon a wind. The Constitution came
down, and at ten-minutes past four, this eventful
action began, by the Guerrière firing a few guns
at the Constitution, more with a view to try the
distance, than for any effective attack. At fifteen
minutes past four, the American hoisted his colours,

and opened his fire : the Guerrière wore several times to avoid being raked, and the action was continued, as both ships ran off the wind, the Constitution on the larboard-beam of the Guerrière, endeavouring to cross her bows; but which Captain Dacres for some time prevented : thus far, the two ships had fought with an equal chance of success, when the day was decided by one of those accidents to which ships of war are ever liable, and which can rarely be guarded against. A twenty-four pound shot passed through the mizen-mast of the Guerrière, and at twenty minutes past five, the mast fell over the larboard-quarter; the ship consequently came to, against her helm, which was kept hard a-port, and the Constitution had an opportunity of raking her with a very destructive fire. The stern of the Constitution coming in contact with the bow of the Guerrière, the boarders on each side were preparing to rush into the opposing ships, but were prevented by the motion, and the uncertainty of the number who might be able to reach the decks of the enemy at one time. While the bow guns of the Guerrière, and her small-arm men, were firing into the Constitution, the latter, with a numerous company of well-trained marines, did great execution among the officers and crew of the Guerrière, whose bowsprit at that moment striking the taffrail of the Constitution, slacked the fore-stay of the Guerrière, and the fore-shrouds on the larboard or weather side being mostly shot away,

the mast fell over on the starboard side, crossing
the main-stay; the sudden jerk carried the main-
mast along with it, leaving the Guerrière a defenceless wreck, rolling her main-deck guns in the
water. The American, as soon as the Guerrière's
masts fell, removed to a distance, lying by for a
short time to repair her damages. Captain Dacres,
though severely wounded, still kept the deck,
and with his brave officers and crew, exerted himself to clear the wreck, and get the ship before the
wind. The spritsail was loosed, and a small spar
being lashed to the stump of the foremast, in three-
quarters of an hour a topmast-studdingsail was set
on it, and she was going off before the wind. But
valour, skill, and exertion were alike fruitless; the
spritsail-yard went in the slings, the haul-yards of
the jury fore-yard were shot away, and the motion
of the ship was so quick and so violent, that it was
impossible to work a great gun: she had several
shot-holes between wind and water, the Constitution had taken a position to rake her, without the
smallest chance of the Guerrière returning a shot,
and the officers concurring in opinion with the
Captain, the colours were struck.

Mr. Ready, the second lieutenant, commanding
on the main-deck of the Guerrière, was killed,
with fourteen men; the captain, first lieutenant
(Mr. Kent), and sixty-one seamen and marines
wounded. This number made nearly one-third of
the crew with which he went into action. The
third lieutenant, second lieutenant of marines, two

midshipmen and twenty seamen were away in prizes. All the officers, and every midshipman capable of taking charge of a watch (except one), were wounded. The comparative force of the ships will be best shewn by the accompanying table; and when all the circumstances are taken into consideration, it will be allowed that the Guerrière was most nobly defended, against a ship very nearly double her force; and that the sentence of the court-martial, by which Captain Dacres, his officers, and ship's company were honourably acquitted, was no more than a just tribute to their valour and misfortunes. Captain Dacres, as a proof that the lords commissioners of the Admiralty approved of his conduct, was, before the conclusion of the American war, appointed to the Tiber, a new frigate of forty-four guns, which he commanded for five years.

CONSTITUTION.

	Guns.	Men.	Boys.
Main-deck········	30 24-pounders	476	
Quarter-deck·····	24 32-pounders		
Forecastle ········	2 long 18-pounders		

GUERRIERE.

	Guns.	Men.	Boys.
Main-deck········	30 18-pounders	244	19
Quarter-deck ·····	14 32-pounders		
Forecastle ········	{ 2 32-pounders		
	{ 2 long 9-pounders		

Lieutenant Kent was promoted to the rank of Commander.

The Guerrière could not muster more than seven men to a gun, and in some instances only five, the number of her small-arm men was not above thirty, while her enemy had more than sixty, besides twelve riflemen in each top.

Captain Dacres, on going into action, gave permission to seven American seamen (all he had on board), to retire from their quarters. Of this they availed themselves. Had the Englishmen on board the Constitution received the same indulgence, it is probable the ship would have been taken into Halifax.

On the morning after the action, it was discovered that the Guerrière was so completely a wreck, that it would be impossible to take her into port; she was therefore set on fire and burnt. The conduct of Captain Hull, of the Constitution, to Captain Dacres, and his officers and crew, was that of a humane and gallant enemy, with one exception only, which we are about to mention. Soon after his arrival at Boston, Captain Hull resigned the command of the Constitution; was made a Commodore, and a Commissioner of the Navy, of the United States.

It appeared in evidence on the court-martial, that there were many Englishmen on board the Constitution, and these were leading men, or captains of guns. The officers of the Guerrière knew some of them personally, and one man in particular, who had been captain of the forecastle in the Eurydice, a British frigate, then recently come from England. Another was in the Achille at Trafalgar; and the third lieutenant of the Constitution, whose name was Reed, was an Irishman. It was said, and we have no reason to doubt the fact, that there were two hundred British seamen on board the Constitution, when she began the action.

Captain Dacres, while lying wounded in his cot, heard one of them say to an American boatswain's mate, "Don't strike me! you Yankey, if it had not been for us, you would never have had the Guerrière;" and so fearful was Captain Hull that the remnant of the Guerrière's crew would be tempted by the number of their countrymen on board to make some desperate effort, that he kept his prisoners manacled and chained to the deck during the night, and a greater part of the day.

We have been more than usually minute in giving the particulars of this ill-fated action, not only with a view of rescuing the character of a brother officer from undeserved censure, but to efface an impression that our navy was declining, and our officers and men deficient in their duty! The inference is erroneous, founded on a supposition, that if two ships happen to be called frigates, the lesser one, being manned and commanded by Englishmen, ought to take the greater, though a ship very nearly double her force, in size, guns, and men: we need scarcely enter into any argument to prove the fallacy of such an expectation. A ship five feet wider, and twelve or fifteen feet longer, has much more room for fighting her guns, is steadier on the water, higher above its surface, and less vulnerable to the shot of her enemy, as her sides and her masts are so much thicker, while the shot of her adversary are proportionably smaller. If to these advantages we add nearly double the number of men, and the stoutest of them Englishmen, we think the capture of the Guerrière is fairly accounted for.

As we are to relate other naval actions between our ships and those of the United States, some more fortunate, but none more gallant, we intend this reasoning to apply to the whole of them; we shall therefore have little more to do, than state the facts.

In July the Americans invaded the western provinces of Upper Canada. The war was carried on with the utmost rigour on both sides, yet without any declaration on our part; the port of Halifax was crowded with prizes, of the most valuable nature, though till the following year no commission was granted for their trial or condemnation. Much of their cargoes was stolen from them by nightly plunderers, and much afterwards consumed in expensive litigation, while the hulls of the vessels drifted from their anchors, and were scattered in careless profusion round the harbour. This apparent indifference on the part of government to the interests of the seamen, was the cause of great desertion and discontent. According to the Gazette numbers, no less than one thousand four hundred sail of ships of war, privateers, and merchant - vessels, were taken, in the course of the short space of two years and a half; and by accurate calculation it appears that British vessels taken by the Americans were fully equal in number, and perhaps of greater value.

On the 27th of September, Admiral Sir John Warren arrived at Halifax in the St. Domingo, of seventy-four guns. He took on him not only the command on the North American station, including Newfoundland, but also that of the Windward and Leeward Islands and Jamaica; and was vested with the powers of a minister plenipotentiary.

Sir John Warren was accompanied by the Poictiers, of seventy-four guns, commanded by Sir John P. Beresford: some noble frigates also arrived on the coast from England, intelligence having been received that Commodore Rogers had sailed with a squadron to destroy our Newfoundland trade. Captain Broke was sent after him, with the Shannon, Nymph, and Tenedos, of thirty-eight guns, and Curlew, brig. Sir John Warren sailed soon after for the Chesapeake, with a very strong squadron. In November, Vice-admiral Sawyer returned to England. Another action, of as mortifying a nature as the last, was fought between the Frolic brig sloop of war, of eighteen guns, and the Wasp, called also a sloop of war by the Americans, but as much superior to her opponent in point of size, scantling, and number and quality of her crew, as the Constitution was to the Guerrière; to which may be added, that the Frolic was a disabled vessel, only half manned.

Captain Whinyates, of the Frolic, was on his passage home from the bay of Honduras with a convoy, on the 16th of October, 1812. Having come through the gulf of Florida, and being informed of the war with America, he encountered a gale of wind, which dispersed his convoy, carried away his main-yard, and sprung his main-top-mast: he was short of his proper complement of men, and of his crew one-third were fit subjects for invaliding. Thus circumstanced, on the 18th of October, after having collected six sail of his convoy, he fell in with the Wasp, an American sloop of twenty guns, eighteen thirty-two pounders and two long twelve-pounders, and one hundred and thirty-eight men.

Captain Whinyates, like a gallant officer, and conformably to the maxim of Nelson, first made the signal to the convoy to disperse or provide for their own safety; after which, when they were at such a distance as to ensure their escape, he came to the wind and engaged his enemy. This action, like that of the Guerrière's, was also decided by an accident. The fire of the Frolic was so spirited, that in a few minutes the fore-topmast of the Wasp fell over the side, and unfortunately almost at the same moment, the gaff-head of the Frolic, which having no square mainsail, wanted after-sail to keep her to the wind. This allowed the Wasp

to take a raking position, and the decks of the
Frolic were swept of her gallant officers and men
with comparative impunity, but nothing could
induce Captain Whinyates to surrender, as long
as there was a chance of victory : when the Frolic
had scarcely twenty men unhurt on her decks,
the crew of the Wasp boarded from their own
vessel, and struck the British colours. Captain
Whinyates surrendered his sword to an enemy
that could not but respect his valour. The Frolic
had fifteen officers and men killed; her first lieutenant and master mortally wounded; Captain
Whinyates, the second lieutenant, Mr. B. Wintle,
and forty-three men wounded with more or less
severity : some of these died in consequence. The
British brig was entirely disabled. The Wasp,
which had one hundred and thirty-seven stout
men, was supposed to have eight men killed, and
as many wounded, but their numbers were carefully concealed. The action was scarcely ended,
when the Poictiers, of seventy-four guns, hove in
sight, retook the Frolic, and captured the Wasp.
In number of guns, and weight of metal, the two
sloops were nearly equal; the superiority of the
Wasp lay in her size, the number and quality of
men, and scantling of her timbers. A court-martial
decided the merit of Captain Whinyates, by declaring that he had done all that could be done to
defend his vessel, and he was therefore honourably
acquitted, with all his officers and crew. Captain
Whinyates at the time of fighting this action was

a post-captain, but did not know it: he received his commission on his arrival in England.

Another severe mortification awaited us, in the capture of the Macedonian, a British frigate, similar in size and rating to the Guerrière, that is to say, an eighteen-pound frigate, with a complement of two hundred and eighty-four men.

On the 12th of October, 1812, in lat. 29° N. and long. 29° 30″ W. this frigate, commanded, by Captain J. S. Carden, fell in with the United States, an American frigate of the largest class. Both ships mutually steered a course to close with each other. The Macedonian set her fore-topmast, and top-gallant studding-sails: it was blowing strong: Captain Carden, as the enemy approached, took in his studding-sails, and was under a plain sail before a shot was fired. The British frigate, sailing faster than the American, would soon have been alongside of her, but in the first or second broadside the Macedonian lost her mizen-topmast, and gaff-haulyards. This produced an equality in the rate of sailing, and the United States kept her enemy in one position on the quarter in a running fight. The first man killed on board the Macedonian, was y a forty-two pound carronade shot,—a proof that, contrary to numerous reports, he commenced action within range of carronade, and indeed so close, that Captain Carden attempted to lay his enemy on board, in which he was disappointed only by his lee-forebrace being shot away,

which brought his ship up in the wind, and probably saved the lives of most of his crew; for it
would be the height of presumption to suppose
that the very reduced numbers on board the Macedonian, could have contended against the crew
of the United States in a personal conflict, as an
assailing enemy. It need scarcely be noticed that
Captain Carden has been accused by a very in-
competent judge of running down to bring his
enemy to action, in a heedless and confident manner. He ran into action as his brother officers had
done, and will do again, to fight his enemy, and
decide the day as quickly as possible: how could
Captain Carden have closed sooner, and what right
had he to suppose his ship's company deficient in
the practice of gunnery, when he was confident
that every pains had been taken to instruct them?
Captain Carden was ignorant of the action between the Guerrière and Constitution, and having
exerted himself to the utmost to defeat his enemy,
was compelled to surrender, after his mizen-mast
and topmasts were shot away, and his ship a mere
wreck: his conduct has therefore been most cruelly
misrepresented. The Macedonian had thirty-six
men killed; thirty-six severely, and thirty-two
slightly wounded. A court-martial acquitted him,
his officers and crew, of all blame for the loss of
the ship. Mr. David Hope, the first lieutenant,
was severely wounded in the head, towards the
close of the action, but being carried below, he
immediately returned to his duty. This officer

was highly complimented for his gallantry, and is now a commander. He is the same whose conduct we noticed as first lieutenant of the Freya at Guadaloupe, in the year 1810. The guns of the United States, according to the official report of Captain Carden, were, on the main-deck, thirty long twenty-four pounders; forecastle and quarter-deck, twenty-two carronades forty-two pounders, and two long twenty-four pounders, making fifty-four guns, besides a traversing carronade and howitzers in her tops : her complement of picked men amounted to four hundred and seventy-six. She had the scantling of a seventy-four, and was, in a gale of wind or bad weather, equal to almost any two-decked ship.

Captain Carden received his sword from Rear-admiral Sir Henry Hotham, the president of the Court, who took occasion to pay him a very hand-some compliment on his gallantry; and as the Court was composed of men of honour, of the naval profession, it is to be presumed that an investi-gation of four days would have put them in pos-session of the facts, and that they would return a verdict according to their oaths.

Commodore Decatur, who commanded the United States, behaved to his prisoners in a man-ner so honourable and humane, as to entitle him not only to the thanks of Captain Carden and his officers and men, but also to the grateful record of history. The Commodore, who was an orna-ment to his country, lost his life in a duel with a brother-officer: they fought with muskets; both shots took effect, but one only inflicted a mortal wound.

The year 1812 terminated with the loss of another British frigate, the Java, of thirty-six guns, eighteen pounders, commanded by Captain Henry Lambert, one of our most distinguished officers, whom we had occasion to mention with peculiar honour in the East Indies, as Captain of the Psyche and St. Fiorenzo. The Java, on her way to the East Indies, had sailed from England late in the year. She was newly equipped, with a crew composed of different portions of the men of other ships, and a sad mixture from the guard ships at the Nore, and in Hamoaze: such at the close of the war were the generality of our crews. She had but a small proportion of seamen, and nineteen of her men were away in a prize.

On the 29th of December, when off St. Salvador, on the coast of South America, the Java fell in with the Constitution, commanded by Commodore Bainbridge. At first, the Constitution, on making out the Java to be a British frigate, stood away from her under all sail upon a wind. The Java pursued and gained on her; when the American hoisted her colours, shortened sail, and bearing up, placed herself on the lee-bow of the Java. At ten minutes past two she began to fire, when half a mile distant from her enemy, giving her larboard broadside. This was not returned by the Java, until close upon the weather-bow of the Consti-

tution, when a desperate action ensued. The
American avoided close fighting, and fired high to
disable the Java, in which he too well succeeded:
by cutting away the head of her bowsprit, and
most of her running rigging, he obtained the weather gage, and at length raked the Java, with a
heavy and destructive fire. Captain Lambert had
ordered his ship to be laid on board the enemy,
but at the very moment, his foremast fell, and soon
after the main-topmast, while the stump of the
Java's bowsprit passed over the Constitution's taffrail. It was now easy to perceive that the day
was gone; the only hope was by boarding, and
that the enemy was too wary to allow; having all
his masts, and being perfectly under command,
he took his own distance. At half-past three,
Captain Lambert received a mortal wound in the
breast, and was carried below. The command
devolved on Lieutenant Henry Ducie Chads,
the first lieutenant. Many of the guns of the
Java were disabled: two or three were all that
could be brought to bear until a quarter-past four,
when her mizen-mast falling, she broke off a little,
and brought her starboard guns to bear, and the
enemy's rigging being much cut, she could not
avoid shooting a-head, which brought the two
ships fairly alongside of each other. In this position, they continued engaging until thirty-five
minutes past four, when the Java's main-yard went
in the slings; and she was frequently on fire, owing
to the wreck hanging over her guns on the fighting

side. The American now made sail a-head, and remained out of gun-shot for one hour, while the Java lay an unmanageable wreck, with nothing standing but her mainmast, and that expected to fall every moment. The Java was however not yet given up, though in a condition in which few would have thought a defence practicable; still, like the Guerrière, they rigged a small jury-foremast, cleared the wreck from their guns, and spared no exertion to be ready to renew the action: a small sail was set on the bowsprit: the weather half of the main-yard remaining aloft, the main tack was hauled on board, and the helm put up in hopes of getting before the wind, but the ship rolling very heavily, the mast fell, and nearly covered with its wreck the whole of the starboard guns. Thus circumstanced, what more could be done by the bravest? a useless sacrifice of those who, while a hope remained, freely devoted themselves to the cause of their country, would have been an ungrateful return for their patriotism; and as the Constitution approached within hail to rake them, the officers of the Java agreed with Mr. Chads, that it would be proper to surrender, and at five minutes past five, the colours were struck. No sooner were the wounded men taken from the ship, than the American captain, seeing *she could not float*, set her on fire, and she went down. The reader will be struck with the remarkable similarity between this action and that between the same American frigate and the Guerrière: that of the Macedonian and the United States bears also very strongly on the question; and the result of the whole forms a mass of undeniable evidence, proving that neither courage, discipline, or seamanship, were wanting on our side, but that these frigates were taken, simply because they were opposed to ships as much their superior in every respect as a British first-rate is to an eighty gun ship. The killed on board the Java amounted to twenty-two, viz. five mates and midshipmen, a clerk, and sixteen seamen and marines; besides the captain, who died a week after. The first lieutenant, master, and seventy-five seamen, Lieutenant Davies, of marines, two sergeants, two corporals, and seventeen privates, were wounded.

Captain John Marshall, of the royal navy, a passenger, Lieutenant James Saunders, of the navy, and Captain Wood (aide-de-camp to Lieutenant-general Hislop, who was also on board), were wounded.

Mr. Chads wrote a very modest, unassuming letter, accounting for the capture of the Java, in which he detailed the action in the language not only of a seaman, but of a scholar and a gentleman. He spoke of the support he had received from Lieutenant-general Hislop, Major Walker, and Captain Wood; of Captain John Marshall, R. N.; of the Lieutenants Hetherengham and Buchanan; of Mr. Robinson, the master, and Lieutenants Mercer and Davies, of the marines: and of the Lieutenants Aplin and Saunders, R. N. who were passengers: he diffidently offered a tribute of praise to his gallant and lamented Captain, whose remains were interred with military honours at St. Salvador. Commodore Bainbridge behaved with great kindness to the officers of the Java; but Mr. Chads states that the crew were plundered of every thing by the Americans, and confined in irons. This latter instance of rigour might only have been an effect of caution, as Captain Broke was obliged to confine the Americans, and Captain Hull the crew of the Guerrière. A monument in St. Paul's cathedral deservedly commemorates the name of Captain Henry Lambert as a young and deeply-regretted naval hero.

The Constitution received in this action so much damage, that a very little more resistance, had it been possible to have made it, would have at least reduced her to a wreck, if not have compelled her to submit to an eighteen-pound frigate. Her foremast, mizen-mast, and main-topmast, were much cut, as were her yards and rigging. She had ten men killed and forty-six wounded, four of whom died within the week. The Commodore and his fifth lieutenant were also wounded.

The remaining officers and crew, who survived from the Java, were speedily conveyed to England, where, in the month of April following, they were brought to a court-martial for the loss of the ship. The trial took place on the 13th of April. Sir Graham Moore, one of the best judges of naval merit in our service, was the president of the court.

After all the evidence had been gone through, and the defence concluded, the prisoners were *most honourably acquitted*, and Rear-admiral Moore thus addressed Lieutenant Henry Ducie Chads:

I have much satisfaction in returning you your sword. Had you been an officer who had served in comparative obscurity all your life, and never before heard of, your conduct on this occasion has been sufficient to establish your character as a brave, skilful, and attentive officer.

Lieutenant Chads was promoted to the rank of Commander, on which list he still continues.

CHAP. II.

1. .Debates in parliament on American war—Motions of Marquis Wellesley and Lord Darnley against ministers—Lord Melville's reply as to the state of the navy—Treaty with Sweden, and union of Sweden and Norway—Losses of the French in the Russian campaign—Letters of Admiral Tchitschagoff —Prussia and Austria join the allies—Successes of their arms —Lord Wellington defeats the French at Vittoria, and enters France—Capture of Cuxhaven, Stadt, and Gluckstadt—Position of the allied armies—Counter-revolution in Holland—Prince of Orange embarks on board the Warrior, and lands in his dominions.

2. *Channel.*—Capture of the Argus, American brig of war, by the Pelican—Capture of the Weser and Trave, French frigates—Defence, capture, and re-capture of the fortress of Castro.

3. *Mediterranean.*—Various gallant boat-services and attacks on the enemy—Noble conduct of Captain Black, in the Weazle—Attack on the Col de Belaguer—Storming of St. Sebastian—Capture of Fiume by Rear-admiral Freemantle—Operations in the Adriatic—Capture of Cattaro, D'Anzo, and Lucca —Attack on Leghorn fails.

4. *North America.*—Action between the Hornet and Peacock —Non-descript frigates sent out—Despondency of the British nation on the supposed decline of its marine—Action between the Shannon and Chesapeake—Observations on the clock-machines and torpedoes—Horrible plot of some Americans to blow up the Ramillies—Destruction of a lieutenant and ten seamen—Capture of the Boxer gun-brig—Death of Captain Blythe—Operations on the coast of North America conducted by Rear-admiral Cockburn—Destruction of Havre de Grace—Capture of Kent Island—Proceedings on the lakes —Actions with American flotilla—Capture of the British vessels Detroit and Queen Charlotte.

5. *West Indies.*—Successful voyage of Rear-admiral Durham to Barbadoes—Capture of the Alcmene and Iphigenie, French frigates—Action between the Amelia and Arethuse.

THE war with America was the question which engrossed the attention of the British parliament. On the 18th of February, Lord Castlereagh delivered to the house of commons a most able, luminous, and satisfactory account of the whole correspondence and the transactions which had led to the commencement of hostilities. His Lordship's speech was founded on the declaration of his Royal Highness the Prince Regent, dated on the 19th of January preceding. This declaration completely refuted and disproved every assertion of Mr. Madison, in his message to the senate of the 4th of November, 1812.

Lord Castlereagh observed " that the Americans, in their complaints against this country, had assumed, that Great Britain had impressed fifteen or twenty thousand citizens of the United States; but upon particular inquiry by the Admiralty it had appeared, that out of one hundred and forty-five thousand seamen employed in the British service in January, 1811, the whole number claiming to be American subjects, amounted to no more than three thousand three hundred, of whom not more than one in four could prove their citizenship; so that the real number would have been reduced to one thousand six hundred or one thousand seven hundred men," the whole of whom, his Lordship might have added, were discharged, as soon as their claims were proved. " Nor could the house of commons believe," said his Lordship, " that for such a consideration as one thousand seven hundred seamen, his Majesty's government would irritate the feelings of a neutral nation, or evade public justice." Having convinced the great. majority of the house of the moderation and propriety of the measures pursued by the government, his Lordship concluded, by moving an humble address to his Royal Highness the Prince Regent, assuring his Royal Highness of the entire approval of the resistance which had been opposed by the British government to the unjustifiable pretensions of America, being satisfied that those pretensions could not be admitted, without surrendering some of the most ancient, undoubted, and important rights of the British empire.

On the 12th of March, the Marquis Wellesley, no longer in office, made his motion relative to the retreat of the British army, under Lord Wellington, from Burgos, at the latter end of the preceding year; contending that Lord Wellington had not been supported by a sufficient supply of troops to enable him to face the enemy. His Lordship was answered by Earl Bathurst, and the Earl of Liverpool, and his motion lost by a great majority.

The motion of the Earl of Darnley, in the house of peers, on the 14th of May, met a similar fate. His Lordship, in calling the attention of the house to our naval disasters, on the coast of North America, particularly alluded to the action between the Peacock and Hornet. He disapproved of the small force on the coast of America, at the commencement of hostilities, when it had long been obvious that a war must ensue; and contended, that a force of five sail of the line, seventeen fri-gates, and an adequate number of small vessels, should have been stationed to blockade the ene-my's ports. His Lordship remarked on the length of time which had elapsed between the declaration of war on the part of America, on the 18th of June, and the granting of letters of marque and reprisals in this country, on the 13th of October, and ob-served, that more than two months elapsed after this last date before "any orders were given to blockade the Chesapeake and the Delaware, but Rhode Island *and* Newport remained open, and in the *last* the American frigate was refitted which took the Macedonian." Who would not suppose from this statement that these were two harbours? Yet we can affirm, that there is but one; New-port being the name of the town and harbour of Rhode Island. The licences granted by the Bri-tish government to the American commerce, were strongly and justly reprobated; and his Lordship concluded by saying, that a case had been made out loudly demanding investigation; the motion was seconded by Earl Stanhope.

Lord Melville contended, that although it was easy to foresee hostilities, yet a general opinion prevailed, that a revocation of the orders in coun-cil would have satisfied the American government. With respect to the lapse of time between their declaration of war and ours, the delay had been admitted, in hopes that America would have altered its determination. His Lordship denied that it was the duty of ministers to have kept a fleet always on the coast sufficient to have blockaded the ports: " the public service in other parts of the world," his Lordship said, " would not have admitted of it." With respect to the extraordinary dimensions of the American frigates, his Lordship said, and we think with very great propriety, " that we were not to alter the classes of ships in the British navy, merely to meet those of America; that it was far better to send out seventy-fours for that purpose." We are sorry this wise determination was ever departed from, by building or altering those non-descripts, of which we shall speak in another place. The motion of Earl Darnley was lost by a large majority, in favour of ministers.

On the 11th of June, the treaty then recently concluded between Great Britain and Sweden, was laid before Parliament. By this treaty it appeared, that the King of Sweden was to employ thirty thousand men in direct operation on the continent against the common enemy; they were to be commanded by the Prince Royal of Sweden, in concert with the troops of Russia. His Britannic Majesty acceded to the convention between these two powers, as far as it related to the annexation of Norway to Sweden, promising to afford his assistance, if necessary, towards the accomplishment of that object.

The reasons assigned for this arrangement were,

that the French government had occupied Swedish Pomerania, and menaced the empire of Russia. The contracting parties had engaged to make a diversion with from twenty-five to thirty thousand Swedes, and thirty-five thousand Russians, on some part of the coast of Germany ; but as the King of Sweden could not, consistently with the safety of his dominions, make such a diversion, while he must regard Norway as an enemy, the Emperor of Russia engaged either by negotiation, or by force, to unite Norway to Sweden. The King of Denmark was to be indemnified by territory on the south side of the Baltic, more contiguous to his dominions. Sweden received from us a subsidy of £1,000,000 sterling. Guadaloupe was ceded to her in full sovereignty, his Swedish Majesty granting to Great Britain, for twenty years, the right of entrepot in the ports of Gottenburg, Carlsham, and Stralsund, for all commodities, on an ad valorem duty of one per cent. The date of the treaty is the 24th of March, 1812.

Denmark and Norway were at first highly indignant at this transfer. Norway was disposed to resist; and, in consequence, her ports were declared, by a British order in council, of 1814, to be in a state of blockade ; but she soon after submitted, and the treaty was finally carried into effect, to the great regret of all who are acquainted with the manners, habits, and sentiments of that excellent people.

The year 1812 closed on Napoleon with the loss

in his Russian campaign of forty-one generals, one thousand two hundred and ninety-eight officers, one hundred and sixty-seven thousand men, and one thousand one hundred and thirty-one pieces of cannon. Memel, with immense stores, fell into the hands of the allies. The Prussian general, D'Yorck, with fifteen thousand men, was cut off from the French army, and compelled to remain neuter, and Prussia almost immediately became the enemy of France. On the 6th of January, 1813, Witgenstein, the Russian general, entered Konigsberg, the French flying in the utmost confusion, leaving behind their sick, cannon, and baggage. Tchitschagoff and Platoff entered Marienwerder, from which Murat and Victor narrowly escaped. The Russian Generals soon after took Marienburg and Elbing, and, crossing the Vistula, pursued the French in every direction. Platoff invested Dantzic. Napoleon, in the mean time, flying from his distressed army, as he had done in Egypt, got back to Paris, and directed his agents to make out the best story they could to tranquillize the public mind.

The following extracts of two letters written by Admiral Tchitschagoff, an officer of distinction greatly attached to this country, give in few words a perfect idea of the losses and the sufferings of the French army. This officer, though an admiral in the Russian service, acted on this occasion as a General, and we think with very great success:

Wilna, the $\frac{19}{27}$ December, 1812.

This was begun at · · · but could not be finished there; since that time I have been chasing Bonaparte till he got out of our frontiers. He has lost nearly all his guns, baggage, shot, and powder, and three-quarters of his army. He has saved himself, with some of his guards only; all the rest were left behind, in the most wretched state possible, famished, exhausted, and half frozen. The road he has passed is covered with dead—frozen or killed. I am sure there never was such a scene of human misery witnessed, as in the countries he has gone through. His ravages can hardly be described. His people have been burned in the very cottages they set fire to, or frozen in those in which they had destroyed doors and windows, and which otherwise might have served to shelter them. I hope he will not attempt any thing more against a country which is so strongly guarded by its position, and by its climate. The nation has shewn a great hatred for the French, and has strongly contributed to their expulsion. They were destroyed whenever the peasants could get at them. This campaign must have cost him at least three hundred thousand men, and certainly a great loss of confidence, and a diminution of that terror, which other nations had of him. If every one does his duty now, the world may be delivered of its tyrant, and every nation recover its independence.

St. Petersburg, the $\frac{1}{13}$ June, 1813.

The last time I wrote, I mentioned only that I had quitted the army without saying why. I can tell you something more of it now. Whilst I was coming from Moldavia to act with the troops that were to be opposed to Napoleon, who was already between me and Moscow and Petersburg, our communication was rather difficult, and therefore many people said what they thought about the state of my army, and greatly exaggerating our advantages over Bonaparte, reducing the number of the enemy, and augmenting mine, according to their own fancies. In short, it was so well managed, that on the point where I met Napoleon he was said to have had twenty thousand men, and about twenty-four guns only, and I eighty thousand men; but in fact he had one hundred and twenty thousand, and more than three hundred guns, when I had only twenty-five thousand to oppose him. The truth of this was proved afterwards at the place where I first met him at the passage of the river Beresina; there we found no less than thirty thousand bodies, and I made about as many prisoners, besides what were frozen upon the road from thence to Wilna, yet Napoleon passed with nearly fifty thousand through that town. The ignorant and the mischievous, at first clamorous, are now silent. The truth will be better known hereafter; but as I did not wish to expose myself to such stupid and absurd judges, I retired from the service.

Prussia and Austria once more joined the allies. The French evacuated Pomerania, and, retreating towards the Elbe with the swarm of Douaniers from the shores of the Baltic, were encountered by a Danish army. Morand, the French general, thus opposed and pursued, was glad to escape across the Elbe, leaving his cannon behind him. Hamburgh received General Tettenborne with open arms, on the 18th of March. The Russians and Prussians fought side by side against the French, at Lunenberg, which they took by storm, and made two thousand three hundred prisoners. Here General Morand was killed. Blucher was called to the head of the Prussian armies; and every hour brought fresh accounts of victory to the British capital; but the French, under Davoust, again got possession of Hamburgh, and grievous were the cruelties practised by that ferocious general. In the month of June, an armistice was concluded between the Emperor Alexander and Napoleon, affording both parties time to recruit their forces.

Hostilities recommenced in August, when the Austrian army took the field in favour of the

Allies. Tremendous conflicts succeeded before
Dresden, in which Napoleon had intrenched himself with one hundred and thirty thousand men.
An assault was made on the 27th of August.
General Moreau, who had joined the Allies, was
mortally wounded, and the loss on both sides was
considerable, without any decided results. On
the 30th, Vandamme was defeated at Kulm, by the
troops of Russia and Prussia, lost ten thousand
men, sixty pieces of cannon, and was himself,
with six of his generals, taken prisoner. Blucher
had, on the 22d, defeated Marshal Macdonald near
Goldberg, taking eighteen thousand prisoners, and
one hundred and three pieces of cannon. The
Crown Prince of Sweden, Bernadotte, with the
Swedish, Russian, and Prussian troops united,
defeated the French army of seventy thousand
men, under Marshal Ney, taking eighteen thousand
prisoners, four hundred waggons, and fifty pieces
of cannon.

Napoleon, in the month of October, concentrated
his forces in and about Leipsic, to the amount of
one hundred and eighty thousand men. On the
17th, 18th, and 19th, he fought the famous battles
in which he was utterly defeated; Leipsic was
taken, himself escaping only two hours before the
enemy got in.

In proportion as he lost ground in the north,
his prospects in the south became still more
desperate. The losses on the Elbe were supplied
in some degree by draughts from Spain, whence

he took near thirty thousand veteran troops, and this after the Marquis of Wellington had defeated King Joseph at Vittoria. That glorious victory was obtained on the 21st of June, when Joseph, with Marshal Jourdan and the great body of the French forces, were completely overthrown and dispersed, with the loss of baggage, cannon, provisions, treasure, waggons, and cattle. Joseph crossed the Bidassoa and entered France, followed by the victorious Wellington, who planted the British banners on "the sacred soil."

Captain Arthur Farquhar, of the Desirée, of thirty-six guns, had the command of the British vessels employed in the Elbe and Weser, and in the reduction of the fortress of Gluckstadt. The enemy was at that time flying from the neighbourhood of those rivers in the utmost confusion, pursued by the combined armies. Holland was effectually freed from the hated presence of the French soldiers.

By an order in council, dated the 27th of November, 1813, the blockade of the rivers Elbe, Weser, and Ems, was discontinued; the provinces of East Friesland, the state of Kniphausen, the duchy of Oldenburgh, and the duchy of Bremen, were declared to be no longer under the control of France. Bremerleehe, or Castleburgh, on the Weser, having a French garrison of two hundred and sixty men, and thirteen pieces of ordnance, surrendered to the combined British and Russian forces on the 23d of November. Captain Farquhar, in La Desirée, contributed to the capture of this place.

The French had been driven from Cuxhaven, and regained possession, more than once; but on this occasion, with the assistance of Captain Farquhar, their expulsion was final. The works were very strong: they had twenty-six heavy guns, and four thirteen-inch mortars, with a garrison of three hundred men. The city of Stadt, in the same river, was taken by the Russians. The army of the Crown Prince entered Holstein on the 28th of December. Davoust retreated on Hamburgh. Captain Farquhar, crossing the Elbe from Cuxhaven, ascended to Gluckstadt on the right bank, and co-operated with the Swedes in the reduction of that fortress, the siege and bombardment of which commenced on the 24th of December. Captain Farquhar's squadron lay in the river, and reduced the place to great distress: the assailing batteries fired red-hot shot, a mode of warfare very unusual with us, since the siege of Gibraltar. While the British naval force thus harassed the town by night and day, and had frequently set it on fire, a detachment of the army of the Crown Prince of Sweden sat down before it, and protected the batteries from a sortie. A British rocket corps assisted at the siege; and the place finally surrendered on the 4th of January, 1814. This event released the army of the Crown Prince from before a fortress, which he could not with safety have left in his rear, and enabled him to neutralize the army of Denmark by a suspension of hostilities.

Ten gun-boats and two sloops of war were taken from the enemy on this occasion. There were in this fortress two hundred pieces of cannon, with an immense quantity of military stores.

Thus the tide of war set strong against the Usurper's power: the Elbe, the Rhine, and the Bidassoa, the Danube, the Po, and the Guadalquiver, no longer controlled the advance of the conquerors; every boundary was passed, and France became a prey to foreign invaders, after having for twenty-two years desolated Europe. The armies of Russia, Prussia, and Austria, were ready to cross the Rhine in December, in the neighbourhood of Basle. The Allies commanded the Elbe and Weser; the Duke of Wellington at St. Jean de Luz, entered France between the sea and the Pyrenees; the Austrian armies were in Italy, on the shores of the Adriatic and the banks of the Mincio. The island of Schoenen surrendered to Lord George Stewart on the 7th of December, the French garrison becoming prisoners of war, and on the 9th his Lordship, with great promptitude, obtained possession of the island of Tholen, and its battery, commanding the entrance to the Keetan.

The fleet of France lying in the Scheldt at this time, consisted of—

Ships.		Guns.	
3	....of....,	80	half manned and equipped
4	....	80	in ordinary
8	....	74	partly manned and equipped
5	....	74	in ordinary
2	(frigates)	44	
12	gun-brigs.		

In Flushing—1 ship of eighty guns; 3 frigates of forty-four, not manned.

In the road of Flushing—4 frigates of forty-four guns, manned and ready for sea.

These ships were extremely ill put together, and not sea-worthy. We shall hereafter give an account of the farther disposal of them.

The North Sea fleet was commanded by Admiral Young, who had his flag in the Impregnable, of ninety-eight guns. He had with him fifteen sail of the line, and during the whole of the winter kept his station off the mouth of the Scheldt. On the 17th of December, Commodore Owen landed at Tergoes with a party of marines from the fleet, and distributed the proclamations of the Prince of Orange to his subjects. He was received with the loudest acclamations. The French garrisons every where retreated, and the Dutch flag displayed on all the forts, assured his Highness of a welcome reception. Thus, after all our efforts in favour of Holland, the time of her emancipation drew near. The Dutch, encouraged by the disasters of the French on the Elbe and Vistula, and the retreat of the army of Napoleon, threw off the yoke, and recalled his serene highness William, prince of Orange, now king of the Netherlands. The prince embarked on board the Warrior, of seventy-four guns, at Deal, on the 26th of November. The ship was commanded by Captain Lord Viscount Torrington. The Orange flag was hoisted at the main-topgallant-mast head, and saluted by the

Warrior, and all the ships in the Downs. The
prince sailed on the following day for his native
land, from which he had been an exile nineteen
years. On the 30th, the Warrior came in sight of
the coast of Holland, when they had the satisfaction to perceive the Dutch flag displayed on the
steeple of the Hague, and generally throughout
the country. The French, however, still held
the little fortress of the Brill; the prince therefore landed at Scheveling, where he was received
by his subjects with the most affecting marks of
returning attachment to a family from which they
derived their independence. The prince, soon
after his landing, presented Lord Torrington with
a gold-hilted sword, as a mark of his royal approbation.

In the Channel an action was fought between
two vessels of nearly equal force, the one British,
the other American. This action, immediately following that between the Shannon and Chesapeake,
completely restored the British navy to the good
opinion of its country, which it had most unde-
servedly lost.

Captain John Fordyce Maples, commanding
the Pelican, of eighteen guns (sixteen thirty-
two pounders, two long sixes), and one hundred
and twenty men, was ordered by Vice-admiral
Thornborough to cruise in the St. George's Channel, for the protection of the trade, and to seek
for an American sloop of war supposed to be on
the coast. On the 12th of August, at dawn of

day, Captain Maples got sight of the enemy, then setting fire to an English merchant-brig. Both vessels sought each other, and both were equally well prepared. The British vessel gave three cheers, and at half-past five, began a close and a bloody action, which continued forty-five minutes, when Captain Maples laid his brig alongside of the enemy, and was in the act of boarding as she hauled down her colours. She proved to be the American sloop of war Argus, of eighteen twenty-four pound carronades, and two long twelve pounders, having at the commencement of the action one hundred and twenty-seven men: of these about forty were killed or wounded, and among the latter their gallant and lamented commander, W. H. Allen, who died from the amputation of his left thigh, and was buried with every mark of respect at Plymouth. Two only were killed on board the Pelican, and five wounded. Captain Maples was promoted to the rank of post-captain, and was subsequently honoured with the junior order of the Bath.

The Weser, French frigate, of forty-four guns, and three hundred and forty men, was gallantly engaged by the Scylla and Royalist, commanded by the Captains M'Donald and Bremer. After watching, chasing, and fighting her for four days, she surrendered in the presence of Captain Cole, of the Rippon, of seventy-four guns. This frigate had left the Texel, in company with La Trave, of similar force, which was captured on the 25th of

the same month, by Captain Tobin, in the Andromache, of thirty-eight guns. Having been previously disabled in her masts and rigging, she had
no prospect of escaping, and struck her colours
very soon after the action began.

The defence of the sea-port town of Castro, on
the north coast of Spain, although it ended in the
surrender of that place to the French army of
thirteen thousand men, was so honourable to the
British and Spanish arms, that we shall give a few
of the particulars, as stated in the official letter of
Captain R. Bloye, of the Lyra, to Lord Keith. The
enemy had been twice repulsed from its walls,
when they again appeared before it in the month
of April. It was at that time a place of no strength;
the garrison consisted of an irregular body of Spanish royalists, under the command of Don P. D'Al-
varez, who, after having made a vigorous sortie,
was reduced to act solely on the defensive; in this
he was ably assisted by Captain Bloye, who had
under his orders the Sparrow and Royalist brigs
of war. On the 7th of May, the French had established a battery to the westward of the town, and
a twenty-four pound carronade was landed from
the Sparrow, on a small island, within point-blank
shot. On the following morning, the two adverse
batteries began to fire on each other; and the single gun of the Sparrow was directed with so much
effect, as to render the embrasures of the enemy
untenable. The Spaniards, in the castle, plied
them at the same time with continued discharges

of artillery. The enemy approached in another position, and brought a heavy gun within one hundred yards of the castle; to counteract which, a twelve pounder was mounted by the British seamen; but it unfortunately burst, after a few discharges. The Spaniards, encouraged by the presence of their allies, defended the place with obstinacy; while the French seized every opportunity of adding to their number of troops and battering train, by sea and land conveyance from Santona and Portugalette. Off the latter place, Captain Bloye directed the Royalist and Sparrow to watch by turns, while he remained to afford assistance to the besieged; every effort on the side of the French was met by a corresponding movement on that of the allies; but numbers at length gained the day. A practicable breach was effected in the walls; and at nine o'clock at night, three thousand men rushed into the town, through the breach, and over the walls. They were received with firmness, and every inch of ground disputed from house to house, until the garrison were driven into the castle, whence they embarked in the British boats by companies, under showers of musketry, and reached the Lyra, Royalist, Sparrow, and Alphea schooner. While this was going on, the enemy endeavoured to enter the castle, but were kept out until all the guns were thrown into the sea; they however got in before the train was fired, which would have blown the castle down; but not before every soldier, and

most of the inhabitants, were embarked in safety
by the British officers, and their intrepid seamen
and marines.

Captains Bloye, Bremer, and Taylor, received
the greatest praise for their good conduct at this
siege.

The French having gained possession of the
place, committed barbarities too shocking to be
detailed; but did not long enjoy their conquest.
The British cruisers intercepted all the supplies;
and on the 22d of June, the French garrison were
forced to retire to Santona. Captain Taylor, of
the Sparrow, seeing this movement, took possession of the castle, without giving them time to
destroy the works and artillery, which they attempted to do. Fourteen prisoners, who were
taken in the place, were carried to Bilboa, and
there executed by the Spanish authorities, as a
punishment for their cruelty to the innocent inhabitants of Castro.

Among the young officers who distinguished
themselves on the coast of Spain, the name of
Captain Timothy Scriven deserves to be recorded.
This officer, in a schooner called the Telegraph, of
sixteen guns and sixty men, attacked, on the 13th
of October, the French national corvette, Flibustier,
of twenty guns, and one hundred and sixty men,
then lying at anchor under the batteries of Bayonne,
and so near the shore as to enable the Frenchmen
to save themselves in their boats, after a severe
action of three-quarters of an hour, having set their

vessel on fire. The boats of the Telegraph boarded instantly, but could not save her from the flames; she mounted sixteen twenty-four pounders, two long nines, a brass howitzer, and four brass three pounders. She was bound to Santona, and had on board treasure, arms, and ammunition, for the relief of that garrison.

In the month of January, Captain William Hoste, of the Amphion, sent Lieutenants O'Brien and Hood, with Lieutenant Haig of the royal marines, to attack a division of gun-boats off Otranto. They boarded and captured five sail, armed with heavy guns, and manned with from thirty to forty men each.

The boats of the Havannah frigate, Captain the Honourable G. Cadogan, were sent, in the month of February, to attack a convoy of twenty-five sail, which had taken refuge under some guns. Lieutenant Lumley, who commanded the party, destroyed the battery, and took, sunk, or burnt four gun-boats, and the whole of the vessels collected. This convoy was from Venice, laden with ordnance stores.

In the same month, Captain Tritton, in the Kingfisher sloop of war, captured one armed trabaccoli, and drove nine on shore, which were totally destroyed, on the island of Corfu; and in the following month, Captain Cadogan destroyed a large trabaccoli, carrying three nine pounders, and small arms. The next morning, the 23d, he captured five other armed trabaccolis, and destroyed five feluccas.

Captains Napier and Mounsey, in the Thames and Furieuse frigates, with a body of troops, consisting only of the second battalion of the 10th regiment of infantry, took the little island of Ponza, near Naples. This island has a small harbour, about a quarter of a mile in breadth, and a mole, which was defended by ten pieces of heavy cannon, and two nine-inch howitzers. Waiting till the wind suited, Captain Napier ran the two ships in, and anchored across the mole-head, sustaining the fire from the enemy for half an hour, before their position enabled the British ships to return a shot; but the moment the guns could be brought to bear, the ships engaged on both sides, while Colonel Coffin landed, and marched directly for a tower on the heights, to which the enemy had retreated, and whence they sent down a flag of truce to say that they had surrendered.

The Honourable Captain G. G. Waldegrave, in the Volontaire, destroyed some strong batteries at Morgion, near Cape Croisette, landing his marines and seamen at Sormion, under the command of Lieutenant Isaac Shaw. That young officer ascended the hills, came on the forts in the rear, and took them after a short resistance. In one fort were five thirty-six pounders, in the other two twenty-four pounders; he threw the guns over the cliffs into the sea, spiked a mortar, destroyed the ammunition, and took the lieutenant and his guard prisoners. While the first lieutenant was thus employed, Lieutenant Sayer, of the same ship, though opposed by two field-pieces, boarded and took eleven sail of vessels laden with oil, and burned three others.

Captain Thomas Usher, of the Undaunted, destroyed the battery of Carey, near Marseilles. Lieutenant Tozer, with a party, landed, and drove the enemy from their palisadoes, took four twenty-four pounders, a six pounder, and a thirteen-inch mortar.

Captain Edward Brace, of the Berwick, of seventy-four guns, in company with Captain Napier (removed from the Thames to the Euryalus), attacked a convoy of the enemy at Cavalacci. Lieutenant Sweedland, first of the Berwick, with Captain Mathews, of the royal marines, landed, gained possession of the fort, and turned the guns on the convoy, and an armed xebec. The latter only attempted to escape, but Captain Napier pushed the Euryalus so close in shore, as to cut her off. She mounted ten long nine pounders, and had ninety-five men, who reached the shore. Twenty-two vessels, of different descriptions, found in the harbour, were either taken or destroyed, the guns spiked, and every thing worth bringing away was embarked.

Captain Charles Adam, of the Invincible, acting in conjunction with the Baron de Erroles, attacked the ports of Ampollo and Perello. Two of his

boats armed with carronades, and a Spanish felucca, were sent under the orders of Lieutenant
Corbyn, first of the Invincible, to attack Ampollo,
which they surprised, killed the centinel, and turned the two eighteen pounders in the tower on the
guard-house.   The guard fled to Perello, which,
though at two leagues distance, was taken by the
same officer, and a detachment from the Spanish
army. Two small privateers, which had been
highly useful to the enemy, were taken; and his
means of communication with the Col de Belaguer,
a strong fortress near Barcelona, were considerably
abridged.

In the month of May, the enemy had again
fortified the post of Morgion; and again it was
attacked, under the orders of Captain Moubray, of
the Repulse; of seventy-four guns, who directed
Lieutenant Shaw, of the Volontaire, to land, accompanied by Captain Ennis, of the royal marines,
and one hundred men of that corps; the boats of
the Undaunted, and a party of men from that ship;
together with the launches, armed with carronades.
This force, with the same valour and promptitude
as on the former occasion, took the fort, spiked
and destroyed the guns, and brought away six
vessels with cargoes.

The island of Augusta, on the coast of Dalmatia,
and not far from Lissa, surrendered to Captain
B. W. Taylor, of the Apollo, and Lieutenant-colonel Robertson, with two hundred and fifty infantry.
The same force took Carzolo. They also captured

seven vessels, laden with grain; and retook all the church plate, and other valuable property, which the French of the republican school had shipped to carry away. This was, of course, restored to its proper owners.

In the month of April, Captain James Black, in the Weazle brig, of eighteen guns, discovered a convoy close to the land off the island of Zirona, making for the ports of Tran and Spolatro. Seeing the British vessel in chase of them, they separated; the greater part, with ten gun-boats, bore away for the bay of Roscalini, and at half-past five, A. M. anchored in a line about a mile from the shore, and hoisted French colours, the wind blowing strong at S. E., directly into the bay. At six o'clock, A. M., the Weazle was brought to anchor, with springs on her cable, within pistol-shot, and engaged them for twenty minutes, when the enemy cut their cables, and ran closer in shore. Here they again anchored, and renewed the action: Captain Black cut, and followed. Three heavy guns now opened on the Weazle, and two or three hundred small-arm men from the heights above their heads. The action continued with fury till ten o'clock, when three of the gun-boats struck their colours, two were driven on shore, and one sunk. Four more gun-boats now came down to their assistance, and anchoring outside of the Weazle, obliged her to engage on both sides; but these soon after ran in, and joined the others; and the whole eight, from behind a point of land, whence their mast-heads only could be perceived from the Weazle's decks, covered her with grape-shot. The day was going hardly with the British vessel, five of her men were killed, and twenty wounded; with difficulty she could man four guns, and keep a few seamen and marines at the small arms; still the gallant Chief continued the fight till three, p. m., although his grape-shot had long been expended. The enemy ceased firing for forty minutes, and then began again, and continued without intermission till half-past six in the evening: the firing now entirely ceased on both sides. During the day, the enemy had received considerable supplies of troops, who kept up an incessant fire upon the Weazle. The sloop was almost a wreck, within a few yards of a lee-shore, not a rope or sail but what was cut to pieces, her masts crippled, many shot in her hull, five between wind and water, both pumps shot away between decks, and with difficulty she could be kept free by constantly baling at both hatchways. Would not many a brave officer have been deemed to have performed his duty nobly, had he, under these difficulties, been content to keep his ship from falling into the hands of the enemy? But Captain Black thought nothing was done while the French flag was flying in his presence. At dark, he sent in his boats, and burned, besides the gun-boats, eight sail of the convoy, bringing out their anchors and cables for the use of the Weazle, and without which she would in all probability have gone on shore, as her own were shot to pieces. All night the laborious crew were employed in warping their vessel out from the land, from which, at daylight, on the 23d of April, they were distant only one mile, when they were again attacked by the remaining gun-boats, who took a raking position; nor could the broadside of the Weazle be brought to bear upon them. The whole of this day, and the succeeding night, was passed in warping out.

On the 24th, a battery was still to be passed, and the brig still warping out. This opened upon them about noon, and the gun-boats began again to rake them astern, while musketry from the shore flew thick about them; nor was it till five o'clock in the afternoon of the third day, that the gun-boats ceased firing, and the Weazle was safe out of the bay. Captain Black was himself among the wounded, as was Mr. Whally, his first lieutenant. What might not be expected from such men in a ship of the line?

Captain Charles Adam, in the Invincible, was directed by Rear-admiral Hallowell, to co-operate with Lieutenant-colonel Prevost, in the siege of the Col de Belaguer, on the road between Tortosa and Tarragona. It is situated in a most difficult pass, and the only way by which cannon could be brought into Catalonia, without going round by Lerida. It was at that time armed with twelve pieces of cannon, and surrounded by heights almost impassable, but on which these officers contrived to establish their batteries.

The force intended for the investment, consisted of the riflemen of De Rolles' regiment, and some other light troops, which were landed from the Invincible, on the 3d of June, with four pieces of artillery. These being mounted on the heights, were placed under the command of Lieutenant Corbyn, of the Invincible, who, with a detachment of seamen from the ship, kept up an admirable fire, diverting the attention of the enemy from another party of the besiegers, who had landed five twenty-four pounders. Captain W. F. Carroll, of the Volcano bomb, and the seamen and marines from the ships of war, were incessantly employed in getting the heavy guns up the heights, and completing the breaching battery; and by the evening of the 5th, two eight-inch mortars, and two twenty-four pounders, were brought to the foot of the hill, with a large quantity of ammunition. It was not till the morning of the 7th, that the two mortars began to play, supported by the battery of Lieutenant Corbyn; and at seven in the morning, the Governor, seeing the perseverance of his enemies, surrendered, on condition of being allowed to march out with the honours of war.

The siege of Tarragona, and the progress of the British arms in the neighbourhood of that place, was checked in the month of June; and circumstances of a nature peculiarly unpleasant between the two services occurred, on the embarkation of the British troops. As entering into details on this subject, would naturally lead to a renewal of a controversy, now happily terminated, we pass over with more than usual precipitation that part of the Peninsular history, trusting to the candour of the future military historian to do justice at least to the exertions of the navy, and particularly to those of Rear-admiral Sir Benjamin Hallowell.

On the north coast of Spain, the enemy continued to lose ground, being forced by the Spaniards and English to evacuate the fortress of Guitaria, together with the castle, town, and port of Passages.

The siege and storming of St. Sebastian, forms one of the most brilliant epochs of the Peninsular war. The British army, in its rapid progress towards the confines of Spain, was forced to reduce this strong hold, which, both by land and sea, was highly important to the cause of the allied armies. The island of Santa Clara, lying at the mouth of the harbour, and close to the town, was stormed on the night of the 26th of September, by a party of seamen, marines, and infantry, under the orders of Captain Cameron, of the 9th regiment, and Lieutenant the Honourable James Arbuthnot, of the Surveillante, assisted by Captain Henderson, of the royal engineers, Lieutenant Bell, of the royal marines, and Captain John Smith, of the Beagle. The only landing place lay under a flight of steps, commanded by a small intrenchment thrown up on the west point, and completely exposed to the fire of grape-shot from the whole range of works on the west side of the walls of the town. This strong and important little post, was

defended by one officer and twenty-four men,
who, assisted by the fire from the town, killed
two of the assailants, and wounded seventeen,
after which they surrendered; and the approaches
of the British army, under the Duke of Wellington,
were considerably facilitated by this gallant exploit. Breaches had been made in the walls of
St. Sebastian, on the 30th of August. On the
31st, two divisions of boats from the ships of war
in the bay, having been previously arranged for
the purpose, under the command of the Captains
Galway of the Dispatch, and Bloye of the Lyra,
made a feint to attack the back of the rock, which,
as had been anticipated, diverted a great part of
the enemy's force from the point really assailed.
The sloops of war weighed at the same time, with
a slight breeze; and the Dispatch and the boats
received a heavy fire from the batteries. As the
tide fell, the British troops, under Sir James Leith,
advanced to the assault; and, after a murderous
struggle in the breach, the town of St. Sebastian
was carried. The citadel, into which the garrison
retreated, still held out. Among the naval officers
most distinguished for their share in this memorable siege, were Captains R. Bloye and John Smith,
the Lieutenants the Honourable James Arbuthnot
and O'Reilly, of the Surveillante. Ships of the
line could not be brought near enough to act with
effect, or find safe anchorage. The frigates lay
out of gun-shot. The sloops of war and gun-boats
only could bring their fire upon the works. The

ships which were employed upon that service
were—

Ships.	Guns.	Commanders.
Surveillante	44	Captain G. R. Collier
Revolutionnaire	44	
President	44	
Magicienne	36	
Andromache	32	

[The five frigates at anchor off St. Sebastian.]

Ships.	Guns.	Commanders.	Where stationed.
Sparrow	16	Captain Taylor	Off the Bidassoa
Lyra	16	—— Bloye	In the harbour of St. Sebastian
Beagle	18	—— J. Smith	In the harbour of St. Sebastian
Dispatch	18	—— Galway	Off the mouth of the Bidassoa
Challenger	16		

Constant gun-brig, Lieutenant Stokes, and Nimble cutter, in
the Bidassoa, with some schooners and gun-boats.

The castle of La Motte, or citadel of St. Sebastian, capitulated on the 10th of September, to
Lieutenant-general Sir Thomas Graham, after a
bombardment from fifty-four pieces of ordnance.
One thousand seven hundred men were made
prisoners.

The capture of San Sebastian, at that season of
the year, was important to the farther operations
of the war; and the small but repeated disasters of
the French flotilla, from Trieste to the Texel, produced a vast difference in the general result of the
Peninsular campaigns.

Fiume, in thé Adriatic, from its commercial
importance, and military strength, attracted the
attention of Rear-admiral Fremantle, who, in the

month of May, collected a squadron to attack the
place.   The ships were the Milford, seventy-four
guns, flag; Elizabeth, seventy-four; Eagle, seventy-four, Captain Charles Rowley; Bacchante,
forty-four, Captain William Hoste; and Haughty,
gun-brig.   The Rear-admiral anchored off Fiume,
on the evening of the 2d.   The Eagle silenced a
battery to which she was opposed, and the signal
being made to storm, Captain Rowley, in his gig,
led the first division of marines to the attack, and
hoisted the British colours on the battery, while
Captain Hoste, with the marines of the squadron,
spiked the guns of another fort, which had been
silenced by the Milford and Bacchante.   Captain
Rowley, leaving a party of marines to turn the
guns of the battery he had taken against those
which still held out, with the remainder of his
men, entered the town, receiving the fire of the
inhabitants and military from the windows and
tops of the houses, and a field-piece placed in the
centre of the great street.   The Lieutenants Lloyd
and Nepean, with the marines and seamen, attacked this gun, and the enemy retreated with it
until they came to the great square, when they
made a stand, taking post in a large house.   At
this moment Captain J. D. Markland came up,
with the boats of the squadron, armed with carronades, and opened his fire on the house, when
the enemy fled in every direction out of the town.
Captain Hoste joining with his division that under
Captain Rowley, the conquest of the place was

complete. The two remaining batteries were taken. The Governor, and every officer and man of the garrison having run away, the public stores, and all the shipping in the harbour, fell into the hands of the conquerors. It should be recorded, that although the place was taken by storm, no violence was offered to the peaceable inhabitants; nor were they plundered of any article of their private property. Ninety vessels were taken, but the smaller ones were restored. Great quantities of ordnance, ammunition, and provisions, were brought away or destroyed. Porto Ré and Ormagro suffered the same fate; and Captain Harper, in the Saracen, sloop of war, took the island of Zapano by surprise, making prisoners the greater part of the garrison. In July, Captain Rowley, with the boats and marines of his own ship, took the fortress of Farasina: the storming party was led by the Lieutenants Greenaway and Hotham, and Lieutenant Lloyd, of the marines. The Honourable Captain Cadogan, in the Havannah, frigate, captured another convoy of ten sail of vessels, under the town of Vasto. This service was conducted by his first lieutenant, Mr. Hambley.

In the month of August, Captain Usher, of the Undaunted, with the Captains Coghlan, Sir John Sinclair, and the Honourable R. Spencer, attacked the batteries of Cassio, near Marseilles, which they took by storm, destroyed them, and brought out from the mole, or burnt, all the vessels they found there. The citadel battery was carried by escalade by Captain Coghlan,* and the marines, who drove the French before them at the point of the bayonet. Two large gun-boats were taken, and one destroyed, with twenty-five sail of vessels. Captain R. H. Mowbray, of the Repulse, landed the marines, under the command of Lieutenant Harris and Captain Innis of that corps, and took the town of Vernazza, burning five vessels lying in the harbour.

In the same month the Austrians entered Fiume, and established a communication between their army and our squadron.

The small actions in the Adriatic, which occurred so frequently during the latter part of the war, become too numerous to admit of being severally detailed. The boats of the Apollo, Cerberus, and Bacchante, in the course of the summer, nearly annihilated the trade of the gulf of Venice. Rear-admiral Fremantle, who had the command in that division of the Mediterranean, remained in St. George's harbour, in the island of Lissa, detaching and spreading his active cruisers in every direction.

* It has been stated in the second volume of this work, that Captain Coghlan was impressed into the service. This is incorrect; he was induced to enter into the navy by the persuasion of Lord Exmouth, who, when the Dutton, Indiaman, was wrecked in Plymouth Sound, saw and justly appreciated the merits of this singularly gallant and deserving officer. Captain Coghlan belonged at that time to a merchant-vessel lying at Plymouth, and had been one of the first to get on board the Dutton to save the crew.

The boats of the Cerberus, Captain T. Garth, conducted by Lieutenant John Wm. Montagu, with Lieutenant Nares, attacked eleven gun-boats supported by soldiers on the cliffs, and took two of them by boarding. Captain Hoste, in the Bacchante, chased a large convoy off Guila Nova : these consisted of ten gun-boats and fourteen sail of merchant vessels : they anchored or grounded, and the beach a-stern of them was lined with musketry, and two field-pieces. From these the boats sustained a heavy fire until they were fairly alongside of their enemy, when the crews were driven from the vessels with great loss, and the whole were taken or destroyed.

Rear-admiral Fremantle wrote to Sir Edward Pellew, the Commander-in-chief of the Mediterranean fleet, acquainting him with the fortunate events which had put us and our allies in possession of the coast of the Adriatic. "The Imperial flag," he says, "was flying on the whole coast of Istria, and Croatia was almost entirely up in arms against the French; Ligne, Porto Ré, and Fiume, had the Austrian flag flying." The Croats in the French army hearing of the success of the Austrians, changed their character, and became our allies. One thousand five hundred were marching with six hundred French troops from Pola to relieve Fiume, when the Croats rose on the French, made them prisoners, and sent them to General Nugent, who commanded the Austrians at Fiume.

The people of Croatia swore never more to admit the French into their country : one hundred and fifty of them in garrison at Lusin spiked the guns, obliged the French commander to pay them their arrears, and then sent the French.garrison to Istria, giving up the island of Lusin to the natives and from Lissa to Trieste the islands were nearly clear of the French.

The daring Captain Black, of the Weazle, surprised the garrison of Ragosniza, with the boats of the Milford and his own : he left the ships after dark, when seven leagues from the land, and having passed the sea battery unperceived, landed at the back of the island, and at daylight the enemy heard their cheers, and saw them on the hill above their heads. Captain Black and his men rushed down, took their fort, which was open in the rear, and in which they found six twenty-four pounders, and two seven and a half-inch howitzers. A captain, subaltern, and sixty soldiers, were taken prisoners, and the boats returned to their ships. Captains C. Rowley and Hoste, in the Eagle and Bacchante, took Rovigno, on the 2d of August, destroying the forts, and burning, sinking, or bringing away every vessel in the harbour.

Captain the Honourable G. Cadogan, burnt or took seven sail of gun-boats, and armed merchant-vessels, on the coast of Manfredonia. In the month of November, Captains Harper and Black, in the Saracen and Weazle brigs, landed, and took the island of Mezzo, near Ragusa. This conquest was effected by the marines and seamen, who, headed by their captains, after infinite labour, mounted some guns (which they carried with them) on the top of a rocky mountain, whence they commanded the castle.

Rear-admiral Fremantle had now by his able measures and active co-operation with Count Nugent, the Austrian general, established the Allies in every strong post on the coasts of Istria and Dalmatia. On the 21st of September he arrived at Capo d'Istria, at the head of the Adriatic, and soon after proceeded to Trieste, leaving the Elizabeth, of seventy-four guns, off Dwino. While the Milford, at Trieste, lay at anchor, with her stern near the shore, the Rear-admiral was surprised by the French opening a masked battery on the ship with a field-piece and a howitzer. Captain Markland got springs on his cables, hove his broadside to the shore, and in a quarter of an hour demolished the battery. A shell exploded on the poop of the Milford, but did no damage. After this, Captain Markland was sent on shore with the marines, and in conjunction with Count Nugent, laid siege to the castle of Izonzo, against which they established two batteries, mounting twelve guns, and from which a heavy fire was kept up the whole day. The enemy was driven from a post called the Windmill, which was immediately occupied by the Austrians.

Captain C. Rowley had advanced a long thirty-

two pounder to within two hundred yards of the
Spanza, a strong building with one gun, and loop-
holes for musketry, which stood on a hill, with a
wall fourteen feet high surrounding it. On firing
the first shot from the thirty-two pounder, the
ground gave way, and the gun fell six feet below
the platform. It was fine to see (says the honest
Admiral, in his dispatch) Captain Rowley and his
people immediately get a triangle above the work,
and the heavy gun with its carriage run up to its
place again, in the midst of a shower of grape and
musketry, which did considerable mischief, and
occasioned severe loss to our brave men; but the
perseverance of Captain Rowley was crowned
with success. The enemy surrendered the Spanza:
and the castle soon followed. This place was
very strong, and garrisoned by eight hundred
Frenchmen; mounted forty-five large guns, forty
mortars, and four howitzers. Thus, by the timely
co-operation of the British squadron with the
Austrians, these fruitful provinces were liberated
from oppression. The British Rear-admiral and
the Austrian General, mutually praised each other.
The number of British seamen killed, amounted
only to ten, and of the wounded to thirty-five.
The number of merchant-vessels taken in the harbour was fifty; and Trieste was, by the aid of
Britain, once more restored to the house of Austria.

Although the scale, of naval war was not extensive in point of numbers engaged, or the force
employed, the Adriatic produced in the year 1813

the most interesting scenes, in the display of valour, of resources, and of discomfiture to our inve-
terate enemy. The islands on the eastern shore of
the gulf of Venice are numerous, strongly fortified,
and afford excellent anchorage. Bonaparte was
aware of the advantages of such a country. The
coasts of Istria, Croatia, Dalmatia, Albania, and
Greece, supplied soldiers to the French army,
seamen to her fleet, and naval stores for her ships
of war. From Trieste to Corfu on the east side,
and from Venice to the point of Otranto on the
west, the trade was carried on with vigour by the
enemy, and opposed with the most daring enterprise, and the completest success, by the British
cruisers. Of this we have already adduced proofs;
but more remain yet to be told.

Captain Hoste, in the Bacchante, whose name
has so often appeared in the annals of the Mediterranean, arrived off Ragusa on the 12th of
October, where he joined Captain Harper, in the
Saracen, and a detachment of troops under the
command of Captain Lowen. With this little
force Captain Hoste forced the narrow passage
between Castel Nuovo and the fort of Rosa, and
found excellent anchorage three miles above the
first-named place. Captain Harper most gallantly
attacked and took the island of St. George, making
the whole garrison prisoners. The capture of
this post was highly important to farther successes; it commanded the approach to the town
of Cattaro, a strong place belonging to the Ve-

netians. The forts of Rosas and Castel Nuovo, in
the Bocca de Cattaro, surrendered by capitulation,
and the French had nothing left but Fort St. John,
about fifteen miles up the river. Into this they
retreated with six hundred men.

Farther to the north-west lies the excellent port
and castle of Zara, which, in the month of December, surrendered to the Honourable Captain
G. Cadogan, in the Havannah, with a sloop of war
(not named by the Admiral), and a party of Austrian troops. The castle stood a bombardment of
thirteen days from the batteries erected against it
by the allies; and in his dispatches, Rear-admiral
Fremantle says, "Captain Cadogan, with the
crews of a frigate and sloop of war, has accomplished as much as required the services of the
squadron united at Trieste."

Two attacks on the enemy's vessels, by British
officers and boats from the ships of war, deserve
to be recorded. Captain E. S. Dickson, of the
Swiftsure, of seventy-four guns, sent Lieutenant
William Smith, with the boats of that ship, in
pursuit of a French privateer. The enemy was
cool and collected, well manned and prepared: he
reserved his fire until the boats had begun, when
a bloody ad desperate conflict of ten minutes
terminated in victory on our side, but was purchased with the lives of a gallant officer and four
men: four officers and eleven men were wounded.
The loss of the enemy was about equal. The
name of the vessel was the Charlemagne, of eight

guns, and ninety-three men, stored for a six months' cruise.

Captain E. R. Sibley, of the Swallow, sloop of war, sent his boats under the command of Lieutenant S. E. Cook, in chase of a privateer, off the mouth of the Tiber; and although the vessel ran close under D'Ango, and was supported by numerous batteries, and two gun-boats, they boarded and carried her, keeping her in tow until she was brought out. She was called La Guerrière, mounted four guns and had sixty men.

D'Anzo was taken on the 5th of October, by Captain G. H. L. Dundas, in the Edinburgh, of seventy-four guns, assisted by Captain the Honourable H. Duncan, in the Imperieuse, with the Resistance, thirty-eight, Swallow, Eclair, and Pylades, sloops of war. The ships were brought against the batteries with great judgment, and a storming party landing at the same moment, the enemy fled, after a short resistance, leaving twenty-nine sail of vessels in the mole, which were brought out without any loss: twenty of them were laden with timber for the dock-yard at Toulon. This successful enterprise seems to have been attributed with much justice to Lieutenant Trevers, of the Imperieuse, who, in a very gallant manner a few nights before, had, with a boat's crew, stormed a tower of one gun, and brought away the guard, from whom he acquired the information which led to the attack. Captain William Mounsey, of the Furieuse performed an exploit of a similar nature at Marinelo, where a convoy of nineteen sail were observed at anchor. This place is about six miles to the eastward of Civita Vechia: here he attacked them, and under the fire of batteries and five hundred troops, brought out fourteen sail, and sank two, with the loss of twelve men killed and wounded. One of these vessels was a gun-boat, carrying a long brass twenty-four pounder, and four swivels: two others were armed vessels; and the rest laden with merchandise.

On the 5th of November, the British fleet under the command of Sir Edward Pellew, had a slight action with that of Toulon. Our ships had been blown off in a gale, and standing in shore towards Cape Sicie. The enemy's fleet of fourteen sail of the line, and seven frigates, was seen coming out with the wind at E.N.E. They were between Cape Bruno and Cape Carcaviene. A sudden shift of wind to N.W. gave Sir Edward Pellew a prospect of bringing their rear to action. The Caledonia, Boyne, and San Josef, were some distance a-head, and would probably have cut off a three-decker with a Rear-admiral's flag flying, but the wind headed them, and they could not fetch nearer than to exchange some distant shot, and the enemy got back into the harbour of Toulon. The Caledonia, San Josef, Scipion, Boyne, Pompée, and Pembroke, had each two or three men wounded: one man was killed by accident. Sir Edward Pellew says, in his public dispatch, that he should have thought the affair not worth mentioning, had he not been convinced that it would be grossly misrepresented in the columns of the Moniteur.

If France was daily losing ground on the continent, she owed it in a great measure to the loss of her fleets. Her coasts, now defenceless, offered an almost unresisting prey to the first invader. Distracted with numerous and incessant calls for assistance, their armies knew not which way to turn. The naval force of Britain, so multiplied and so expert from long practice, had acquired an intimate knowledge of their harbours, their bays, and creeks: our officers knew the depth of water, and the resistance likely to be met with in every situation.

Early in December, Captain Josias Rowley, in the America, of sixty-four guns, collected a squadron, consisting of the Armada, of seventy-four, Edinburgh, of seventy-four, Imperieuse and Furieuse, of forty-four, Mermaid, of thirty-two, and Termagant, of eighteen guns. On board of these ships he embarked an Italian levy of one thousand men, commanded by Colonel Catanelli, an officer whose valour appears highly conspicuous amidst the degradation of his country. With this force Captain Rowley attacked Via Reggio, landed the troops and field-pieces; drove the enemy from the town, and took the batteries. Colonel Catanelli pushed to Lucca, which he took the same night. Captain Rea, of the royal marines, with forty of

his men, took a strong castle to the northward of
Reggio, walled, ditched, and regularly fortified.
This place was capable of holding one thousand
men. Captain Rowley ordered it to be destroyed,
and it was blown up. Colonel Catanelli having
returned with his men from Lucca, was attacked
on the evening of the 12th by a column of six
hundred French troops, cavalry and infantry, from
Leghorn. These he completely routed, taking
from them three field-pieces and howitzers; killing,
wounding, and making many prisoners. Supposing they could reach Leghorn by sea, before
this party could return to it by land, Captain
Rowley and the Colonel agreed to proceed thither
immediately, and arrived on the following day at
three o'clock, when a part of their troops and guns
were landed without opposition, but bad weather
prevented them from getting the remainder on
shore. By this time the corps of the enemy, which
had been defeated at Via Reggio, having been re-
inforced, came up, and attacked the marines and
seamen of the squadron under the orders of the
Honourable Captain Dundas, of the Edinburgh,
by whom the enemy was completely defeated; but
the attack on Leghorn failed, owing to the strength
of the fortifications, and an overpowering French
force within the walls : the troops and seamen
were therefore re-embarked, during a temporary
suspension of hostilities.

In North America, we have at the commencement
of the year 1813 one more melancholy action to

relate. It was fought between a British and an American sloop of war, in which the latter was victorious. We shall never attempt to diminish the credit due to an enemy, where no false claim is set up by him. Captain Lawrence was a gallant young officer; but his assertion respecting his *blockading* the Bonne Citoyenne must receive the most formal contradiction. Captain Pitt Burnaby Green, had he had no more than the Hornet to contend with, would have taken her, or perished in the attempt; but his duty forbade his engaging the Hornet, while the Constitution was looking on. The correspondence upon this subject is printed at large in the Naval Chron. 1813; vol. i.

After the destruction of the Java, the Constitution and the Hornet continued till January off St. Salvador, when they separated; and Captain Lawrence says, he was driven from the blockade of the Bonne Citoyenne by a British seventy-four. He next proceeded off Demerara, and on the 24th of February, 1813, fell in with the British brig of war Peacock, of eighteen guns, commanded by Captain William Peake. The force of the Peacock was sixteen thirty-two pound carronades, and two long sixes, with one hundred and twenty men and boys: that of the Hornet was eighteen thirty-two pound carronades, two long twelves, and a complement of one hundred and forty men. This we believe to have been nearly the force of the two vessels: the tonnage about equal. Captain Peake, without a moment's hesitation, brought his enemy to action. The American captain received him with valour and steady courage, laid the Peacock on board on the starboard quarter, and by a superior fire killed her captain, and about thirty of her men. In fifteen minutes the action was concluded, the Peacock struck, and made the signal of distress. The Americans were very active in saving the wounded; but after bringing both vessels to an anchor, the Peacock went down in five and a half fathoms water, taking with her thirteen of her own crew, and three of the Americans. For his conduct in this action, Captain Lawrence received the merited praises of his countrymen: he was soon after removed to the command of the Chesapeake, that ill-fated ship, the continued source of disaster to her country.

No sooner were these defeats of our frigates and sloops of war known in England, than the government saw where the fault lay, and willing to apply a remedy, flew from one extreme to the other. Our eighteen pound ships being too slight, a heterogeneous body was constructed, a frigate only in name, but not in fact. Such were the Lancaster, the Java, the Leander, and the Newcastle, ships of sixty guns, carrying twenty-four pounders on their main-deck, and having one complete tier of thirty-two pound carronades from stem to stern, along the gangways, quarter-deck, and forecastle. The Majestic, Saturn, and Goliath, three seventy-four gun ships, were cut down and armed in the same manner. In such ships no honour could have been gained by taking the President; and disgrace would have attached for surrendering to an American seventy-four. They were wretchedly manned, and the guns on their gangways, like one-third of their crew, would have swelled the triumph of an enemy, without contributing to the defence of the ship, in which they were only lumber.

The British navy, depressed by repeated mortifications, had in some measure lost its spirits, and the dissatisfaction expressed in the public journals of the empire produced, as no doubt many of the writers intended, a feeling of discontent and disgust in the bosoms of our seamen. This melancholy impression was removed by the fortunate and gallant action fought on the 1st of June, 1813, between the Shannon, of thirty-eight guns, eighteen pounders, and the American frigate Chesapeake, of the same force in guns, but superior in the number of her crew. Captain P. B. V. Broke, an officer of great good sense and determined resolution, had long been watching the Chesapeake as she lay in Boston harbour, whence Commodore Rogers in the President, with the Congress, another large frigate with twenty-four pounders, had escaped, during a fog, on the 13th of May, passing by the Shannon and Tenedos. Finding the Chesapeake alone remained, Captain Broke detached the Tenedos to cruise off Cape Sable, while he continued close in with Boston, and on the 1st of June, sent in a challenge to Captain Lawrence, of the Chesapeake, to come out and fight him, promising that no other ship should interfere, whatever might be the event of the battle, and requiring the same pledge from Captain Lawrence. Whether it was in compliance with this challenge, or in obedience to his orders, that the American captain thought proper to put to sea, is uncertain.

The day was fine, with a light air of wind, when the Shannon, with a blue ensign at the peak, stood in towards Boston, exercising her great guns, but without firing. At eleven o'clock the Chesapeake loosed her sails: at twelve o'clock the Shannon was lying to, Cape Anne bearing N.N.E. half E. twelve or fourteen miles. At half-past twelve the Chesapeake weighed, and set royals and studding-sails: at one, the Shannon stood out, under her topsails, to gain a little more offing, the enemy, with fifty or sixty pleasure boats, and a privateer schooner, coming out of Boston roads. At forty minutes past three, the American frigate fired a gun, and hauled up, intimating that she was not to be led farther from the land, on which the Shannon's fore-topsail was laid aback, and the Chesapeake again steered for her. At four, Boston light-house W. by N. six leagues, the enemy still coming out, under topgallant-sails, jib and foresail, having taken in his studding-sails, and sent his royal yards on deck. He had three ensigns displayed; one of unusual size in the main rigging, one at the peak, and one at the mizen-topgallant-mast head: an American jack at the main, and a white flag at the fore, on which were written the words, "Sailors' rights and free trade." At ten minutes past five the Shannon beat to quarters, filled her fore-topsail, kept her main-topsail shivering, set her jib and spanker, and was going about two miles an hour. At forty-five minutes past five, the enemy hauled up within two hundred yards of the Shannon's weather-beam, and gave three cheers. On this Captain Broke addressed his ship's company, told them that that day would decide the superiority of British seamen, when well trained, over other nations; and that the Shannon would shew in that day's action, how short a time the Americans had to boast, when opposed to equal force. The two ships being now not more than a stone's throw asunder, the Chesapeake about one point abaft the starboard beam of the Shannon, whose guns were most deliberately and exactly pointed, as the object varied its position, at fifty minutes past five, the action commenced by the Shannon giving her broadside, beginning with the aftermost guns on the starboard side. The enemy passing too fast a-head to receive more than a second discharge from the aftermost guns, the boarders were ordered to prepare, when the Chesapeake, attempting to haul her foresail up, fell on board the Shannon, whose starboard bower-anchor hooked the larboard mizen chains of her opponent. Here a sharp fire of musketry took place between the marines of both ships: when this had lasted a few minutes, the enemy appeared to flinch, and Captain Broke, at the head of his boarders, mounted the forecastle car-ronade, and leapt on the quarter-deck of the Chesa-peake, followed by Lieutenant Watt, Sergeant Mo-lineux, Corporal Osborne, and the marines. This division was supported by the main-deck boarders

under Lieutenant Falconer, third lieutenant, and Mr.
Smith, a midshipman.   Captain Broke, followed by
about sixty of his people, put to death all that
opposed his passage round the gangway, and drove
the Americans below, while the bow guns of the
Shannon, under the command of Lieutenant Wallis,
made dreadful havoc on the main-deck of the enemy.
Mr. Comahan, a midshipman of the Shannon, placed
himself on her main-yard, whence, with musketry,
he killed or wounded nearly all the men stationed
in the main and mizen-top of the enemy.

Captain Broke, in the mean time, with the boarders, had cleared the enemy's quarter-deck, though a
little impeded by their fire.   Our men gave three
cheers, rushed forward, and, carrying all before
them, united on the forecastle, and drove the crew
of the Chesapeake below. It was in making a charge
along the larboard gangway, that Captain Broke
nobly saved the life of an American seaman who
called for quarter; but the villain, suddenly snatch-
ing up a cutlass, gave his deliverer that blow on the
back of his head, which had nearly proved fatal at
the time, and from the effects of which he has never
recovered.   The Shannon's people instantly cut the
miserable man in pieces.   The Americans were ral-
lying on the main-deck, when the English made
another desperate rush among them; and in fifteen
minutes from the commencement of the action, the
British flag had supplanted that of America, and the
Chesapeake was a prize to the Shannon. While this
contest was proceeding, the two ships had separated;

and a small British blue ensign had been hoisted at the gaff-end of the Chesapeake. Lieutenant Watt, first of the Shannon, unfortunately wished to exchange this flag for a large white ensign which he had brought with him for that purpose. The people on board the Shannon perceiving that the firing still continued, and that the blue ensign was hauled down, concluded that the enemy had overpowered the small party of Englishmen then on board. Under this natural but fatal error, they directed their fire at the Chesapeake's quarter-deck, killed Lieutenant Watt, and three of the Shannon's men, and wounded some others; nor was it till the small blue ensign was re-hoisted, that the firing ceased. The crew of the Chesapeake being driven into the hold of their own ship, a marine sentinel was placed over the main hatchway: the Americans treacherously fired up from the hold and killed him. On this, our men poured down a heavy fire on them, until they again called for quarter, and promised to deliver up the offender. The prisoners were now secured and handcuffed on the orlop-deck. Many of them were drunk and riotous, but the others tranquil and well-behaved. At seven in the evening, the pleasure-boats and the privateer which had accompanied the Chesapeake to the scene of action returned to the afflicted town of Boston, where balls and suppers had been foolishly prepared, for the anticipated victors, and their British captives. The action was one of the most bloody and determined ever fought between two ships of their class, in so short a time.

The loss on board the Shannon, out of three hundred and thirty men, was three officers and twenty-three men killed; Captain Broke, two officers, and fifty-eight men wounded: eighty-seven total. On mustering the crew of the Chesapeake on the following day, they found she had begun the action with four hundred and forty men, of whom, the second lieutenant, master, marine officer, some midshipmen, and ninety seamen and marines, were killed; Captain Lawrence mortally wounded: the first and third lieutenants, some midshipmen, and one hundred and ten men were also wounded; making a total of killed and wounded between the two ships of nearly three hundred men, or twenty men for every minute the ships were in action.

The capture of the Chesapeake by a ship of the same number of guns, and weight of metal, but inferior in number of men by one hundred and ten, was proof sufficient that all our preceding losses had been solely caused by the encounter of ships unequally matched. Trusting that America and Great Britain will know their true interests too well to be again embroiled, let us conclude by observing that both ships did their duty, though some fault was found with one or two of the officers on board the Chesapeake. The Shannon and her prize arrived at Halifax on the 6th. Captain Lawrence had died on the 4th, and was buried with the honours of war at that place: the body was taken up a month after, and conveyed, at the express request of the American government, to Boston, where it was again interred in grateful solemnity. Captain Broke shortly after returned to England in the Shannon. On his arrival he was created a baronet, and received with every mark of respect. The same valour unsuccessful alongside of the Constitution and United States, was received with coldness and unmerited neglect by all those who were not perfectly acquainted with the merits of the cases, and the relative force of the contending ships.

It was never the wish of the writer of these pages to perpetuate animosity between Great Britain and America; facts are only recorded for the instruction of our successors, and to guard them against a recurrence of similar evils.

The clock-machine and fire-vessels, we admit, were introduced by the English : we disapprove of them, and lament that they were ever used, as adding unnecessarily to the horrors of war. But even these machines were conducted by valour; and though the projector declined exposing his own person, Englishmen were found who could make the coffins fast to the cable, and lay a fire-ship on board the French flotilla before Boulogne. So far the warfare was manly, because a risk was incurred by the assailants. America also, in her turn, used a clock-machine, which had very nearly destroyed the Plantagenet, of seventy-four guns. This was no more than what we had a right to expect, and what was foretold by the Earl of St. Vincent on their first introduction. But these instances can never be pleaded in justification of the base and cowardly plot by which a gallant young officer, and ten British seamen, belonging to the Ramillies, were blown into the air.

Captain Sir Thomas Hardy, of the Ramillies, was off New London, in June, 1813, when his boats captured a schooner, making for that harbour; the crew had left her. The vessel was brought close to the Ramillies : Sir Thomas Hardy ordered her to be placed alongside of another prize. Lieutenant Geddes, and thirteen men, were in the execution of this order, when, about half-past two, the vessel blew up, and the Lieutenant, with ten of his men, perished; three men only escaped, but were dreadfully scorched. Such was the effect of a wicked and cruel artifice, planned by American merchants of New York, and sanctioned, we fear, by the government. It had been reported, that the Ramillies was short of provisions; they had therefore placed some articles of this description in the hatchway, in hopes the vessel might have been taken alongside. In the hold were stowed several barrels of gunpowder; trains were laid to explode at a given time, by means of clock work. A quantity of arsenic among the food would have been so perfectly compatible with the rest of the contrivance, that we wonder it was not resorted to. Should actions like these receive the sanction of governments, the science of war, and the laws of nations, will degenerate into the barbarity of the Algerines ; and murder and pillage will take place of kindness and humanity to our enemies. Every honourable mind in America will blush for his country, when he reads this account, and detest the authors of such diabolical treachery.

The steam-vessel, called the Fulton (from the name of the inventor), appears to have been a very formidable floating-battery, with the power of loco-motion, at the rate of five miles an hour. Without the aid of masts or sails, she could preserve her position on the quarter of a ship, for any time, in calms or light winds. She had thirty thirty-two pound guns on one deck, her sides were five feet thick, and being covered over like the tortoise's back, bade defiance to the shot of an enemy. For the defence of rivers, and still waters, she answered every purpose; and could have been encountered only by a vessel of similar construction. As she was not produced till after the conclusion of the war, she never came into action; but experiments were made, and her powers appeared to be very surprising.

On the 5th of September, 1813, the Boxer, a gun-brig, commander Captain Samuel Blyth, was captured by an American schooner, of nearly double her force in number of men, and greatly superior in guns and in size. The action was fought off Portland, in the United States. The first broadside from the American killed Captain Blyth, and two of his men; the main-topmast of the Boxer was shot away at the same time; and the enemy being by this means enabled to keep a raking position, the Boxer very soon became a wreck, and a prize to her adversary. The Americans chose to call this a wonderful achievement, and to insist, that the Boxer had one hundred and four men at least. This was inferred also by Commodore Hull (who ought to have known better), because he counted ninety hammocks on board of her; each man in the British navy being allowed two, that he may have a clean one ready to put his bedding into. We have no wish to deprive the Americans of the honour they may claim by this victory; but they certainly on this, and every other occasion of the like nature, greatly overrated the force of their enemies.

The forces on the coast of North America had been augmented in the latter end of the year 1812; a marine battalion, of two thousand men, raised from the ships of war, had been formed and disciplined by their own officers. Rear-admiral Cockburn sailed from Cadiz, in the Marlborough, of seventy-four guns, and arrived at Bermuda in January, 1813; he was shortly after joined by Sir John Warren, and the two Admirals, with the forces under their orders, proceeded to the Chesapeake, which they reached on the 3d of March, up to which period nothing had been attempted against the Americans, beyond cruising off their ports. The manner of carrying on the war was now entirely changed. Surveys were made, and excellent charts procured from American vessels; by which means, our officers soon became very expert pilots. The Rear-admiral, having obtained the consent of the Commander-in-chief, ran into Hampton roads, cleared the James river with his boats, and spread dismay throughout

·Virginia. The Constellation, an American frigate,
lying at the mouth of the Elizabeth river, waiting an opportunity to get to sea, was forced to return
to Norfolk; and the Americans sank a large ship in
the channel, to obstruct the passage of our ships.

The Rear-admiral, followed by the Commander-
in-chief, in the St. Domingo, next went up the northern branch of the Chesapeake, and took many vessels, some of them armed for war. Having reached
nearly as high as Annapolis, he was detached by Sir
John Warren, with two frigates, some brigs, and
small craft. He carried the Marlborough as high as
the depth of water would permit, then left her, and
hoisted his flag on board the Maidstone, with Captain Burdett, and proceeded to the upper part of the
Elk river, at the head of the Chesapeake: here he
destroyed a battery, and a large depôt of military
stores. At French Town, the inhabitants being perfectly inoffensive, and not assisting the soldiers in the
defence of the works, no injury whatever was done
to them; but it was not always in the power of the
Rear-admiral thus to mitigate the horrors of war.
The Americans are particularly skilful in the use of
the rifle, with which the peasantry and inhabitants
of the villages along the shores of the Chesapeake
would frequently fire upon our boats; and many of
our men being killed by this bush-fighting, the Rear-
admiral publicly declared, that whenever the inhabitants, not being military, should so conduct themselves, he should deliver up their towns, farms, and
stores, to military execution, and consider the peo-

ple, when in his power, as prisoners of war; but that, on the other hand, every kindness and indulgence should be shewn to such as attended only to their own agricultural or mercantile pursuits. The people of French Town, confiding in these assurances, saved themselves, and their property. Cattle were purchased from the estates, regularly paid for, and sent down to the fleet; and the American farmer was as secure from our depredations, as if he had been a British subject. But the people of the town of Havre de Grace, at the entrance of the Susquehana, confiding too much in their own strength and valour, fired on our boats as they passed. The Rear-admiral, true to his word, attacked the place in the morning of the 3d of May, with two hundred seamen and marines; and, after a smart skirmish, took their battery, turned the guns against the town, drove the people into the woods, and gave up those houses to plunder, whose owners had taken up arms against us; at the same time, affording security and protection to such as had taken no part in these acts of hostility. The Americans had a large cannon-foundry about four miles from Havre, where they cast guns for their ships of war. This the Rear-admiral destroyed, together with fifty-one new pieces of cannon, and many large depôts of government stores. After giving this memorable lesson to the Americans, and being on shore the whole of the day, on the high road between Baltimore and Philadelphia, the Rear-admiral re-embarked his men, and returned to his ship.

The Americans had collected a small but very mischievous force in the Rappahannock : it consisted of four schooners, of the most superior construction, either for sailing or fighting. They were the Arab, of seven guns and forty-five men; the Lynx, of six guns and forty men; Racer, of six guns and thirty-six men; and the Dolphin, of twelve guns and seventy-eight men. These vessels, all moored in a close line, for mutual support, were boarded and brought out by the boats of the squadron, under the orders of Lieutenant Puckinghorne, of the St. Domingo, who greatly distinguished himself on this occasion, as did the Lieutenants Urmston and Scott, of the Marlborough, Bishop, of the Statira, and Lidden, of the Maidstone.

On the 6th of May, Rear-admiral Cockburn went with his boats to the Sassafras river, on which stand two places, called George Town, and Frederick Town; and having warned the people of what had happened at Havre de Grace, and invited them to be peaceable, he proceeded to attack the forts. The inhabitants joined with the militia in their defence; and, after a smart engagement, were beaten, and the places given up to plunder. These three examples sufficed to convince the Americans both of the power and the clemency of their enemies; and the Rear-admiral had no farther occasion to resort to the cruel necessity. From that moment no country, having become the theatre of war, ever suffered so little from the presence of a hostile army. On the 7th of May, the Rear-admiral rejoined Sir John Warren, who carried the fleet down to Lynhaven bay, where he left Admiral Cockburn with a squadron to keep up the blockade, and went with the rest of the ships to Halifax.

Returning again on the 19th of June, Sir John Warren brought with him a land force, under the command of Colonel Sir Sydney Beckwith. This consisted of one regiment of infantry, some few marines and artillery, and some companies of Frenchmen, who had been permitted to enter into the British service. With this force, to which were added some seamen from the squadron trained to small arms, the Rear-admiral and Colonel Beckwith made an attack on the town of Norfolk, in Elizabeth river, a well fortified place, containing a naval arsenal, and a government store. The Rear-admiral hoisted his flag on board the Barossa, Captain J. A. Gordon, and anchored off the mouth of Elizabeth river, with three other frigates, some gun-brigs, and smaller vessels. The troops landed on the 22d of June, in the morning, and moved towards Craney Island, a post which it was necessary to take, in order to secure the passage for the ships of war, and to enable them to reach the Constellation. The boats of the squadron, under the command of Captain Pechell, of the St. Domingo, endeavoured to reach and to storm this island; but being unacquainted with the channel, they grounded on the mud, and became exposed to a heavy fire of grape, which sank three of the largest of the boats, and killed and wounded about ninety men. The rest retreated; and Sir Sydney

Beckwith declaring that the troops under his orders were inadequate to the undertaking, they were re-embarked, and returned to their ships.

After this unsuccessful attempt upon Norfolk, it was determined to attack Hampton, a fortified town, and military post, on the shore of Hampton roads, opposite to the mouth of Elizabeth river. This was undertaken on the 25th of June, by the Rear-admiral, with the armed boats of the squadron, and Colonel Beckwith, with the troops. The place was taken by a joint attack, after a sharp action; but no great advantage seems to have arisen from it; and the French troops behaved so infamously, that Sir Sydney Beckwith declared, with great truth, that he should feel much stronger without them: accordingly, such as had not deserted to the enemy, were re-embarked, and sent to Bermuda. The Colonel kept possession of Hampton till the 27th, when it was given up to the Americans.

On the 1st of July, Rear-admiral Cockburn shifted his flag to the Sceptre, of seventy-four guns, which had been sent out for him; and the enemy having collected a small naval force at Okrakoke, in South Carolina, he volunteered to go and attack it. Having obtained permission of the Commander-in-chief, and received on board of his small squadron a detachment of the 102d regiment, under Colonel Napier, he sailed on the 3d, and anchored on the 11th of July off the port. There was not depth of water sufficient for a ship of the line, or even a frigate, to approach; the troops were therefore put into the

boats the same evening, and by daylight they had
got within the harbour, and so near the enemy's
vessels, as to receive from them a hasty though in-
effectual fire: they instantly boarded and carried
them. One was called the Anaconda, a fine brig,
of twenty guns; the other the Atlas, a schooner, of
twelve guns. The Chiefs having landed, and collected a supply of cattle and other necessaries from
the surrounding country, and got their prizes over
the bar, evacuated Okrakoke on the 16th of July,
and returned to the Chesapeake, where nothing had
taken place during their absence.

It was next decided, to land and take possession
of Kent Island, for the purpose of refreshing the
troops. With this object, the squadron moved from
the entrance of the Potowmac, and ascended the
Chesapeake. The Sceptre, gaining the lead, with
the Barossa, far outstripped the Commander-in-
chief; and at dawn of day on the 5th of August, the
Rear-admiral, with a party of the 102d regiment, the
marines, and a few seamen from both these ships, had
landed, and in a few hours they were in quiet possession of the island. The troops were put on shore,
and procured a supply of all those refreshments so
necessary to the preservation of their health. They
remained here till the 22d, when they were re-embarked, and returned to Lynhaven bay. While we
were in possession of this island, our boats made
many excursions into the neighbouring creeks and
inlets, always returning laden with spoil, or having
destroyed some fort or store of the enemy.

On the 6th of September, Sir John Warren sailed with the principal part of the forces to Halifax; leaving Rear-admiral Cockburn in the command of the Chesapeake bay and anchorage.

In the mean time, some events had occurred on the lakes of Canada, which require to be noticed. The naval force employed there was not equal, in some respects, to that of America. The command of the land forces, and the government of the Canadas, were intrusted to Lieutenant-general Sir George Prevost, an officer whose character has been shamefully traduced by party writers; and, by a refinement of cruelty, his memory attacked before the tears of his family were dried up for his loss. The naval force was commanded by Captain Sir James Lucas Yeo, who had the temporary rank of Commodore. The American army had received some severe checks from ours under the command of General Brock and Sir Roger Sheaffe. Commodore Yeo sailed from Kingston, on Lake Ontario, on the 3d of June, to assist the land forces, cut off the supplies of the Americans, and draw their squadron from their port. On the 8th of June, the hostile squadrons met at Forty Mile Creek. Our gun-boats came near enough to drive the enemy from their batteries, and compel them to leave their provisions, guns, and stores: all the American batteaux, with their materiel, were also taken.

On the 8th of August, Commodore Yeo, in the Wolfe, discovered the enemy's squadron at anchor off Fort Niagara. They consisted of thirteen sail;

ours of only six, though much larger vessels. They
weighed, and offered battle, which the Commodore
gladly accepted; but before they were well within
gun-shot, the Americans fired their broadsides, and
sought the protection of their batteries. A breeze of
wind, towards the evening, enabled the British squadron to close; and at eleven o'clock at night, to engage that of the United States. The Wolfe got
alongside of the General Pike and the Madison,
both which ran away, firing their stern-chase guns,
and leaving two of their schooners in possession of
the Commodore: each of these mounted one long
thirty-two pounder, and one long twelve pounder,
with a crew of forty men. The General Pike, which
escaped with the Madison, is said to have mounted
twenty-eight long twenty-four pounders, and to have
had a crew of four hundred men. The enemy retreated after this affair to Sacket's Harbour. Our
squadron received no other injury than a few shot
through their sails, and some rigging cut away.

The success of the Americans by land was not so
great as might have been expected, when the proxi-
mity of their resources, compared with ours, was
duly considered. In that inclement season, the month
of December, the armies kept the field; and the
flotillas on Lakes Ontario and Erie cruised against
the enemy,

The American generals Hamilton and Wilkinson,
were obliged by the British forces to retreat with loss,
both in Upper and Lower Canada. A division of
gun-boats, under the command of Captain Pring, of

the royal navy, advanced from Lake Ontario into Lake Champlain, cutting their way through the ice for many miles. Reaching the neighbourhood of Platsburg, they burned and destroyed the enemy's stores and ammunition, and retired without loss.

The flotilla on Lake Erie was commanded by Captain R. H. Barclay, a young officer, whose courage led him to attempt more than prudence would have justified, under any other circumstances than those in which he found himself: his squadron only half manned, without stores, his men on two-thirds allowance, and not a day's provisions in the port of Amherstberg, where he lay blockaded by an American squadron of superior force. In this critical situation, Captain Barclay, guided by the wishes of Major-general Proctor, with whom he was directed to consult and co-operate, determined to attack the enemy, let the event be what it might. He had been led to expect a reinforcement of seamen from the fleet on the coast, but they did not arrive, and every hour's delay rendered the state of his squadron more desperate. On the morning of the 9th of September, the American flotilla appeared in Put in Bay, and Captain Barclay bore up to engage them. A change of wind brought the American squadron to windward, and they came down upon him with a determination to fight. The name of Captain Barclay's ship was the Detroit. About noon, he brought the American Commodore to action; two American schooners, with very heavy long guns, engaged him at the same time. The Queen Charlotte and Lady Prevost were cut to pieces by the American schooners. Captain Finnis, of the Queen Charlotte, was killed early in the action, and his death was the fore-runner of destruction to the British squadron. Captain Barclay, who, long before this action, had lost an arm, was again severely wounded; and every officer about him being either killed or wounded, it became necessary to surrender both the Detroit and the Queen Charlotte to the United States ship St. Lawrence, Commodore Parry. In number and weight of guns, the two squadrons were nearly equal; but the Americans had every advantage in the number and quality of their men.

Captain Barclay, and all the other officers, were honourably acquitted for the loss of the ships; and great care was taken to reinforce the squadrons on the lakes. On shore we were more fortunate. Fort George capitulated to General Drummond, who, on the 9th of December, took Fort Niagara by storm, with small loss on our side; the enemy had near four hundred men killed, wounded, or taken. Major-general Riall took Black Rock and Buffalo, two strong posts be-longing to the Americans, who, in the depth of a Canadian winter, must have deplored the mad-ness of a government which had thus wantonly plunged them into the horrors of war.

A drawn battle, of an unusually desperate cha-racter, occurred on the coast of Guinea, in the month of February, 1813, between the Amelia, a British frigate, of thirty-eight guns, commanded

by the Honourable Frederick Paul Irby, and the
Arethuse, of the same size, commanded by Commodore Bouvet, a French officer, of great merit.
The Arethuse was cruising in company with Le
Rubis, a frigate of the same force, off the Isles de
Loss, where they had destroyed the Daring, a
British gun-brig, and many other vessels. The
Tweed, sloop of war, was expected on the coast,
with a convoy, and large supplies. As it therefore
became the duty of Captain Irby to get sight of
the enemy, and draw them off the coast, he sailed
from Sierra Leone on the 4th, and on the 6th found
both the ships at anchor off the Isles de Loss, with a
Portuguese ship, of twenty guns, which they had
taken. The Amelia steered for the Rubis; the
Arethuse, which was at some distance from her
consort, weighed, and closed with her. Unwilling
to engage both the frigates, as his own was scarcely
more than half manned, Captain Irby stood off to
sea for the night, and in the morning he had only
the Arethuse in company. Both ships now mutually sought an action, which commenced within
pistol-shot, and continued for four hours, the ships
sometimes touching each other, the water smooth,
and the winds very light; at length both being
equally disabled, the Arethuse sheered away, and
the Amelia was unable to pursue. The Rubis was
expected to join, and had she done so, the British
frigate must have fallen. Her first, second, and
third lieutenants, with Lieutenant Pascoe, of the

Daring, and forty-seven men lay dead; Captain Irby was severely wounded, as were all his officers, and about ninety-five of his men; making a total of one hundred and forty-five killed and wounded, of a crew of less than three hundred men, exhausted with sickness and fatigue. The carnage on board the Aréthuse was equally great; one hundred and fifty was the number stated to the minister of the marine as killed and wounded. The Rubis, it appeared, had run on shore in the Isles de Loss, and was wrecked. Each of these ships had on board a crew of three hundred and seventy-five men.

On the 9th of October, Captain Watkin Owen Pell, of the Thunder bomb, while on his passage from Spithead to the Downs, fell in with a French lugger, off the Owers light. The appearance of the Thunder being precisely that of a merchantship, the enemy supposed her to be so, and to favour the deception, Captain Pell steered as if he intended to run on shore. The unfortunate Frenchman fell into the snare: running close upon the larboard quarter of the Thunder, he hailed, and desired her to strike; his decks being full of men, and prepared for boarding, he put his helm up for that purpose, and Captain Pell put his down, giving a broadside, and a volley of musketry; at the same moment the lugger fell on board of the Thunder, and was taken. She was called La Neptune, pierced for eighteen guns, had fourteen mounted, and had on board sixty-three men, of whom four were killed, and ten wounded. The Thunder had only two men wounded.

Captain Dashwood, of the Snap brig of war, of sixteen guns, had a rencontre with five large French luggers, which, had they supported each other, might have given him some embarrassment. Captain Dashwood very gallantly laid himself alongside of the nearest, and in ten minutes took her. She was called Le Lion, of sixteen guns, and sixty-five men, of whom five were killed, and six wounded.

CHAP. III.

Sir J. C. Sheı broke and Rear-admiral Griffiths—Death of Sir
Peter Parker—Affairs on the Lakes—Defeat of British flotilla
before Platsburg, and death of Captain Downie—Retreat of
Sir George Prevost—Defence of his conduct—Expedition of
Rear-admiral Cockburn to Cumberland Island—Capture of
St. Mary's.
5. *West Indies.*—Capture of the Alcmene and Iphigenie by
Rear-admiral Durham—Gallant Action of Captain Lennon,
in the Hibernia.

IT is a pleasing part of the duty of an historian,
after having related the successes of the wicked
and unprincipled conqueror, after exposing his
falsehood—his deceit—his political wiles, to trace
him up to the hour of adversity, to the inevitable
retribution, which as surely awaits crime, as darkness follows the departure of celestial light.

The Rhine, no longer the boundary of France,
was forced and violated by hostile armies, from
Basle to Dusseldorf; the immortal Blucher passed
at the fortress of Kaub, so well known to the British tourist. The Emperors of Russia and Austria,
and the King of Prussia, met at Basle on the
14th of January, while the respective generals
and armies of these monarchs pressed on, and over-
ran the eastern frontier of France. Bonaparte saw
his danger, but was too proud to own it.

Hamburgh was not yet released from the cruel
oppressor, Davoust. The city of Dantzic was evacuated on the 2d of January; the French garrison
became prisoners of war, and the place was entered
by Duke Alexander, of Wirtemburg, at the head
of sixteen thousand Russians and Prussians.

The Crown Prince of Sweden commanded a

powerful army of Russians, Prussians, Swedes, and Danes, this last named power having joined the coalition; the forces of the Prince occupied Cologne, Brussels, Mons, Namur, Avesnes, and Rheims. The British army, under Sir Thomas Graham, acting in conjunction with the Prussian general, Bulow, drove the French into Antwerp with loss. Bonaparte now thought it time to place himself once more at the head of his armies: for this purpose, he arrived at St. Dizier, on the Maine, on the 27th of January.

In Italy, the prospects of Napoleon were still darker. There is no true friendship among the wicked. Murat, a man of low birth, who had been raised by his master to the high rank of king of Naples, now turned against his benefactor, and joined the Emperor of Austria, with forty or fifty thousand men. In the month of January, the Austrian forces occupied both banks of the Mincio. Negotiations for peace had been begun between France and the Allies, but were broken off on the 18th of March.

On the 5th of January, Captain Rainier, in the Niger, of thirty-eight guns, and Captain Pipon, in the Tagus, of the same force, captured off the island of St. Antonio, the French frigate La Ceres, of forty-four guns, and three hundred and twenty-four men, commanded by the Baron de Bougainville. The chase continued for the distance of two hundred and thirty-eight miles. The prize was lately from Brest, and bound on a cruise.

A frigate action, of an interesting nature, was fought in February, 1814, between the Eurotas, a British ship, of forty-four guns, eighteen pounders, and La Clorinde, of the same force. The two ships met on the 25th of the month, in lat. 47° 40′ N., and 9° 30′ W. Captain Phillimore, of the Eurotas, a newly fitted ship, instantly sought a close action with his adversary; and, at five o'clock, passed under her stern, hailed, and gave his broadside. Luffing under her lee, and passing a-head of her, he received that of the Frenchman, which shot away his mizen-mast. Captain Phillimore ordered the helm to be put down, to lay the enemy on board: this manœuvre failed, the wreck of the mast impeding the action of the rudder. The fight continued, and once more the Eurotas raked the enemy, after which the two ships lay broadside and broadside, until twenty minutes past six, when the main-mast of the Eurotas, and the mizen-mast of the French ship, both fell. At fifty minutes past six, the enemy's mainmast, and the fore-mast of the Eurotas, fell; and ten minutes after seven, the French ship slackened her fire, and with her fore-mast standing, succeeded in getting out of gun-shot of the Eurotas.

Captain Phillimore was severely wounded with a grape-shot in the shoulder, in the early part of the action, but kept the deck till the enemy was defeated, and had run away, when he suffered himself to be carried below, ordering his first lieutenant, Mr. Smith, to rig jurymasts, and to make sail

after the enemy. The fore-mast and main-mast,
then lying nearly fore and aft the decks, were
quickly disengaged from the ship; and before
twelve o'clock the next day, this gallant young
officer, with a raw ship's company, had succeeded
in rigging jury-courses, topsails, staysails, and
spanker, had cleared his decks for action, was
going six knots and a half, and coming fast up
with his enemy, who had not then cleared away
any part of his wreck. Victory would probably
have declared in favour of the Eurotas; but
it was anticipated, by the appearance of the
Dryad, of thirty-six guns, Captain Galway, and
the Achates sloop of war, Captain Morrison.
The French Captain presented his sword to Captain Galway, who very honourably refused it, observing, that that mark of respect was due to
Captain Phillimore. La Clorinde mounted forty-
four guns, though we should call her no more than
an eight-and-thirty: she had three hundred and
sixty men, of whom one hundred and twenty were
killed or wounded; the Eurotas had twenty killed,
and forty wounded.

On the 26th of March, Captain Sir Michael
Seymour, in the Hannibal, of seventy-four guns,
with the Hebrus, Captain E. Palmer, and the
Sparrow brig, of ten guns, fell in with two French
frigates, off the Isle of Bas. Both these ships appeared to have been disabled: they separated on
seeing our squadron. One was pursued and taken
by the Hannibal; she was called La Sultane,

mounted forty-four guns, and had three hundred men. The other, chased by the Hebrus, was brought to action the same night by that vessel, and very gallantly taken after a contest of two hours and twenty minutes. She was called L'Etoile, was of the same size as her consort; and had the same number of men, of whom forty were killed, and seventy wounded. The Hebrus had twelve killed, and ten severely wounded, with some others slightly hurt. Captain William Sargent served as a volunteer on board the Hebrus, and was subsequently promoted to the rank of post-captain for his good conduct.

On the 1st of September, an action was fought off Cape Clear, between the British brig sloop of war Avon, and the American brig of war Wasp, both large class vessels. The American had, however, greatly the advantage in size and number of men, and had two more guns. The action lasted two hours and twenty minutes. The Avon had forty-two men killed and wounded, and was sinking when the Castilian brig came in sight, and after giving the Wasp a broadside, hastened to the relief of the Avon. The Honourable Captain Arbuthnot, her commander, was severely wounded; the first lieutenant, Mr. Prendergast, mortally; and the sloop sank as soon as the last officer had quitted her. The Wasp received comparatively little damage.

Ships.	Guns.		Men.
The Avon · · · ·	16 32-pounders and 2 long sixes		120
The Wasp · · ·	18 32-pounders	2 long twelves	140

On the 20th of February, the Marquis of Wellington reached the banks of the Adour, where his
progress was nearly arrested for want of boats to
transport his army across the river. The mouth
of the Adour is obstructed by a bar on which the
sea breaks with terrific violence. Rear-admiral
Penrose had his flag in the Porcupine, of twenty-
four guns, and directed the operations of the boats
and small craft, attempting to enter the river. At
a distance were seen the British troops passing
over from the south to the north side, and indi-
cating by the lengthened operation the extreme
distress they were in for assistance from the ships
of war. Stimulated by every thing which could
inspire a Briton, Captain O'Reilly, in a Spanish
boat, with a good pilot, made the first attempt:
his boat was overset; but with his people he
escaped to the shore. Lieutenant Debenham, in a
six-oared cutter, succeeded in crossing the bar.
He was followed by Lieutenant Cheyne, of the
Woodlark, gun-brig, in a Spanish boat, manned
with British seamen. After him came Lieutenant
Chesshyre, who was the first officer that hoisted
the British colours in the Adour. "Many other
boats," says the excellent and gallant admiral,
"followed in rapid succession; the zeal and science
of the officers triumphing over all the difficulties of
the navigation." Some lives were lost in this
daring but necessary enterprise, more honourable
than the best fought action at sea, inasmuch as the
motives were more urgent for the success or pre-

servation of the British army. Captain Elliott, of the Martial gun-brig, was drowned, with four of his seamen; Mr. Norman, his surgeon, killed. Mr. Henry Bloye, master's mate of the Lyra, with five of his men, was drowned; and four boats were lost, with all their crews.

Rear-admiral Penrose, in conjunction with the British land forces under Sir John Hope, crossed the Adour below Bayonne, on the 23d and 24th of February, and formed a complete bridge over that river, at the same time that they invested the city of Bayonne. Early in March, Marshal Beresford was ordered by Lord Wellington to. move directly on Bordeaux, the first city which openly displayed its reconciliation with the persecuted house of Bourbon. Marshal Beresford having reached the city on the 12th, was met by the loyal inhabitants with every demonstration of joy. The Duke D'Angouleme accompanied the British general; the white cockade was displayed, and Louis XVIII. was proclaimed.

Rear-admiral Penrose followed the motions of this corps, and on the 21st of March, with his flag in the Egmont, of seventy-four guns, he let go his anchor in the Gironde.

Paris was now threatened in her turn with hostile arms and internal commotion. The great day of the 30th of March, laid open her gates to the Allies; and Bonaparte beheld, as the fruits of his ambition and cruelty, his bitterest enemies mount guard at the Thuilleries. On the 2d of April, the senate declared that Napoleon had forfeited his throne. To this he submitted, and chose the island of Elba as the place of his retreat and seclusion: himself and the empress Maria Louisa were to retain their rank, and to be allowed an income of two millions and a half of francs, about £100,000. The provisional government of Paris offered the throne to Louis XVIII. which he gladly accepted. Thus, after the storms of the revolution, after destroying the altars, thrones, and every ancient and honourable institution, did France suddenly return to reason; and Europe looks back on the frightful scenes, as one awakened from a horrid dream.

While these things were passing at Paris, Lord Wellington pursued Marshal Soult to Toulouse, where the French general shut himself up, ignorant of what had been done at Paris. Round the walls of this romantic city, a bloody and a useless battle was fought on the 10th of April, in which a victory, dearly bought, remained with the Allies. This battle is the more to be lamented, since by a little diligence in forwarding the dispatches, the whole might have been prevented. On the 12th, his Lordship entered Toulouse.

How it happened that neither the Marquis of Wellington nor Marshal Soult, the only generals in France at that time opposed to each other, should not have been made acquainted with the events which had taken place in the capital between the 31st of March and the 9th of April, is a question which we decline solving. That a courier with common speed might have gone from Paris to Toulouse in three days, with ease, and to Bayonne in about the same time, is certain; yet two murderous battles were fought at these places on the 10th and 14th of April; and it is very probable that the French general in Bayonne (if not Soult also) was perfectly acquainted with the capitulation of Paris.

On the 9th of April, Rear-admiral Penrose acquainted Lord Keith, the commander-in-chief of the Channel fleet, that the Gironde and the Garonne, as high as Blaye, were quite cleared of the enemy's force, the batteries on both sides being either taken or destroyed. When the Rear-admiral entered the Gironde, he drove before him the Regulus, a French ship of eighty guns, and three brigs of war.

The Centaur, of seventy-four guns, arriving soon after to reinforce him, the Rear-admiral prepared to attack the enemy, who had anchored under the protection of the batteries at Blaye. At midnight on the 6th of April, the French ships appeared in flames, and were burnt to the water's edge. Captain Coode, of the Porcupine, reached as high up the Garonne as Pouillac, where his boats, under the orders of Lieutenant Delop, captured and destroyed the enemy's flotilla.

Rear-admiral Lord Amelius Beauclerc, in the Royal Oak, of seventy-four guns, lying in Basque Roads, received a letter from the general of divi-

sion, Baron de Raffiniere, commander-in-chief at
Rochelle, stating that, in the name of his division,
he had acknowledged his Majesty Louis XVIII. and
had hoisted the white flag; and he proposed to the
Rear-admiral a suspension of hostilities, until farther orders should be received from their respective
governments.   To this proposal his Lordship immediately assented, as far on the coast as the
authority of Louis XVIII. should be acknowledged.
Declarations and proposals to the same effect were
sent off to Rear-admiral Sir Harry Neale, who lay
at anchor with his squadron in Douranenez bay.
On the 14th of April, the white flag was displayed
at Brest, and a universal declaration in favour of
the Bourbons was made throughout France.   Sir
Harry Neale, under these pleasing assurances, consented to a general suspension of hostilities.

On the 20th of April, Louis XVIII. made his
public entry into London.   On the following day
his Majesty proceeded to Dover, where every
preparation had been made for his reception.
Vice-admiral Foley, who commanded in the
Downs, was instructed to have his squadron in
readiness to do honour to the king of France.   A
scene was now preparing between the two coasts,
which, for interest, exceeded any thing of the kind
that ever was exhibited in Europe.

His Royal Highness the Prince Regent proceeded himself to Dover, to attend the embarkation.
The Duke of Clarence hoisted the Union at the
main, on board the Jason, commanded by the

Honourable Captain W. King, to escort the royal yacht to the opposite coast; a squadron of frigates, and sloops of war, was placed under his Royal Highness's directions. Some Russian ships of war also composed part of this memorable and triumphant escort. The Board of Admiralty repaired to Dover, and hoisted their flag on board the Royal Sovereign yacht, which was prepared for the reception of the King of France.

On Sunday morning the King held a levee, at which his Majesty was pleased to confer the order of the St. Esprit, on his Royal Highness the Duke of Clarence.

At one, p. m. the tide serving, the yacht got under weigh, and his Royal Highness the Prince Regent took a most affectionate leave of his Majesty, the Duchess of Angouleme, and the princes of the blood royal, and landed at the pier head.

As soon as the Prince Regent had quitted the yacht, the royal standard of England, and the flag of the Admiralty, which had been flying, were struck. The royal standard of France, surmounted by a British pendant, was hoisted at the main, and saluted with twenty-one guns, by the castle, the batteries, and every ship of the squadron. The Royal Sovereign proceeded to sea, followed by the other yachts, in which the royal family and suite were embarked. As the Royal Sovereign passed the outward pier head, his Royal Highness the Prince Regent, who stood at the extremity, gave the signal for three cheers, which was obeyed with enthusiasm by his subjects, who thronged every part of the shore. This last mark of affection was received by the royal family of France with unutterable feelings of gratitude and attachment to the prince and the nation.

In two hours and fifteen minutes the royal yacht entered the harbour of Calais, and France received from the British navy the descendant of the Capets, Louis le Desiré. Such was the termination of the great struggle between France and England, which had continued, with the exception of the truce of Amiens, for twenty-one years.

Sir Edward Pellew, who in the month of February was off Toulon, saw in the morning of the 13th, three sail of the line and three frigates, under a rear-admiral, standing to the southward. Captain George Burlton, in the Boyne, of ninety-eight guns, was so fortunate, with every possible exertion, as to succeed in getting into action: he ran alongside of the Romulus, which was an eighty-gun ship, the sternmost of their line. A severe running fight ensued, and so near to the rocks was the enemy driven, that the Admiral, who was close up, saw she could not be stopped without running the Boyne and the Caledonia on shore; he therefore commanded Captain Burlton to desist. The Boyne had two men killed and forty wounded. The French boasted very much of this action; and in 1818, displayed to the author the " celebrated Romulus," lying safe in the basin of Toulon, after her engagement with the British fleet. The

Romulus certainly acquired much honour by the action.

The Urania, a French frigate, having been chased into Brindisi by the Cerberus, Captain Taylor, of the Apollo, sent a message to the municipality, to know in what situation he was to consider the port, as he had learned that the Neapolitan government had joined the Allies; he could not, therefore, understand why protection was afforded by it to this frigate. The French Captain, supposing the Apollo was coming into the harbour to attack him, landed his powder, and set fire to his ship; she was entirely consumed. The town of Cattaro surrendered to Captain Hoste, of the Bacchante, on the 5th of January, after ten days cannonading from the batteries erected by that officer, and Captain Harper, of the Saracen; and the Boca de Cattaro was perfectly cleared of the French intruders.

Captain Taylor, as the last act of his valuable life, took the little island of Paxo; in this he was assisted by Lieutenant-colonel Church, with a small body of troops. Paxo is situated close to Corfu, and was occupied with a view to an attack on that island. Captain Hoste took Ragusa, a very strong place to the northward of Cattaro, which gave the Allies the complete possession of every place in Dalmatia, Croatia, Istria, and the Friuli, with all the islands in the Adriatic. After this conquest, Rear-admiral Fremantle returned to England, and gave the following brief summary of his services in the Adriatic:—

Names of Places.	No. of Guns.	No. of Men in Garrison.	By what Ships taken.
Agosta and Curzola	124	70	Apollo, Imogen, and a detachment of troops
Zussana	..	39	The boats of the Saracen
Fiume and Porto Ré	97	..	90 vessels, 500 stand of arms, besides military stores, by the Milford, Elizabeth, Eagle, Bacchante, & Haughty
Farrazina	5	..	Eagle
Isle of Mezzo	6	59	Weazel and Saracen
Ragosnizza	8	86	Boats of Milford and Weazel
Cittæ Nòva	4	..	Elizabeth and Bacchante
Rovigno	4	..	Tremendous
Pola	50	..	Wizard, party of Milford's marines, and 50 Austrians
Stagno	12	52	And military stores, by Saracen, and party of Austrians
Lessena and Brassa	24	..	Bacchante
Trieste	80	800	Milford, Eagle, Tremendous, Mermaid, Wizard, and Weazel, with 1500 Austrians
Cortellazo & Cavalino	8	90	Elizabeth, and a party of Austrians
Four forts at the mouth of the Po, containing	24	100	And 45 brass guns dismounted, by the Eagle, Tremendous, and Wizard, with 500 English, and 2000 Austrian troops
Zara	110 18 howitzers	350	100 guns dismounted, 12 gun-boats, by the Havannah and Weazel, with 1500 Austrians
Cattaro	130	900	Bacchante and Saracen
Carlobago	12	150	Bacchante and Saracen
Ragusa	158	500	Bacchante, and Austrians under General Mulitinovitch
Paxo	3	122	Apollo
Total	824	3298	
Howitzers	18		
	842		

Captain Sir Josias Rowley, who, for his services in India, had been recently created a baronet, was ordered by the Commander-in-chief to assist in the reduction of Genoa. He received on board his ships Lord William Bentinck, and the forces under his command. On their arrival, they found that Captain the Honourable G. H. L. Dundas, in the Edinburgh, with the Rainbow, and some flotilla, had co-operated with the advance of the British army, joined by a strong detachment of our forces from Sicily. On the 13th, the small vessels drew near the town; and on the 17th, the whole of them opened their fire, and landed the seamen and marines previously to the storming; the enemy fled from their batteries, and deserted the whole of the sea line, without the walls, which was instantly taken, and the guns turned upon the place. Things were in this position, when Sir Edward Pellew, with five sail of the line, came to an anchor before the town, and Genoa was again in possession of the British forces. Captain Edward Brace, of the Berwick, of seventy-four guns, and Captain Hamilton, of the Havannah, with Captain Rea, of the marines, and many other officers, were distinguished on this occasion.

The ships and vessels of war taken here were important; the Brilliant, of seventy-four guns, ready for launching, another of seventy-four guns, not named, in frame, with two brigs of war, of eighteen guns, and two of sixteen. On the 22d of March, Captain Hoste, in the Bacchante, took possession of Parga, at the request of the inhabitants, who struck the French flag.

On the 12th of April, Captain Brisbane, of the Pembroke, of seventy-four guns, with the Aigle and Alcmene frigates, chased on shore under the guns of Port Maurizio, in the gulf of Genoa, a French convoy of twenty sail of vessels, four of which, with the cargoes of fifteen others, they brought off. The vessels had been scuttled by the crews, and were destroyed by our people.

The few remaining troops and garrisons of France serving in Spain capitulated. On the 24th of March, Ferdinand VII. arrived at Gerona, and on the 6th of April entered Saragossa. About the same time the Pope returned to his dominions.

The unhappy Napoleon, after embracing his eagles, and some few of his military companions, set out from Fontainbleau for the place of his exile, and took the road to Marseilles. Off this port was stationed Captain Thomas Usher, in the Undaunted, of thirty-eight guns, with the Euryalus, Captain Napier.

Captain Usher had been prepared some days before for a change in the south of France. On the night of the 21st of April, when off Marseilles, the illuminated horizon in the N. E. indicated some joyful event. The two frigates approached the batteries, but perfectly prepared for action; the British colours displayed in their usual situations, and the royal standard of France at the main-topgallant-mast head. Coming within range, a shot was fired by the French, which struck the Undaunted, but hurt no one. Captain Usher wore, and stood out, hauling down the French flag only: a second shot struck the ship under her counter. The Undaunted was immediately brought within point-blank shot of the battery, which stood on an island, and after a few broadsides, the enemy quitted their guns. A boat was seen rowing out of the harbour, with a flag of truce. The Mayor and municipality had come to inform Captain Usher of the happy change which had taken place, by the appointment of a provisional government, in the absence of the Bourbons; they also apologized for the conduct of the officer in the battery; but this Captain Usher assured them was unnecessary, as he had already done justice to his insulted flag; and to prove that he had the most perfect confidence in the loyalty of the people, he anchored the two frigates under the walls of the town. The Captains went on shore in their barges: when they approached, the people plunged into the water, and taking them on their shoulders, carried them to the Hotel de Ville, while the air resounded with " Vivent les Anglois." In the midst of this affecting scene, Colonel Campbell arrived, and stated, that Napoleon being on his way to the island of Elba, he (Colonel Campbell) requested the assistance of Captain Usher to convey him thither; this, in pursuance of the instructions from Lord Castlereagh, Captain Usher consented to. Frejus was fixed upon as the place of embarkation, and there the Undaunted arrived on the 23d of April. About two o'clock, Captain Usher met Colonel Campbell, who conducted him to Napoleon. The Emperor was dressed in a frock uniform, he wore a star, and had a book in his hand: he asked the Captain many questions, as to the anchorage, and other points of nautical information.

While preparing to embark, the Dryad, a French frigate, arrived. Captain Moncabret waited on Napoleon, supposing the Emperor would prefer his ship for the voyage; but Napoleon informed him that he chose to go in the Undaunted. The French Captain put to sea immediately after this mortifying decision; and it was arranged, that Napoleon should embark on the following day; but being indisposed in the forenoon, he ordered his carriage at seven o'clock, at which hour he quitted his hotel, accompanied by Captain Usher, Count Bertrand, and Baron Koëler. The Russian and Prussian Envoys, and Colonel Campbell, followed in their own carriages. It was a bright moon-light night; the scene was solemnly grand, and deeply interesting; a regiment of cavalry was drawn up on the beach. When the carriage stopped, the bugles sounded, and Napoleon, stepping out, embraced his friends, then took the arm of Captain Usher, and entered the barge of the Undaunted. The officer who commanded the boat was Mr. Smith, fourth lieutenant of the Undaunted, nephew to Sir Sidney Smith; he had been a midshipman with Captain Wright, in the Vincejo. The arrangement of his commanding the boat was accidental, but the coincidence was a strange one. On coming alongside, Napoleon walked up with ease, bowed to the officers on the quarter-deck, and instantly went forward to the forecastle among the seamen, minutely examining every thing, and making many observations, which could not fail to be interesting from a person of his remarkable distinction.

During the voyage, Napoleon spent the greater part of the day on deck, and was not the least seasick; he looked at the coast of Corsica with intense interest through a telescope, and related many anecdotes of his former days. He wished Captain Usher to go into Calvi, for which port he appeared to be a pilot: he was even playful in his remarks, proposing to Baron Koëler to take a walk with him on the cliffs; the Baron whispered to Captain Usher, that he knew the Emperor too well to trust himself in his company alone.

Passing the island of Capraja, famous for its anchovy fishery, a deputation came off, requesting the Captain would take possession of the island, which he did. Napoleon talked with the deputies, who were greatly surprised to find him on board an English ship of war.

Elba appearing in sight, the Emperor inquired what colours were flying on the batteries. When within four or five miles of the harbour of Porto Ferrajo, Colonel Campbell, and Lieutenant Hastings, first of the Undaunted, with the foreign ministers, went on shore as commissioners to take possession of the island, and make the proper arrangements for receiving its future Sovereign.

On the 30th of April, about eight o'clock in the evening, the frigate anchored at the harbour's mouth. A deputation of the inhabitants waited on their Emperor; he was on deck, at his usual hour, and indefatigably inquisitive. At seven, A. M., the Undaunted weighed, and ran into the harbour, anchoring abreast of the town. After breakfast, Napoleon requested Captain Usher to cause two flags to be made by the ship's tailors; they were to be white, with a horizontal red stripe, on the stripe three bees, as the arms of the Emperor. One of the flags was hoisted at one, P. M., and saluted by the Undaunted, and a French corvette lying in the harbour. At two, on the 3d of May, Napoleon landed, and took upon himself the government of the island. He particularly requested, that two officers of the Undaunted, two officers of marines, and two sergeants, might accompany him, and remain on shore. One of the sergeants, selected by himself, slept at the door of his bedchamber. Four hundred men, of his vielle garde, were, by the treaty of abdication, permitted to accompany him in his exile. Not arriving so soon as was expected, he expressed his suspicions that they would not be permitted to leave France; but when he learned that English transports were provided for their reception, his mind was at ease,— a high compliment to the national honour. The transports arrived early in May. Napoleon was delighted, sent out pilots to meet them, and prepared barracks for the men, and stables for his horses. At seven in the morning, the vessels were secured in the harbour, and the troops landed, under the command of General Cambrone, and were paraded by Napoleon. One half of the Undaunted's crew were sent on board the transports; and at four o'clock, all the horses, carriages, and baggage, were landed, and the transports reported ready for sea. When Napoleon was informed of this, he seemed much surprised, and pointing to some of his own subjects, said, " These fellows would not have done in eight days, what you have done in eight hours; moreover, they would have broken my horses' legs, which, by the expertness of your sailors, have not received even a scratch." Bonaparte dined at seven, after which, he usually walked in his garden with Captain Usher till eleven; his conversation, says the gallant Captain, " was most interesting, and he was in high spirits." Having completed his arrangements, Captain Usher demanded an audience of leave. The Emperor was grieved at the thoughts of losing the Undaunted and her Captain, and used every argument to induce him to prolong his stay, but in vain. When he took leave, the Emperor was visibly affected; the attentions and kindness which he had received from that excellent officer, had evidently wrought a change in the sentiments of Napoleon in favour of England. Captain Usher rightly conceived, that the duties of hospitality demanded of him every soothing act which could tend to alleviate the afflictions of a conquered enemy, and of fallen grandeur. We must now take leave of Napoleon, while we conclude the history of the war in other parts of the world.

On the 14th of January, a treaty of peace was signed between Great Britain and Denmark, after a war of six years and three months. All the foreign settlements of Denmark were to be restored to her; but the island of Heligoland, at the mouth of the Elbe and Weser, was reserved to the King of England in full sovereignty. The island of Anholt was restored to Denmark. His Danish Majesty consented at the same time to make peace with Russia, Sweden, and Prussia, as the allies of Great Britain, and to furnish ten thousand men towards the common cause; the King of Great Britain paying a subsidy of £400,000. sterling, for the maintenance of them. The King of Denmark bound himself to abolish the slave trade; he was to receive a proper compensation for Norway; and all former treaties between Great Britain and Denmark were to be renewed.

The definitive treaty between England and France was signed on the 14th of May, in the same year. France was to return to the limits of 1792, with some modifications. The course of the Rhine, from the point where it becomes navigable, into the sea, and vice versa, to be free. Holland was to be placed under the sovereignty of the house of Orange, with an increase of territory. The States of Germany to be independent, and united by a federative bond. Switzerland to govern herself. Italy, beyond the limits of the house of Austria, to be composed of sovereign states. Malta, and its dependencies, to belong to his Britannic Majesty.

The eighth article of this treaty was the most remarkable, as relating to colonies. All those taken by us from France were to be restored, as they stood in January, 1792, with the exception of Tobago, St. Lucie, the Isle of France, Roderigue, and the Sechelles. The Spanish part of St. Domingo, ceded to France by the treaty of Basle, was to be restored to his Most Catholic Majesty. Sweden restored Guadaloupe, and Portugal French Guayana, to France. France engaged to erect no fortifications in India, and only to place in her establishments such a number of troops as would secure the maintenance of the police. France to have the right of fishing on the banks of Newfoundland.

The fifteenth article particularly refers to the division of the ships and naval stores found in the arsenals of such maritime places as should be restored by the second article of the convention of Paris. By this article, the ships of war and naval stores were to be divided between France and the country in which the said places are situated; two-thirds to France, and one-third to the power enti-

tled; but this article was not to extend to such
places as were in the power of the Allies before the
23d of April; and the vessels and arsenals belonging to Holland, particularly the fleet in the Texel,
were not included in this article; Antwerp to be
thenceforward solely a commercial port. The King
of France, by one of the additional articles of the
treaty of Paris, engaged to use his utmost endeavours at the then approaching Congress, to procure
the abolition of the slave trade. The reader is here
only offered an outline of this celebrated treaty, as
far as it relates to maritime and commercial rights;
but the whole is worthy of perusal, as being conceived in terms more congenial to the love of peace,
and the genuine spirit of Christianity, than any on
record. We will not claim exclusive merit for our
beloved England; but we will venture to say, that
since the records of men were committed to parch-
ment, no nation ever shone with more resplendent
lustre than Great Britain at the treaty of Paris.
Peace was proclaimed in London on the 17th day
of June, 1814. The Allies were all included in the
general pacification.

Captain David Porter, in the Essex, American
frigate, who had been very successful in his depredations on our trade in the northern hemisphere,
had gone round Cape Horn, in 1813; and Captain
Hillyar, in the Phœbe, of thirty-six guns, with
Captain Tucker, in the Cherub sloop of war, of
eighteen guns, had long been in search of him off
Valparaiso, a Spanish port, and open roadstead,

where the most rigid neutrality was enforced by the government; and as Captain Porter was sensible of the superiority of his enemies, he kept his ship very close to the batteries.

Captain Hillyar had nearly five months of anxious search for the Essex. At length he got sight of her in the road of Valparaiso, and six weeks more were passed in watching her movements. On the 28th of March, the American frigate got under weigh, with the hope of escaping from a long and involuntary confinement. The Phœbe and Cherub chased; the Essex, endeavouring to weather them, carried away her main-topmast, and anchored very close to the shore, beyond the limits of neutrality. Strong and baffling winds for some time prevented the Phœbe coming to close action. Having got springs on his cables, Captain Hillyar made the signal to Captain Tucker to keep under weigh, expressing at the same time his own determination of anchoring alongside of the enemy. At thirty-five minutes past five in the evening, the action began, and lasted until twenty-five minutes past six, when the American being disabled, struck her colours. Captain Porter's conduct was perfectly honourable: he defended himself against a very superior force; his ship was twice on fire, and many of his crew in this extremity jumped overboard. The number on board the Essex at the commencement of the action could not be ascertained, as no ship's books, nor any papers, except charts, were found on board of her. Captain

Porter stated that his crew amounted to two hundred and sixty. Captain Hillyar received on board one hundred and sixty-one prisoners, of whom forty-two were wounded; twenty-three were found dead on her decks: the others escaped to the shore, or were drowned in the attempt. The Phœbe had her first lieutenant, Mr. Ingram, and three men killed, and seven wounded: the Cherub had one killed and three wounded, among them Captain Tucker. The Essex arrived safe in England, under the command of Lieutenant Pearson, second of the Phœbe, who was promoted to the rank of Commander.

Rear-admiral Cockburn returned to the coast of North America. The Sceptre being found defective, he shifted his flag to the Albion, of seventy-four guns, and went to the Chesapeake, where he learned that Vice-admiral Sir Alexander Cochrane had been appointed to succeed Sir John Warren as commander-in-chief in North America. Sir John was recalled; and the Newfoundland and West India stations were restored to their former arrangements.

Sir Alexander Cochrane, in notifying his appointment to Rear-admiral Cockburn, directed him to get possession of some island in the Chesapeake, which might serve at once as a place of arms and refreshment for the troops, and where our ships of war, and their prizes, might ride in safety, and obtain fresh water.

When the British army under the Duke of Wellington, had marched in triumph from the banks

SIR GEORGE COCKBURN. G.C.B.

MAJOR GEN? OF MARINES.

Drawn & Engraved by Charles Turner

FOR CAPT BRENTON'S NAVAL HISTORY.

London Published Feb? 1 1825 by C.Turner. 50. Warren Street, Fitzroy Square.

of the Adour to the Garonne, he was enabled to
spare a detachment, consisting of the 4th, 44th,
and 85th regiments of infantry, with some pieces
of artillery. These were embarked from Bour-
deaux, and received on board a squadron lying at
the mouth of the Gironde ready for their reception.
The ships were, the Royal Oak, of seventy-four
guns (on board of which the flag of Rear-admiral
Pulteney Malcolm was flying); the Dictator and
Diadem, of sixty-four guns each, but armed 'en
flute;'—the frigates Pomone, Menelaus, Franc
Weser, and Thames; the Meteor and Devastation,
bomb-vessels, and one or two gun-brigs, with
several store-ships and transports. The military
were under the command of Major-general Ross:
they left the Gironde on the 2d of June, and on
the 24th, arrived at Bermuda, where they joined
Sir Alexander Cochrane in the Tonnant, of eighty
guns, who was waiting to collect the fleet. On the
30th they were augmented by the arrival of the
fusileers, a very fine battalion, mustering nine hundred strong. A squadron of six frigates, from the
Mediterranean, arrived on the same day, with the
21st, 27th, and 62d regiments: the two latter
destined for Canada; the former for a reinforcement to General Ross, who now had about three
thousand five hundred men. The fleet sailed from
Bermuda on the 3d of August, and reached Cape
Charles on the 14th. On the following morning
they came to an anchor within the bay of the
Chesapeake.

This was one of the most eventful periods of that impolitic war in which the Americans had been so blindly and so rashly plunged. The slave population of Virginia amounted to about three millions five hundred thousand, of whom a seventh part, at least, might be supposed capable of bearing arms; and as many of them were known, and others suspected, to be ready to rise against their masters, they were worse than an open enemy in the heart of their country. A proclamation issued and circulated by and with the emissaries of the Commander-in-chief, invited them to join the British standard, and throw off the yoke of slavery. Tangier Island was selected by the Rear-admiral for his rendezvous. He anchored the Albion within pistol-shot of the shore, took possession, erected fortifications, built storehouses, and hoisted the British flag, to which the negroes and people of colour flocked in considerable numbers; about one thousand seven hundred were collected, and instructed in their duty by the officers of marines, and soon became very useful to us. These services, however, were not gratuitous. At the treaty of Ghent, their emancipation was one of the most serious grievances complained of, and it was agreed that the question should be referred to the Emperor of Russia, who awarded £250,000 as a proper remuneration to the proprietors.*

The activity and enterprise of Rear-admiral

---

* See the speech of the Right Honourable Frederic Robinson, in the House of Commons, on the 28th February, 1825.

Cockburn, kept the shores of the Chesapeake and
its tributary streams, in a constant state of alarm.
The Captains Barrie, of the Dragon, J. A. Gordon,
of the Barossa, and George Burdett, of the Maidstone, pursued the American flotilla under Commodore Barney up the Patuxent, and forced the
Americans to burn them all.   On the 15th July, the
Asia, of seventy-four guns, arrived with some troop-
ships, and a battalion of royal marines. This enabled
the Rear-admiral to vary his attacks, to prevent
the enemy from combining on any given point,
and finally to defeat, wherever he met with them.
At the same time he conducted himself with the
greatest kindness towards the peaceable inhabitants, gained their good-will, and had not one man
on his missing list,—a fact almost incredible, and
without example in an enemy's country.   The
forces under Major-general Ross, not amounting
to four thousand men, were considered unequal to
any farther operations; but Rear-admiral Cockburn having shewn what he had done with five
hundred marines and seamen, through an extensive
portion of the countries of Virginia and Maryland,
it was agreed that the army should land on the
shores of the Patuxent, and that the Rear-admiral
should accompany the Major-general.   Having
ascended the river as high as Benedict, beyond
which there was not water for ships of war, General
Ross landed on the right bank; while the Rear-
admiral, with his boats and small craft, followed
up the stream.

The Rear-admiral and the Major-general agreed to march directly to Washington. Reaching Bladensberg on the 24th, the enemy was discovered, drawn up on a hill on the opposite side of a river which runs by the lower part of the town. Our men crossed the stream, against a heavy fire of cannon and musketry, and steadily advanced towards the top of the hill, on the centre and flank of the Americans, who fled, leaving on the field most of their cannon and wounded men. After giving their people a short time for refreshment, the chiefs again put them in motion, and entered Washington the same evening, where their arrival was so unexpected, that the dinner-table was laid at the President's house for the entertainment of a large party. A little musketry from one of the houses in the town, which killed the General's horse, was all the resistance they met with. This was quickly silenced; the house burnt; and the people within it put to death; and highly to the honour of the victors, this was the only instance of severity, or injury to private property. The troops were withdrawn from the scene of temptation: detachments were immediately sent to destroy all the public works and stores. These were, the arsenal, with two hundred pieces of cannon, and an immense quantity of small arms and ammunition; a frigate of the largest class, ready for launching; a sloop of war; a stock of timber, for the construction of ships of the line; the President's house, the barracks, and the dock-yard. These were all consigned to the flames, or rendered useless, on the nights of the 24th and 25th of August; and it was calculated that the American government sustained a loss of near four millions sterling.

While these transactions occupied the attention of Mr. Madison in the capital, Captain James A. Gordon, in the Seahorse, of thirty-eight guns, with Captain Napier, in the Euryalus, of thirty-eight guns, and three bomb-vessels, ascended the Potowmac, a distance of fifty miles: after the most incredible labour, the bombs reached the town of Alexandria, into which they threw their shells. The garrison retreated. Captain Gordon proposed the terms on which he was willing to spare the town from the fate of Washington. They were thankfully accepted. The forts were destroyed, with all their artillery; the shipping, with all the merchandise, brought away; and the squadron retreated with twenty-two prizes deeply laden.

When passing the flats and intricate navigation of the Potowmac, the squadron met with many obstructions, which were surmounted, and served only to display the professional character of Captains Sir Alexander Gordon, Napier, H. L. Baker, Alexander, Bartholomew, Keenah, and Roberts, who commanded the frigates and bomb-vessels.

The terms dictated by Captain Gordon, to the town of Alexandria, and enforced to the very letter, are here offered as a model for future negotiators.

1. All naval and ordnance stores, public or private, must be immediately given up.

2. Possession will be immediately taken of all shipping, and their furniture must be sent on board by the owners without delay.

3. The vessels, which have been sunk, must be delivered up in the state they were in on the 19th of August, the day the British squadron passed the "Kettle Bottoms."

4. Merchandise of all descriptions must be immediately delivered up; and to prevent any irregularities, the merchants have the option of loading the vessels generally employed for that purpose, and they will be towed off by us.

5. All merchandise which has been removed from Alexandria since the 19th instant, to be included in the above article.

6. Refreshments of every description to be supplied to the ships, and paid for at the market price, by bills on the British government.

7. Officers will be employed to see that Articles 2, 3, 4, and 5, be strictly complied with; and any deviation, or non-compliance, on the part of the inhabitants of Alexandria, will render this treaty null and void.

(Signed)   J. A. GORDON, Captain, &c.

At a meeting of the Common Council of Alexandria, on the 29th day of August, 1814, it was resolved, that these terms should be accepted.

While Captain Gordon was advancing up the Potowmac, our army was retreating from the flames of Washington. On rejoining the Commander-in-chief, Rear-admiral Cockburn expressed an opinion that the forces should proceed without loss of time to Baltimore. This proposal was at first rejected, but afterwards, on receiving certain information, it was agreed to, and the fleet, led by the Rear-admiral, reached the mouth of the Patapsco on the 11th of September. The ships and vessels of light draught of water anchored near the point of attack. On the morning of the 12th, the troops were landed, and marched directly to Baltimore. No opposition was experienced for the first five or six miles, though it became evident that the enemy was in a state of activity and alarm, as intrenchments were found newly made, and abandoned.

The Major-general and the Rear-admiral, with some officers well mounted, and the advanced guard of about sixty men, had left the army at some considerable distance, when the Rear-admiral observed, that this was not at all conformable to the practice of their former enterprises, which had been crowned with complete success: in Maryland and Virginia, they had always kept the troops collected, leaving only the flank companies to spread into the woods. Feeling the force of this observation, the Major-general halted, to give the columns time to close. At this moment the enemy concealed in the woods, opened a brisk fire of musketry on the advanced party. Nothing now remained but to push on without hesitation, and return the fire: this was done, and so nobly, that the Americans fled in all directions; but one of their last shot mortally wounded the gallant General Ross, who died soon after on the field of battle. The Rear-admiral instantly sent notice of this event to Colonel Brock, who succeeded to the command of the troops, and joined the advance, which still retained its position. The little army again proceeded, until they discovered the enemy

drawn up behind a large range of thick palings,
about breast-high. While dispositions were making
to attack them, they opened a fire upon the English with field-guns. This discharge produced no
effect on our men, who formed into line, while
a division of light troops, detached from their
right, took a circuitous route to fall upon the left
flank and rear of the enemy. The British forces,
composed of soldiers, sailors, marines, and armed
negroes, and led on by an admiral and colonel, advanced gallantly to the attack. The Americans
kept up a heavy fire until our men reached the
palings and began to break through. At this
juncture the flank company had found their way to
the left and rear of the enemy, who made no farther
resistance, but threw down their arms and ran,
leaving their artillery, and many men killed and
wounded. This, which was called the battle of the
Meeting-house, was a decided victory; and had
our army consisted of ten thousand men, it would
have ended in the capture and destruction of Baltimore. To this place our little army advanced:
they found it strongly defended and fortified; but
notwithstanding these obstructions, it was determined to attack it. In the evening, however, a
dispatch from Sir Alexander Cochrane discounte-
nanced the attempt, and without commanding,
very prudently recommended, the retreat of the
forces. The Commander-in-chief, it soon appeared,
had other and more extensive views.

Captain Coote, of the Boxer, gun-brig, conducted

the boats of La Hogue, of seventy-four guns, the Endymion and Maidstone frigates, up the river of Connecticut, on the 7th of April, destroyed five thousand tons of shipping, three large privateers, ready for sea, a number of boats, and a quantity of naval stores.

Sir Thomas Hardy, in the Ramillies, with Lieutenant-colonel Pilkington, captured Moose Island, and all the other islands in Pass Maquady Bay.

Captain the Honourable Charles Paget, of the Superb, of seventy-four guns, having learned that a ship and brig were lying at a place called Wareham, in Buzzard's Bay, sent his boats, under the orders of Mr. James Garland, his first lieutenant, supported by the Nimrod, sloop of war, as far as the depth of water would admit. Lieutenant Garland burnt two thousand five hundred and twenty tons of shipping, chiefly new, and a cotton manufactory, valued at half a million of dollars.

In the month of September, Major-general Sir John Cope Sherbroke, the Governor of Halifax, and Rear-admiral Griffith (now Colpoys), attacked the enemy's settlements on the Penobscot; they blew up the fort of Castine, destroyed the batteries, burned the John Adams, a ship of war of twenty guns, took some prizes, and returned without loss to Halifax.

Vice-admiral Sir Alexander Cochrane, in September, sent Captain Sir Peter Parker, Bart. in the Menelaus, frigate, up the Chesapeake, to make a diversion above Baltimore. In the zealous performance of his duty, that gallant young officer landed, to attack a force much superior to his own, and in the moment of victory, received a musket-ball in the femoral artery, which caused his death in a few minutes. He was the grandson of the late Admiral Sir Peter Parker, so long and so justly beloved in the naval service.

The fort of Machias, with twenty-four pieces of cannon, was taken by Captain Hyde Parker, in the Tenedos, frigate, assisted by Lieutenant-colonel Pilkington.

In the month of September, our flotilla on Lake Champlain, received a severe defeat from that of America, under their strong batteries of Platsburg. The British vessels employed on this service were, the Confiance, of thirty-six guns, Captain Downie; the Linnet, of eighteen guns, Captain Pring; the Broke, of ten; the Shannon, of ten; and twelve gun-boats. As the army under Sir George Prevost, advanced to the attack of the fort, he requested the co-operation of the navy, which, as usual, was most readily granted. Captain Downie, a very distinguished young officer, had fitted his ship with an expedition truly surprising. On the day of the action she had only been sixteen days off the stocks. Not only his ship, but every other of the British vessels, were only half manned, and by people who, in many instances, had not been more than one or two days on board. Stores of every description were wanting. Captain Downie conceived it his duty to commence an attack on a superior force lying at an anchor, and bore up for that purpose. At seven o'clock in the morning of the 11th of September, the action began, by the Americans firing on our vessels as they approached. Captain Downie reserved his fire. Calms and baffling winds prevented his gaining the position he intended : and after two of his anchors were shot away from his bows, he was compelled to let go a third, at an inconvenient distance from his opponent. The action was fought out of gun-shot from the shore, and Captain Downie was killed.

Captain Pring, in the Linnet, who succeeded to the command, when Captain Downie fell, performed his part admirably; he continued the action until his first lieutenant and the greater part of his men were killed or wounded, and the Confiance had surrendered; when finding it impossible to escape, and useless to contend, he gave up his ship to the United States' ship Saratoga.

The force of the Americans consisted of the ship Saratoga, mounting eight long twenty-four pounders, twelve thirty-two pounders, and six forty-two pounders; brig Eagle, eight long eighteens, twelve thirty-two pound carronades; schooner Ticonderago, four long eighteen, ten twelve, and three thirty-two pounders; cutter Preble, seven long nine pounders; six gun-boats, one long twenty-four, one long eighteen pound carronade; four gun-boats, one long twelve, one eighteen pound carronade.

The Confiance had her captain, two officers, and

thirty-eight men killed; one officer and thirty-nine men wounded.

The Linnet had two officers and eight men killed; one officer and thirteen men wounded.

The Chub, six men killed; sixteen wounded.

The Finch, two wounded. Total, one hundred and twenty-nine.

Sir George Prevost seeing the fall of the little squadron, retreated with his army from before Platsburg. Commodore Yeo, in his letter to the Admiralty, reflected on the General, for having pressed the squadron prematurely and unnecessarily into action. Sir George, wishing to defend himself from this charge, resigned the command in Canada, and returned to England in the most inclement season. On his arrival, he demanded a court-martial, which was ordered at Winchester; but his death put an end to any farther investigation; and Sir James Yeo did not long survive him. It is, however, but justice to the memory of Sir George, to say, that he did not press the squadron to go into action; and that as soon as he saw the battle decided against us, a result which he had not the means of preventing, he rightly considered that storming the fort, and entering the enemy's country, would only have weakened his army by desertion, without the hope of doing any injury to the Americans.

In retreating from before Baltimore, we oberved that the Commander-in-chief had other views, in addition to those connected with the safety of the army. The Admiral had received directions from home, to undertake an expedition against the American settlement of New Orleans, on the Mississippi. This attack had been suggested by Sir Alexander Cochrane, at the time, it would appear, when his Majesty's ministers had thoughts of a similar nature. The object was to form a powerful diversion in the south, to relieve the Canadas in the north. Rear-admiral Cockburn was at the same time to attack Cumberland Island and St. Mary's, on the eastern shore of the Floridas, so as to draw the American army from the Mississippi to the sea-coast on the Atlantic. The combination was ably planned; but partly failed in the execution, from causes which could not have been foreseen by the Commanders-in-chief.

Sir Alexander Cochrane sailed from the Chesapeake on the 19th of September, 1814; and the Rear-admiral went to Bermuda to re-victual and refit his ships: here he arrived on the 26th of October. On the 26th of November he had completed all his repairs, when he sailed again in the Albion for the Chesapeake. On his arrival, he collected all the force he could spare from the duty of the blockade, to attack the town of St. Mary's, the southernmost settlement of the Americans in South Georgia. On the 18th of December, the squadron left the Chesapeake. The rendezvous given out was Cumberland Island. Captain Barrie, of the Dragon, had charge of the troop-ships and transports, on board of which were embarked the marine battalion, the regiment of refugee American negroes, and a corps of marine artillery. In their course to the southward, the Rear-admiral chased and examined every thing he saw, with the view to gain intelligence. This delayed him; and the Dragon, with the convoy, reached the point of destination before the Albion. On his arrival off Cumberland Island, he found the Dragon, and learnt that the marines and black troops had already landed, under the authority of Captain Somerville, of the Rota frigate, who had been ordered to join the expedition with two companies of the 2d West India regiment.

Rear-admiral Cockburn instantly landed, and found the British troops already in possession of St. Mary's, which they had taken after a smart action near Point Peter. The whole force did not exceed nine hundred bayonets: the guns of the ships of war were useless from the shoalness of the water. With this force, the Rear-admiral continued to keep the American army in check, while he completely cleared the great commercial town of St. Mary's of all its merchandise and military stores, which he shipped on board the vessels he had taken in the port. When this work was finished, he received an official communication from Sir Alexander Cochrane, stating the entire failure of the New Orleans expedition: deeming therefore St. Mary's no longer an object of any importance, he blew up the works, and evacuated the place, repairing with his prizes to Cumberland

Island, of which he took possession; as also of St. Simon's, and other fertile islands, which border this part of the coast.

The conclusion of the expedition to St. Mary's, for the sake of perspicuity, is deferred until after the history of the attack on New Orleans, which will be the subject of the next chapter.

Towards the latter end of the year 1813, Rear-admiral (now Sir P. C. H.) Durham, sailed for Barbadoes, in the Venerable, of seventy-four guns, to take upon him the chief command on that station. He had the Cyane, of twenty-four guns, with him; and with the good fortune peculiar to him, he captured, on the 1st of December, the Junon, a French letter of marque, of two hundred and twenty tons, and fourteen guns, with a valuable cargo of silks, wines, and other articles. Proceeding with this vessel on his voyage, on the 16th of January, the Cyane discovered two frigates, to which the Venerable gave chase, and at sun-set having left the Cyane far astern, the Rear-admiral was so near one of the frigates, as to hail, and command her to strike. This the Frenchman declined doing, but putting his helm up, ran with all sail set, on board of the Venerable. She was instantly boarded by Captain Worth, and one hundred men, who hauled down the French colours, killing thirty-two, and wounding fifty, of the crew. She proved to be the Alcmene, of forty-four guns, and three hundred and fifty men. Her consort escaped but for a few hours. Captain Forrest, of the Cyane, pursued and led the chase, until the Venerable had taken out the prisoners, and repaired her damages. The Rear-admiral then made every possible sail on a W. N. W. course; and having run one hundred and fifty miles, he again got sight of the enemy, which, after a chase of nineteen hours more, he came up with, and captured. She was called L'Iphigenie; and was of the same class and force as the Alcmene. Both ships were perfectly new; they had sailed together from Cherbourg, in October; and were victualled for a six months' cruise. The Captains Forrest and Worth, are spoken of by the Rear-admiral in terms of much approbation.

The two French captains, it appeared, had agreed to lay the English line-of-battle ship on board at the same moment. One of them only had the resolution to execute this bold manœuvre, but gained nothing by it. A British ship of the line is at all times difficult to get into; but when her men are at their quarters, and her marines on the poop, it must be a great act of temerity in any two frigates to make the attempt. We think the French will never repeat the experiment.

In the conduct of the masters of our merchant ships, we trace the inherent spirit of Englishmen. The actions of some of these brave men, during the late war, would fill a volume, and, we doubt not, afford much valuable instruction, as well as amusement. The following instance of heroism will be found not unworthy a place in the naval history of Great Britain.

Mr. John Lennon, master of the ship Hibernia, of London, bound to St. Thomas's, in the West Indies, fell in, on the 14th of January, 1814, while off Saba, with two American privateer schooners; one of which, mounting six twelve pounders, and carrying one hundred and twenty men, chased the Hibernia, and about half-past seven brought her to action. Captain Lennon, whose force was only two long nine pounders, and four eighteen-pound carronades, with twenty-two men and boys, prepared to defend himself. With his boarding-nettings up, his guns double shotted, and his small arms loaded, he received his enemy, and six times the gallant crew of the Hibernia compelled them to retire. On one occasion the schooner prepared to lay the Hibernia on board, which the Captain perceiving, put his helm up, with the intention of running him down. This manœuvre unfortunately failed, by the superior sailing of the enemy: the jib-boom of the Hibernia, however, passed through his main-sail, and tore it away from the gaff. An American seaman got on the bumpkin of the Hibernia, endeavouring to board, but was piked by her brave defenders. After a close and noble contention of nine hours, the schooner desisted, leaving the Hibernia with one man killed, and eleven wounded; among the latter, her heroic commander. The loss of the privateer was, from the best information which could be obtained, twenty killed, with forty-two wounded. She was called the Comet. Captain Lennon on the 15th arrived at St. Thomas's, where his gallant conduct was duly appreciated, and handsomely rewarded. He received an address from the merchants, couched in the most flattering terms, and was presented with the sum of fifty guineas for the purchase of a sword : in addition to which, they remitted home by the hands of Captain Lennon the sum of £550 to the merchants at Lloyd's, requesting that one hundred guineas of that sum might be laid out in the purchase of a piece of plate to be presented to the Captain, with a suitable inscription ; and the remainder divided, as Captain Lennon might judge most proper, among his crew. We have often wished that a ship, thus defended, should have a protection from impressment during the war.

The second privateer did not come into action.

The state of Europe at this important moment, is not to be described. England was the pillar of safety to which, under Providence, all eyes were turned. Her noble struggles in the cause of freedom ; her disinterested love of justice ; the sacrifices which she had made, and was still preparing, for the repose of the world ; the valour of her soldiers and sailors; their skill in the art of war, and the generosity with which they exposed themselves to save a sinking enemy, elicited the admiration of a civilized world. The Emperor Alexander, and the King of Prussia, expressed a desire to see a country so renowned. The royal yachts were prepared; and his Royal Highness the Duke of Clarence, as admiral of the fleet, sailed for Calais, to conduct the illustrious visitors to England.

One of the first wishes expressed by their Majesties,

after having seen his Royal Highness the Prince
Regent, was to be present at a naval review, and
visit the celebrated dock-yard at Portsmouth.
Their request was immediately complied with.
On Sunday the 19th of June, his Royal Highness
the Duke of Clarence, as admiral of the fleet,
hoisted the Union at the main, on board the Jason,
frigate, at Spithead, and on the following day the
flag of the Lord High Admiral was hoisted on
board the Ville de Paris. The flag of the Admiral
of the fleet was then shifted to the Impregnable;
and on the 21st, that of the Admiralty was removed to the Bombay Castle, of seventy-four
guns.

. His Royal Highness the Prince Regent left his
palace in Pall-mall at nine o'clock on the morning of the 22d, accompanied by his royal brother
the Duke of Cambridge. On reaching the top of
Portsdown hill, a little after three o'clock, the signal
was communicated to the ships at Spithead, and
to the batteries on each side of the harbour's
mouth, when a salute was fired from the whole.
This ceremony was repeated, when the royal
carriage reached the gate of the garrison, where it
was met by General Houston, the governor, who
presented to his Royal Highness the keys of the
garrison. A triple discharge of artillery, along
the lines and ramparts, announced the entrance
of the Prince within the walls. His Royal Highness was received at the government house by his
royal brother, the Admiral of the fleet, the Board

of Admiralty, and the Secretary of State for the Home Department.

His Majesty the King of Prussia, with the Prince Royal, and the other male branches of the royal family, arrived at half-past seven the same evening, and were conducted to the house of the Lieutenant-governor,

His Majesty the Emperor of Russia, arrived at nine the same evening, accompanied by his sister, the Grand Duchess Catharine, and Count Lieven. His Imperial Majesty and suite were lodged in the Commissioners' house in the dock-yard. On Thursday the 23d, the whole of these royal and illustrious visitors embarked at the king's stairs, in the dock-yard, in a barge prepared for them. In the bow of the barge the royal standard of Great Britain was hoisted, and the procession proceeded to Spithead. On the starboard or right hand side of the royal boat, a barge bore the imperial standard of Russia : another, on the left, bore the royal standard of Prussia. These boats were filled with the suites of their respective sovereigns. His Royal Highness the Admiral of the fleet, in his own barge, and carrying the Union flag, led the starboard line of boats. His Royal Highness was accompanied by the Dukes of York and Cambridge, and the Duke of Saxe Weimar. The larboard line of boats was led by the port Admiral : the rest of the officers of the fleet followed according to seniority. As the Prince Regent passed the garrison, he was saluted with twenty-one guns from the platform; and the same salute was fired by the ships at Spithead. The Admiral of the fleet, the Board of Admiralty, with the Ambassadors of Austria and Prussia, preceded the royal barge, and reached the Impregnable, to be ready to receive their Majesties and the Prince Regent. The yards were manned, and the whole appearance was such as to gratify the most refined taste. Portsmouth was crowded to excess; and Spithead exhibited a scene of gala unknown to former times.

Reaching the Impregnable, the sides were manned by lieutenants; Sir Harry Neale, as Captain of the fleet, received the Prince Regent at the head of the ladder, and, after passing the guard of marines, his Royal Highness was met by the royal Admiral of the fleet. The Union at the main was then struck, and re-hoisted on board the Chatham, of seventy-four guns, and the royal standard hoisted at the main-topgallant-mast of the Impregnable, the Admiralty flag at the fore, and the Union at the mizen. The whole fleet at this moment fired a royal salute; and the batteries on shore returned an equal number of guns. The royal visitors went through every part of the ship, and after partaking of refreshments prepared for them, the imperial and royal visitors quitted with the same order and ceremony, and returned to their respective residences on shore. In the evening, the Prince Regent ente tained the whole of his illustrious guests at dinner, at the government-house, to which naval and military officers, to the rank of post-captain and colonel, were invited. Their Majesties, and the Prince Regent, gratified the people, by exhibiting themselves at the balcony.

On the 24th, their Majesties visited the dock-yard, and then crossed over to Haslar Hospital. On both these great objects, the highest encomiums were justly bestowed; after which, the Emperor returned to his residence, and his Royal Highness the Prince Regent, and the King of Prussia, went on board the royal yacht, where his Royal Highness commanded the signal to be made for the fleet to weigh, which was immediately executed, and the whole stood to sea. When as far as St. Helen's, the royal party, with the exception of his Imperial Majesty, went on board the Impregnable. The fleet went through several manœuvres, and returned to Spithead at seven in the evening. In the evening of the 27th, the royal visitors quitted Portsmouth, his Royal Highness the Prince Regent having first commanded a very liberal naval promotion.

CHAP. IV.

WHAT were the feelings of grief, disappointment, and dismay, experienced by the councils and senate of North America, when they learnt the defeat

of Bonaparte and his armies at Leipsic, it is unnecessary to inquire. The effect produced was,
however, favourable to Great Britain and to peace;
but while our ministers shewed a readiness to
treat, they were also equally prepared to carry on
the war with vigour. We had by the recent events
on the continent a very large disposable force,—
ships in high efficient order; troops and sailors more
than enough to have destroyed every sea-port in
North America. With every means of annoyance,
we had also many motives to wish for a peace;
and while our armies fought on the banks of the
Mississippi, our ministers had put an end to hostilities by the treaty of Ghent.

The expedition to New Orleans appears to have
been simultaneously proposed by his Majesty's
ministers at home, and Admiral Cochrane abroad.
The plans were written out and digested under
the eye of, and in concurrence with, the Admiral,
on his return from America; after which, he again
took his departure for the coast, to await the
arrival of the forces.

It was the earnest wish of the Admiral, founded
on the wisest motives, that the expedition, previously to the attack, should not approach nearer
to the mouth of the Mississippi than Bermudas or
Barbadoes. Such a rendezvous would have concealed from the enemy the place of our intended
landing. Unfortunately neither of these plans were
adopted, and the fleet assembled at Negril Bay,
in the island of Jamaica; the point most contiguous

to the proposed scene of action. This was not the worst. The dispatches, being forwarded to Vice-admiral Browne, the commander-in-chief at Jamaica, did not reach Port Royal till after the death of that gallant officer. They were therefore opened by the senior officer in command, and by means well known to the author of this work, their contents reached the ears of an American merchant resident at Kingston. This man instantly sailed in a schooner for Pensacola, and communicated the important information to General Jackson, who commanded the southern army of the United States, and who at that moment, in consequence of a well-combined manœuvre of Sir Alexander Cochrane, was marching to the relief of St. Mary's, which, it will be remembered, was attacked by Rear-admiral Cockburn, as related in the last chapter.

General Jackson, on hearing that New Orleans was threatened, turned from the defence of St. Mary's, and marched to the westward, for the banks of the Mississippi, assembling about twelve thousand men in and about New Orleans, and throwing up strong entrenchments on either side of the river, below the town.

Another point of great importance to the success of the enterprise, was a large supply of flat boats, and vessels of light draught of water. These Sir Alexander Cochrane had earnestly begged for, and mentioned the Dutch schuyts as the fittest for the navigation of the shoals at the mouth of the Mississippi. These vessels, it was proposed, should at the same time convey a suitable supply of provisions. The inattention to these demands occasioned delay, and led to the farther detection of our plans. By the hiring of small vessels at Port Royal, and the eagerness to collect provisions, the prices for the one and the other were advanced according to the emergency. The whole were in the hands of Jews, who having obtained the secret, had forestalled the market. The great draught of water of the Port Royal boats, which being calculated for the navigation of the coasts of that island, were totally unfit for the shoals on the flat coast of the Gulf of Mexico, was a consideration which had escaped the notice of all but the Admiral. The number of troops originally promised was not equal to the undertaking; and this number, perhaps from unavoidable reasons, had been greatly reduced; warm clothing for the black regiments had been urgently requested by Sir Alexander Cochrane, but none was sent; and these poor natives of the torrid zone perished with cold on the shores of North America, where, on their arrival, they found the oranges frozen on the trees. The diversion of the enemy's force was very judiciously planned by Sir Alexander Cochrane, who depended on the simultaneous attack of the forces under Sir George Cockburn at St. Mary's, while he landed on the banks of the Mississippi, with the main body of

MIRAL THE HON^{BLE} SIR A.LEX.INGLIS COCHRANE, G.

From an Original Picture by Sir Wm Beechey R.A.

Engraved by C Turner for Captⁿ Brentons Naval Hist^y

London Published Augt 1823, by C Turner 50 Warren Str^t Fitzroy Squ^e

the expedition; but the unfortunate disclosure at Port Royal, while it favoured the projects of Admiral Cockburn, blasted the hopes of the Commander-in-chief.

The British fleet under the command of Vice-admiral the Honourable Sir Alexander Cochrane, arrived on the 8th of December, off the Chandeleur Islands, lying to the north of the mouth of the Mississippi. Here is an extensive bay of shoal water, interspersed with numerous islands. The fleet came to an anchor; and the enemy's gun-boats having been prepared for the event, were ready to attack our boats as they advanced. Captain Gordon, in the Seahorse, with the Armide, frigate, Captain Sir Thomas Trowbridge, and La Sophie, sloop of war, Captain N. Lockyer, had been previously dispatched by the Admiral to the anchorage, near Isle aux Vaisseaux. Running along the coast, the Armide was fired on by these gun-boats, which were heavy vessels, carrying a light draught of water; and as they occupied Lac Borgne, through which our boats must pass on their way to the Bayou Catalan, it became necessary to capture or dislodge them, as a preliminary step. To this service, Captain Lockyer was appointed, having under his orders strong detachments of boats, with marines and small-arm men from each ship of the fleet, which had recently been augmented by the junction of Rear-admiral Malcolm, with his division, and a number of transports with troops.

Captain Lockyer, supported by Captain Montresor, of the Manly, and Captain Roberts, of the Meteor, proceeded into Lac Borgne, in search of the enemy; while the frigates and smaller vessels followed as far as the depth of the water would admit, and anchored below the Isles aux Malheureux, where every vessel took the ground.

After a row of thirty-six hours, Captain Lockyer found the enemy's flotilla at an anchor, and having given his exhausted crew a short time to refresh themselves, he advanced to the attack, boarding one vessel, and in spite of the most obstinate resistance, taking her, and turning her guns on the others. Every officer and man exerted himself to the utmost; and in a few minutes the whole flotilla became prizes. They consisted of six large gun-vessels, as follow:

		Guns.	Men.
1.	....	1 long 24-pounder 4 12-pounders 4 swivels	43
2.	....	1 long 32-pounder 6 6-pounders 2 5-inch howitzers 4 swivels	45
3.	....	1 long 24-pounder 4 6-pounders 4 swivels	45
4.	....	1 long 24-pounder 4 12-pound carronades	45
5.	....	1 long 24-pounder 4 12-pound-carronades	45
6.	....	1 long 6-pounder 2 12-pound carronades	20

The loss sustained by our boats was very great!

Seventeen officers and men were killed; and Captain Lockyer, with seventy-six men, wounded. More determined valour was never shewn. Captain Lockyer, for this eminent and highly acceptable service, was made a post-captain. The navigation of the lake being thus rendered clear for our army to land, the disembarkation was begun with all the means possessed by the Admiral. It has already been shewn under what difficulties he laboured, both as to the number of boats, and distance which they had to row.

The Honourable Captain Spencer, of the Carron, Major Forrest, the assistant quarter-master-general, and Lieutenant Peddie, ascertained, on the night of the 18th of December, that the boats could reach the head of the Bayou Catalan, whence a communication might be made to the high road on the left bank of the Mississippi, leading to New Orleans.

On the 16th, the advance under Colonel Thornton was placed in the boats, and, led by Captain Gordon, of the Seahorse, took post on the Isle aux Poix, at the mouth of the Pearl river, where they established themselves on a swampy island; and the boats, including the American gun-vessels recently taken, all returned to the fleet, thirty miles distant, for another division of troops, stores, and artillery. The labour of the navy and of the boats' crews in particular, became now excessive. The weather was bad, the gales strong, and the cold intense. This last fact is singular, and almost

incredible, considering the latitude (29° N.)—the
soldiers, and particularly the blacks, suffered ex-
cessively; nor was it till the 21st, that a sufficient
number of troops could be collected to attempt a
landing on the main with any prospect of success.:
Two black regiments, and the dragoons, were left
on board, for want of conveyance. Although two
thousand four hundred men left the fleet at one
time, only one thousand two hundred could be
transported together from the Isle aux Poix to the
Bayou Catalan, owing to the want of small craft,
the larger vessels which left the fleet grounding
long before they reached as far as the Isle aux
Poix; and leaving this last place to cross the lake
on their way to Bayou Catalan, many more vessels
grounded, some soon after leaving, others midway. They succeeded, however, through all
their difficulties; and about one thousand two
hundred men reached the mouth of the Bayou.
Major-general Keene and Rear-admiral Malcolm,
who had the charge of conducting the army, moved
up that stream, and at daylight effected a landing
at a place where the rivulet, being choaked with
mud, is no longer navigable for boats. In the
course of the day this division took up a position
between that spot and the left bank of the Mississippi, across the main road to New Orleans.
In this situation the exhausted soldiers encamped
for the night, while the seamen returned to the
Isle aux Poix, for another division of troops, when
about seven in the evening, a schooner dropped

down the river from New Orleans, and commenced a brisk fire on our troops in flank, the American army making a simultaneous attack on their front. These were immediately beaten back with considerable loss; and Major-general Keene advanced still more towards the American lines, keeping the river on his left, and the swamp on his right.

Such was the position of the British army on the 25th of December, when Major-general Sir Edward Pakenham, and Major-general Gibbs arrived at head-quarters: the former took the command of the troops. The schooner which had annoyed our army on its first encampment was set on fire by the red-hot shot of our artillery on the 27th, and blew up: and a ship which had come to her assistance, was forced to cut and run up the river.

The American General had thrown up intrenchments from the Mississippi, on his right, to the impassable swamp on his left, a distance of about one thousand yards; this he had fortified with cotton bags, three deep ditches, parallel to each other, and strong palisades, with heavy guns on the ramparts, and his infantry securely posted behind. The redoubts were on a level plain, though the guns were raised by the earth thrown out of the ditches, commanding a perfect range of our gallant army, as it advanced to the attack. Great guns from our ships were brought up by the naval officers, whose indefatigable exertions had achieved the third trip to the fleet, conveying another division of troops, all the artillery, and stores,

A battery of sixteen eighteen-pounders was prepared to oppose that of the enemy; but the attack
was deferred until the arrival of Major-general
Lambert with the reinforcements, then hourly
expected. This officer in fact arrived at the outer
anchorage on the 1st of January, in the Vengeur,
of seventy-four guns, commanded by Captain
T. R. Ricketts, who had under his convoy a fleet
of transports, with the 7th and 47th regiments.
These were brought up by the boats of the fleet
on the 8th; and it was now decided to attack a
fort on the right bank of the river, which the
American General had very wisely placed to protect his flank. This operation was carried into
effect by a wonderful union of labour, science, and
bravery. The canal, which had enabled them to
bring up the troops to within a mile and a half
of the river, was widened and deepened, its course
having long been impeded by an accumulation of
mud and weeds. About fifty gun-boats, barges,
pinnaces, and cutters, having been brought close
to the bank, were tracked up unperceived by the
enemy, and at night the whole were launched into
the Mississippi under the command of Captain
Roberts, of the Meteor, bomb. In these boats
were placed the 85th regiment, a division of seamen under Captain Money, and a division of
marines under Major Adair. The whole force,
amounting to no more than six hundred men, was
under the command of Colonel Thornton, of the
85th, who, just after daylight on the morning of

the 8th, landed on the right bank of the river without opposition, while the armed boats moved up to support him. For about twenty minutes the enemy fought with great bravery; but when Captain Money, with the seamen, charged over the bridge, and the 85th, coming through the wood, charged them in flank, the Americans fled in the greatest dismay, leaving behind them seventeen pieces of cannon, which were found in the battery. Here, then, our army had gained an incalculable advantage. The fort on which the enemy so much relied for the support of his right was taken, and by carrying these guns one thousand yards higher up the river, the whole of their line might have been enfiladed. At the same time our gun-boats, having the entire command of the river, had it also in their power to attack the enemy, whose guns, then just taken, were ready to be turned against them, at the distance of no more than eight hundred yards, the breadth of the river at that place. It was intended that an attack should be made on the enemy's lines in front, at the moment when Colonel Thornton attacked the fort. It has been shewn that this fort *was* gained at daylight, yet Major-general Lambert says in his letter, "The ensemble of the general movement was lost, owing to Colonel Thornton and his division not getting across the river in time. This was not owing to any neglect of the Colonel, or the naval officers, whose exertions were too apparent." The simple fact seems to have been, that the attack on the

enemy's lines in front of our army failed from
causes not explained in the official letters.   The
officer whose duty it was to have had fascines prepared for filling the ditch, had most shamefully
abandoned his post, and was found in the rear,
not one fascine being in readiness, though promised
by 2 A. M.   A general officer rode up to him with
an intention of passing a sword through his body,
but was withheld by an aide-de-camp.   The Lieutenant-colonel was dismissed the service.   Major-
general Pakenham, an officer of the most exalted
bravery, had been accustomed to carry every thing
by the bayonet: his valour and success in this
species of warfare have already been spoken of in
the affairs of St. Lucia and Martinique.   He unfortunately supposed that the American camp was
to be stormed in the same manner as he had taken
Morne Fortuné, and had determined to make the
attempt before daylight, as soon as the firing on
the opposite side of the river should convince him
that the flanking redoubt had been attacked by
Colonel Thornton.   The delay in the advance of
the 44th with the fascines, prevented the attack of
the main army until after daylight, when our
troops advanced within two hundred yards of the
enemy's works.   Here, and not sooner, the want
of the fascines seems to have been felt: but to retreat was now thought impossible.   The gallant
Pakenham rode up in front of his men, cheering
them, with his hat in his hand, when a fire was
opened from every part of the American line, but

not from the battery on the right bank, which had
been by this time attacked and carried, as we have
stated.

The action in front, and on the left bank, was nevertheless continued with great fury, the Americans
keeping up a heavy and well-directed discharge of
grape and musketry. The British soldiers fell in
heaps, and the brave General among the first of
them. Major-general Gibbs, the second in command, was borne off the ground, mortally wounded; and the whole of the British line was thrown
into confusion. At this moment, Major-general
Lambert came up with the reserve, and when
within two hundred and fifty yards of the enemy's
lines, met our troops retreating. Many of our
brave fellows had been shot, or drowned, in the
first ditch, which, for want of fascines, they were
unable to cross.

About eight o'clock an officer reported to General
Lambert the capture of seventeen pieces of artillery in the redoubt on the right bank, by the division under Colonel Thornton, and requested to
know what should be done with them. " Let them
be spiked," said the Major-general, "for I have
not the means of keeping them: we have now two
thousand men killed or wounded." This was as
nearly true as could be ascertained at the time;
but it turned out afterwards that about eight hundred of the wounded being only touched with
buck shot, were in the ranks on the following
day. It was also unfortunate that the gun-boats,

after the glorious success of Colonel Thornton and
Captain Money, had not pushed up to the right
flank of the American army; and if to this had been
added the advance of the American guns, taken
in the redoubt, about one thousand yards higher
up the river, the capture of New Orleans might
have been achieved; or at least General Jackson
would have been defeated; though a very experienced officer who was present, doubts whether
these objects could have been effected by such
movements.

Such, however, was the disastrous appearance of
things, that Major-general Lambert halted the reserve, until he had ascertained the extent of our
loss, and of our remaining resources; having so
done, it was decided to retreat from the shores of
the Mississippi.

It must here be observed, in justice to Sir
Alexander Cochrane, that he had no control over
the movements of the army. It was his duty to
attend to the wishes of the Major-general. Had
our troops passed the first intrenchment, they had
a second and a third to encounter, all fortified in
the same manner, and in fact impregnable, unless
attacked in flank. The position of our army was
therefore such as to warrant the steps that were
taken. The last resource of the Americans would
have been to cut the bank of the Mississippi, and
inundate the ground occupied by the British. The
state of our commissariat was also most alarming;
scarcely a week's provisions remaining in store.

This unfortunate expedition was disastrous, but
not disgraceful, to those employed. Its failure was
not owing to a want of those military virtues by
which the empire has been supported, but to the
neglect of proper precautions in the outset, the
indispensable accompaniments of all enterprise.
Among the causes of defeat may be enumerated,
first, the deviation of the government at home,
from the arrangement agreed on between it and
the Admiral, by changing the place of rendezvous
from Bermuda to Negril Bay: secondly, the di-
vulging of the secret at Jamaica: thirdly, the want
of boats to land all the troops at one time: and the
want of provisions was the fourth. There was one
circumstance, however, connected with this expedition, which should not be overlooked : it certainly relieved the Canadas from the pressure of
war. The attacks on Washington, Alexandria, St.
Mary's, and New Orleans, drew all the American
forces to the southward, and left Sir George Prevost more leisure and means to protect the provinces under his immediate care.

Let us hope that North America will find
her true interests in preserving peace with her
parent state. She becomes the more vulnerable
as her territory extends. With her, education
and refinement do not keep pace with increased
population: an empire so extended and so unin-
formed, cannot long act in unison. The blacks
of the southern states are her most dangerous
enemies; and Great Britain has it in her power,

while she commands the seas, to convulse the continent of America, by exciting and assisting her discontented subjects. Had twenty thousand men been sent from England, as was originally intended, the rising of the slaves in Virginia would have been most probably fatal to the southern states of America.

Having abandoned New Orleans, and embarked all the forces at the Bayou Catalan, the Vice-admiral and Major-general Lambert agreed to attack the American settlement of Mobile, a little to the eastward of the entrance to Lake Borgne. Captain T. R. Rickets, of the Vengeur, with a small squadron under his orders, approached Fort Boyer, situated at the entrance of the bay, and effected a landing with a body of troops, seamen, and marines. In the course of forty-eight hours, he came within pistol-shot of the enemy's works; and the officer commanding the fort agreed to surrender, the troops in garrison becoming prisoners of war. Three hundred and sixty infantry and artillery-men were carried on board the fleet. The fort was found in a very complete state of defence, having twenty-two heavy guns mounted, and a plentiful supply of provisions. The possession of this place was of little importance; and more than counterbalanced by the expenses of the force employed against it. It was given up at the peace with America.

The public discontent was loudly expressed against the Admiral and General, on the failure of this expedition. Had the wisdom of parliament been employed in the investigation of the facts, some discoveries might have been made, which would have turned the national indignation to the proper objects; and the Admiral and General would have been most amply indemnified for the short and unmerited loss of popularity.

After the preliminaries of peace had been signed at Ghent, the American frigate the President, was captured by a British squadron off New York, on the 15th of January. Rear-admiral Henry Hotham lay off that place as senior officer in the Chesapeake, and Captain Hayes, of the Majestic, had with him off Sandy Hook, the Tenedos, of forty-four guns, Captain Hyde Parker; Endymion, of forty-four, Captain Henry Hope; and Pomone, of forty-four, Captain R. Lumley.

Captain Hayes had been stationed off New York, and with great judgment and perseverance had contrived to keep his station during the heavy gales and snow storms, so common to that coast in the winter season. On the morning of the 14th of January, Sandy Hook bearing N. W. fifteen leagues, one hour before daylight, the President and a brig were discovered, and chase was given. The wind failing, the Endymion soon took the lead, and was so fortunate as to get alongside of the President at half-past five in the evening. These two ships so well matched as to their main-decks, having both long twenty-four pounders, fought for two hours and a half, when the sails of the Endymion being cut from the yards, the President got a-head; while the Endymion was repairing her damages, the Pomone came up, at half-past eleven, and on firing a few shot, the enemy hailed to say they had surrendered. It would be unfair to the memory of that excellent man, Commodore Decatur, to say that this was an equal action. It might perhaps have ended in a drawn battle, had not the Pomone decided the contest; but no one will contend that the Endymion had not supported the honour of the British flag, and that she would not, in all human probability, have achieved the conquest without assistance, if we may judge from the carnage on the decks of the enemy, and the damage sustained by him in the action.

The President was the largest frigate at that time in the world, her establishment of guns was—

Main-deck	30 long 24-pounders		
Quarter-deck ...	14 42 pound carronades		
Forecastle	6 42	ditto	1 long 24-pounder
Fore-top	2 brass 6-pounders	These, we presume,	
Main-top	2 ditto	were light howitzers,	
Mizen-top	2 smaller guns	or cohorns.	

The Endymion had eleven killed, and fourteen wounded: the President thirty-five killed, and seventy wounded.

Rear-admiral Cockburn was in the mean while employed at St. Mary's, and having no idea that a peace could be speedily concluded between

Great Britain and America, had fortified Cumberland Island as a place to hold during the continuance of hostilities, and where it would have been in his power to have done great injury to the enemy.

On the 25th of February, he received a flag of truce from General Pinckney, who commanded the American forces opposed to him, intimating that a treaty of peace had been signed and ratified in England, and wanted only the approval of the President of the United States.

The Rear-admiral, in consequence of this communication, rested on his arms until the 2d of March, when official intelligence reached him of the signing of the definitive treaty. He then embarked all his military stores, and the prize goods which he had taken; to this last step General Pinckney objected, and remonstrated, as being contrary to the treaty; but the objections were overruled, and on the 18th of March, the Rear-admiral sailed for Bermuda, and shortly arrived in England, where he was soon called upon to execute a very important mission.

Peace between Great Britain and America was signed at Ghent, on the 24th of December, 1814, The plenipotentiaries were Admiral Lord Gambier, Henry Goulburn, Esq. and William Adams, Esq. on the part of Great Britain. Those of America were, John Quincey Adams, J. A. Bayard, Henry Clay, Jonathan Russel, and Albert Gallatin, Esqrs.

Although generally unfriendly to war, and depre-

cating the horrors of such a state of things, we saw
with regret the termination of a contest provoked
by America, at a time when Great Britain was
struggling not only for her own liberty, but that
of the world. Mr. Madison supposed, by adding
his hostility to that of France, he should ingratiate
himself with Napoleon. In this he was mistaken;
his representatives met with the same indifference
at the Thuilleries, as they had ever done. In addition to the burning of the public works at Washington and Alexandria, and the depredations committed on their coasts, the London Gazette re-
counts the capture or destruction of one thousand
four hundred sail of American vessels. This we
believe to be much under the actual number. Our
losses were equally great in point of shipping, and
probably of more intrinsic value. To these we
might add, the capture of the Levant and the
Cyane, two twenty-gun ships, by the Constitution, after a very honourable defence made by
their captains, Douglas and Falcon. The Penguin,
a brig of eighteen guns, was also taken by the
Hornet. The British captain, Dickenson, fell in
the discharge of his duty, and Lieutenant James
M'Donald, who succeeded to the command, surrendered when no longer able to contend against
a more powerful vessel.

The conduct of the four last mentioned officers,
in the defence of their ships, was highly com-
mendable. Our enemies were elated without any
real cause; these captures being nothing more than

the mere casualties of war, adding no merit to the conqueror. In the rising navy of America the facts were magnified, to give spirits to their sailors and confidence to their officers.

The war has long been happily terminated : it were idle and impolitic to load our quondam antagonists with censure, and useless to convict a few individuals in their navy of partiality and misrepresentation. Let us inquire what advantages America gained by the war? Did she set at rest the question of impressment? or did she define the laws and extent of the power of a belligerent to blockade an enemy's port? These were the ostensible objects for which she went to war (the secret motives are hidden in the breast of Mr. Madison); and they were left as undefined in 1814. as they were in 1794.

Of the number of her citizens forcibly taken to serve in our ships, we have already spoken, and proved shameful exaggerations. The wretched fabrications, promulgated by the basest party writers in both countries, of the cruelties exercised upon American seamen by British naval officers, are unworthy of notice. We have afforded some glaring proofs of the propensity to falsehood among the American sailors. Oaths may be taken by men who have no sense of religion, and received by magistrates whose credulity is equal to their ignorance; but truth, like the waters of the ocean, will ever find its level.

Of the terms of the peace we shall merely give

an outline : they are to be found at large in the Naval Chronicle for the year 1815, vol. i.

All discussions on our maritime rights were to be waved on both sides. American vessels captured by us in retaliation of the Berlin and Milan decrees, were not to be restored. We gave up the province of Maine, but retained the islands in Passmaquady Bay. All the disputed questions were to be determined by Commissioners.

After the victorious allies had advanced into the heart of France, and compelled the emperor Napoleon to abdicate his usurped throne, and retire to the island of Elba, the statesmen who guided the destinies of Europe and the world, supposed they might confide in the promises of a man who, except he had sworn to do evil, never kept his word. The island of Elba, on the coast of Tuscany, and formerly in the territory of the Grand Duke, was fixed on for his abode, with the title of emperor, and a revenue or income of two millions and a half of livres a-year. The king of France, the patient and amiable Louis XVIII. having been seated on his throne by the joint exertions of Great Britain, Russia, Austria, and Prussia, was left to rule his dominions according to the constitution which himself and his people should devise. France began to recover from the desolating effects of internal discord and foreign war, and the ruinous effects of an overgrown army; that army to which she had given birth was nearly proving the monster that should devour its parent.

Profligate, cruel, and rapacious, it could not gratify its appetites without war, nor without the
leader under whom it had fought and deluged the
world in blood.　Napoleon from his rock heard
the complaint of his soldiers, and meditated once
more putting himself at their head.　The moment
he chose for this treacherous enterprise was that
of all others in which he should have remained
tranquil.　The sword was not yet sheathed—the
ships were not all paid off; nor were the armies
disbanded.　The Allies, though unwilling to renew
the war, were not unprepared.　Murat, the creature of Napoleon, governed the kingdom of Naples;
and on this man the cunning and unprincipled Emperor partly relied for support; but the premature movements of the vassal rendered abortive all
the plans of his daring lord. . . . .　..　...　..

The whole army of France, with the greater part
of the population, had beheld the departure of
their idol as a violation of their rights, and secretly
resolved to bring him back.　His return towards
the end of the year 1814, was openly talked of in
France, as an event that would certainly take
place, when the violets were in bloom.　Drawings
of that little flower were sold in Paris, as the symbol of revolt: the profile of Napoleon was ingeniously contrived, and easily discerned in the
vivid colours of its petals. .　. . . .　. .　. ,

Reposing under the promises of his courtiers,
Louis XVIII. was unconscious of his danger,
until the conspirators had closed up every

barrier except that on the road to Ghent. The postmaster-general was sold to the cause of the tyrant, and the body-guard which he had so easily obtained from the good faith of England, was one great instrument of his flight. Napoleon, under a pretext that his revenue had not been paid; that the treaty of Fontainbleau had been violated; and that the allied sovereigns never intended to fulfil their engagements towards him, secretly prepared to gratify his own ambition, and once more to drench the "sacred soil" in the blood of the infatuated people whom he called his subjects.

The court of Elba, during the short reign of the Emperor, had been the resort of numerous English travellers, many of them his professed admirers; for it is remarkable that Bonaparte, who overthrew liberty in Europe, and was the greatest and bitterest enemy to this country, found his chief support and advocates among that party who styled themselves *the friends of the people*. So completely had he cajoled them, that he began to be considered a martyr; his crimes were forgotten in his humiliation; and he became an object of interest and compassion, because his subjection was the effect of the Pitt system.

The squadron of British ships of war stationed in the neighbourhood of Elba, had no particular charge to obstruct the escape of its monarch, who took care to prevent the intrusion of strangers, as long as his designs were in preparation. On the 26th of February, he embarked on board a brig of war, and followed by four or five small vessels, into which he had crowded one thousand soldiers, including his body-guard, and a collection of needy adventurers. With these he landed on the 1st of March, at Cannes, in Provence, and with his followers instantly set out for Grenoble. Nothing could resist the rapid and daring march of the adventurer. The walls of fortified towns seemed to sink into the earth at his approach: the government declared him a traitor, and at the same time prepared to fly before him; Lyons opened her gates; and the princes of Bourbon were rejected with scorn. Marshal Ney, who had equivocally sworn to his deluded monarch to bring Napoleon to Paris, "kept his promise to the ear, and broke it to the sense." The traitor threw himself into the arms of his former patron, the moment he met him. His example was followed by others; and Napoleon, at the head of an army, once more declared himself "By the Grace of God, Emperor of the French." Dreadful period! The same sufferings which Europe had undergone, were about to be renewed. The Allies flew to arms. No treaties, no vows, could bind their enemy; and a war of extermination was begun against the person and power of Napoleon. The navy of England was roused from its short repose, though it had little share in this last struggle. Ships were commissioned, and prepared for sea; but before they quitted their ports, the power of Napoleon was at an end. He entered Paris on the 28th of

March. The king had quitted for Ghent the preceding day. France was almost (at least apparently) unanimous in favour of the conqueror.
The legions assembled, and marched to the northern
frontier, as the most assailable, and the most likely
to be attacked by the Allies, who never, since the
foundation of the world, acted with so much
unanimity and effect. Their declaration, published
at Vienna on the 13th of March, convinced Napoleon and the French nation, that an awful contest was to decide their fate. The empress Maria
Louisa, and her son, were withheld from the presence of their husband and father, who was pro-
scribed as a rebel and a traitor. The declaration
of the Allies was signed by the ministers of every
European power, except Turkey and Naples. In
vain did the flattering addresses of the ministers
of Napoleon deprecate foreign war—in vain declare
that they would only draw the sword in self-
defence : fixed and determined in their purpose to
have no peace or compact with the man who had
no principle, the Allies crowded to their posts.
Belgium was the theatre of the last great scene.
The Rhine was crossed in every department. The
Duke of Wellington, with a large army, was sent
to the Netherlands. The Princes of Bourbon were
not tame and useless spectators of the passing
events. The Duke of Angouleme repaired to
Nismes, in hopes of exciting the people of the
south in favour of his cause; but fear, or disaffec-
tion, had taken possession of their minds. The

Duchess of Angouleme tried the fidelity of the Girondistes. This heroic lady, the daughter of Louis XVI. and Marie Antoinette, supported her character and dignity, in this last ordeal of her fortitude. She addressed the officers in the garrison of Chateau Trompette, who still wore the white cockade: she appealed in vain to their honour and their generosity. "I see," said she, "that you are cowards, and I absolve you from your oaths:" and turning her horse, she rode away, and embarked on board the Wanderer, a British ship of twenty guns, commanded by Captain Dowers. In this ship her Royal Highness sailed from the Gironde for Plymouth, where she arrived shortly after, and held a drawing-room at the Admiral's house. She appeared dejected, but not in despair. There was a firmness of purpose in her eye—a contempt of the world, and patient resignation, which would have commanded esteem, even had she not been known to be the most unfortunate and the most enduring princess on earth.

For the present we must quit the transactions at Plymouth-dock, to which, however, we shall speedily be recalled, to relate facts of no common interest or importance.

The courts of Great Britain, Russia, Austria, and Prussia, not only refused to hold any communication with Napoleon, or his ministers, but bound themselves by the most formal engagements, to defend the restored order of things in Europe, and particularly the treaty of Paris, signed in May,

1814, and those of the Congress of Vienna. They agreed to bring into the field one hundred and fifty thousand men each, and not to lay down their arms until Bonaparte should be deprived of the power of exciting disturbances. The mockery of the Champ de Mai produced no good effect towards the cause of the Usurper. The call to arms resounded once more from Otranto to the Helder: rage on the side of the Allies—despair on that of France—stimulated the minds of the combatants, and prepared the bloodiest day that Europe had ever witnessed. The line of fortresses extending from the German Ocean to the Rhine, had, at the peace of Paris, been garrisoned by British troops, and those of our Allies. The moment the landing and progress of Bonaparte was known in England, large reinforcements were sent over to the Scheldt. The Duke of Wellington had his head-quarters at Brussels: the veteran Blucher, with a large army of Prussians, was at Namur, on the Maese. Bonaparte had his head-quarters at Avesnes, in French Flanders. He left Paris on the 12th of June, determined to give battle to the Prussians and English, before the Russians and Austrians could come to their assistance. The Prussians, notwithstanding their valour and hatred of the French, suffered some severe checks in the neighbourhood of Charleroi and Ligny. The Duke of Wellington, on the evening of the 15th of June, having received information of the near approach of the French army towards the plain between Nivelle and the wood of Soignies, directed the whole of his force upon Quatre Bras. On the 17th of June, the hostile armies came in presence of each other, on the celebrated field of Waterloo, or Mont St. Jean; and at the dawn of day on the 18th, Napoleon is said to have uttered the exclamation, "Enfin je les tiens ces Anglois"—at last I have caught the English. The battle, and its consequences, are recorded in the page of military history. Heaven fought on the side of truth and justice: the tyrant and his legions were defeated. England sustained the field against the whole power of France, from morning until the evening, when Blucher, with his victorious legions, passing between Grouchy's corps and the left of the British army, came upon the right flank of the French, and completed their overthrow. The prodigies of valour performed by our gallant soldiers on that day, are not to be described but by the most eloquent pen. The numbers of dead, of dying, and of wounded, have been variously stated: the best accounts are not exact; but seventy thousand at least may be said to have found their graves on the field of Waterloo,—human sacrifices to the modern Moloch!

Napoleon, after his defeat, hastened to Paris; a ruined gamester, he had staked his crown and lost it. "Unfit to live, and unprepared to die," he became, like another Cain, a fugitive and a vagabond on the face of the earth. He visited and quitted his capital: he sought to gain the sea-

shore, in the Atlantic, that he might escape to
America.   This project would have succeeded
but for the unceasing vigilance of the British squadron stationed in the bay of Biscay.   Reaching
Rochelle, Napoleon embarked on board a French
frigate, called La Saale, and a fair wind on the
13th of July would have taken him from the shores
of Europe, but the exit was denied by the Bellerophon, a British seventy-four, commanded by
Captain Frederick Lewis Maitland.   Supposing that
he might elude discovery in a smaller vessel, he
quitted the frigate, and went into a brig of war
called the Epervier, with all his suite and baggage:
still the watchful Bellerophon prevented his flight.
Learning, at length, from his brother Joseph, with
whom he was in close correspondence, that the
Chambers of Peers and Deputies were dissolved,
he hoisted a flag of truce, and on the 15th of July,
made sail towards the Bellerophon, then lying at
anchor in Basque Roads.   Captain Maitland received him as became an officer and a gentleman:
having no orders to the contrary, he treated him
as a monarch, but offered him no terms.   Captain
(now Sir Henry) Hotham, who commanded the
Defiance, of seventy-four guns, and who was the
senior officer of the squadron, invited him to breakfast on board his ship, and he was there also
received with all the ceremony usually shewn to
a crowned head.   The conduct of these gallant
officers was much criticised, for doing that which
they could not, in justice to their own character

and feelings, have avoided. It was for their superiors to decide how he should be received in
England.

The Bellerophon arrived in Plymouth Sound*
on the 24th of July, and here commenced a very
interesting part of the history of this extraordinary
person.

That the conqueror of nations should be the
guest and the prisoner of a captain in the British
navy, appeared to many a kind of illusion which
fancy could not realize. Plymouth, and its en-
virons, were crowded with company, eager to be-
hold the person of one whom they had so long
dreaded. Boats lay round the Bellerophon so
closely compacted together, that they might be
said to form a stage of some acres in extent. Napoleon often appeared at the starboard gangway,
resting his left arm on the hammocks : in his right
hand he held an opera glass, with which he at-
tentively surveyed every object near him. It was
at this time that his portrait was taken by Mr.
Eastlake, and afterwards engraved by Mr. Charles
Turner. It is by far the best likeness ever presented to the public; and we think it impossible
to produce a more faithful representation.

During the first four days of his stay in Plymouth Sound, the time passed away in conversation; in looking at the diversity and richness of the
surrounding scenery; and in speculations on his

* She went first to Torbay, and immediately came back to
Plymouth.

future destiny. The hope of Napoleon was, to be allowed to pass the remainder of his days in England, with his wife and son. To this he no doubt fondly referred, when, on making the land, he exclaimed, "Enfin voila ce beau pays." A return of post. from London dispelléd the flattering dream. His fate was sealed; by his escape from Elba, he was considered to have violated his faith, and no longer to be depended on: he was therefore degraded from the rank to which he had attained: he was thenceforth to be addressed as General Bonaparte; and the place of his future residence, to the end of his life, was decreed to be the island of St. Helena. The disappointment and rage of Napoleon and his followers, were vented in abuse of the British government and the Allied Sovereigns. Napoleon spoke of escaping from persecution by suicide, but was dissuaded by his friends. One of the ladies of his suite, Madame * * *, attempted to throw herself overboard, and was saved at the moment of execution. The time of departure drew near. The Northumberland, of seventy-four guns, commanded by Captain C. B. H. Ross, and bearing the flag of Rear-admiral Sir George Cockburn, was appointed to convey Napoleon to his last earthly residence. One more effort was made to rescue the Idol from his impending fate: some of his impotent friends contrived to obtain a habeas corpus ad respondendum from the Lord Chancellor, to bring Napoleon as a witness on a pending trial. To serve this legal instrument in due form,

a deputation came to Plymouth; but their secret
had preceded them. Lord Keith, as Commander-
in-chief of the Channel fleet, instantly hoisted his
flag on board the Tonnant, Captain E. P. Brenton;
ordered the Bellerophon to sea; and, to prevent
any unpleasant interview with the agents of the
law, took a fast-rowing boat (it being perfectly
calm) and pulled out into the offing, where he got on
board a sloop of war. The Tonnant could not get
out for some hours after the attorney appeared alongside. The centinels had orders to keep all boats at
a distance. The agent demanded to see Lord Keith.
He was informed that his Lordship was not on
board. He next requested that the Captain would
appear. This was granted : an explanation of the
object of the visit was demanded, and given. It
is quite forgotten under what impression the
captain acted; but he certainly took the agent
for a Frenchman, and in the French language
addressed him; nor would he make use of any
other. The man went away exceedingly dissatis-
fied; and a breeze springing, the Tonnant weighed,
and proceeded to join Lord Keith, off the Berry
Head. His Lordship came on board on the evening of the 3d of August. The Bellerophon was in
company with a frigate, and one or two sloops of
war and cutters. On the 4th, while the squadron
was cruising off the Berry Head, waiting for the
Northumberland, Captain Maitland came on board,
and presented the following letter from General
Bonaparte to Lord Keith :

Protest of Bonaparte, sent to Lord Keith, 4th August, 1815.

Je proteste solemnellement ici à la face du ciel et des hommes, contre la violation de mes droits les plus sacrés, en disposant par la force de ma personne, et de ma liberté. Je suis venu librement à bord du Bellerophon; je ne suis pas prisonnier, je suis l'hôte de l'Angleterre.

Ausitôt assis à bord du Bellerophon, je fus sur le foyer du peuple Britannique; si le gouvernement en donnant des ordres au capitaine du Bellerophon de me recévoir ainsi que ma suite n'a voulu que tendre une embuche, il a forfait à l'honneur et fletri son pavillon.

Si cette acte se consommoit, ce seroit en vain que les Anglois voudroient parler à l'Europe de leur loyauté, de leurs loix, de leur liberté: la foi Britannique se trouvera perdu dans l'hospitalité du Bellerophon. J'en appelle à l'histoire. Elle dira qu'un ennemie qui fit 20 ans la guerre au peuple Anglois, vint, librement, dans son infortune chercher une asile sous ses loix: quelle plus éclatante preuve pouvoit il donner de son estime et de sa confiance? mais comment repondoient on en Angleterre à tant de magnanimité? on feignoit detendre une main hospitallaire á cet ennemie, et quand il se fit livré de bonne foi, on l'immola.

A bord du Bellerophon à la mer, le 4me Août, 1815.

NAPOLÉON.

The authenticity of this document having been doubted, and suspicion expressed in many periodical works of the day, the writer of this work has it in his power to declare, that it is the genuine production of Bonaparte; that as such it was delivered by him to Captain Maitland; and that the ink was scarcely dry when the Captain of the Tonnant, was called in to give an opinion on the meaning of a word contained in it.

Translation.

I protest solemnly, in the face of heaven, and before men, against the violation of my most sacred rights, in disposing, by force, of my person and liberty. I came freely on board the Bellerophon; I am not the prisoner, but the guest of England.

No sooner seated on board the Bellerophon, than I was on the hearth of the British people. If the government, in giving orders to the captain of the Bellerophon to receive me, meant only to ensnare me (tendre une embuche), it has forfeited its honour, and tarnished its flag.

If this act is consummated, in vain will the people of England boast of their fidelity, their laws, and their liberty,—British faith will be buried in the hospitality of the Bellerophon. I appeal to history. She will say, that an enemy who for twenty years had made war against the English people, came freely in his adversity, to seek an asylum under your laws. What more shining proof could he give of his esteem and his confidence? But how did England reply to so much magnanimity? In pretending to hold out the hand of hospitality to that enemy; and when he had in good faith surrendered, they sacrificed him.

Dated on board the Bellerophon, the 4th of August, 1815.

(Signed)   NAPOLEON.

It is no part of our duty to offer any remark on this document; but we think it can scarcely pass unnoticed by the most cursory reader, that Bonaparte, by his escape from Elba, has forfeited every claim to honourable treatment; and the unconditional terms on which he surrendered to Captain Maitland, left the British government free to act towards him as it should judge most conducive to the future tranquillity of Europe.

On the 6th, the Northumberland joined: Sir G. Cockburn waited on Lord Keith, and arranged for the removal of General Bonaparte on the following day. For this purpose the squadron came to an anchor; the Berry Head bearing N. E. by E. $\frac{1}{2}$ E.; the Start point W. S. W. $\frac{1}{2}$ W. one mile and a half distant. On the 7th, a numerous fleet of pleasure

boats and other vessels, surrounded the squadron.
At eight o'clock, Count Bertrand came on board
the Tonnant, and was informed that the baggage
of General Bonaparte must be searched, and that
the General must prepare himself to be removed
to the Northumberland immediately. As soon as
the examination of the trunks was finished, the
barge of the Tonnant was sent with a Lieutenant,
to receive the General. *Lord Keith, we believe,
went also in the boat; but neither his Lordship,
nor Sir George Cockburn, were on the quarter-
deck of the Northumberland, to receive their prisoner. Bonaparte came up the side, clad in his
usual green undress, with white facings, breeches,
and silk stockings. He wore no powder; had very
little hair on the crown of his head; and held his
well-known peculiarly cocked hat in his hand. A
captain's guard received him. The drum beat a
march, the appropriate and established compliment
to a full General. This was a novelty to Napoleon.
He seemed at first a little surprised, but instantly

* Of this fact I am not certain, having no written memorandum.
I write from memory. It was the wish of Sir George Cockburn
that I should go in the boat; but this Lord Keith refused. Sir
George then very kindly desired me, as soon as my Admiral
had left the Tonnant, to go on board the Northumberland, that
I might see and converse with Napoleon. This invitation I took
care to accept, and was in time to see the General come up the
side. I was introduced by Count Bertrand. Napoleon conversed with apparent good humour; asked some questions in
French, to which I replied; but our conversation was inter-
rupted by Lord Keith and Sir George Cockburn, who came up
at that moment, and led him to his apartment. AUTHOR.

recovered himself, bowed to the guard, and then
entered into conversation with the officers near
him. Lord Keith and Sir George Cockburn came
on board while this was going on, and conducted
Napoleon to his apartment. The ship was crowded
to excess. There were near nine hundred people
on board, with provisions, stores, and baggage, in
immense quantities. Very few strangers were
admitted. The Commissioner came from Plymouth, and paid the seamen their wages; and in
the evening the Northumberland stood to the
westward, accompanied by the Havannah and
Bucephalus, frigates, Ceylon, transport, Zenobia,
Zephyr, Ferret, Redpole, and Icarus, sloops of
war. It was not till the evening of the 9th that
the squadron was ready to make sail. The Rear-
admiral had many wants for a voyage to St. Helena;
and the demands of the suite of Napoleon were
not easily satisfied. On the 10th of August the
squadron took its departure from the Lizard, which
at noon on that day bore N.N.E. $\frac{1}{2}$ E. seventeen
miles. They had a very favourable passage to
Madeira, which they reached on the 23d. The
frigates anchored, and took a supply of refreshments, while the Northumberland kept under sail
in the offing. On the 25th they made sail again,
taking a final departure for St. Helena. All the
occurrences of the voyage, and residence of Napoleon at St. Helena, have been related by two
medical gentlemen, who accompanied him in his
exile. These works we have read, but shall not

copy from them. We are guided by the plain and manly journal of Captain Ross, of the Northumberland, which that gallant officer has kindly lent for the purpose.

The Northumberland arrived at St. Helena on the 15th of October, and General Bonaparte landed on the 17th. On the 19th of June, 1817, Sir George Cockburn quitted the island, to return to England, having been relieved in the command by Rear-admiral Sir P. Malcolm, and arrived at Spithead on the 1st of August.

Sir George Cockburn immediately sat off for London, to give an account of his mission, and received from his Royal Highness the Prince Regent, and Earl Bathurst, the highest commendation for the able, steady, and judicious manner in which he had executed the delicate charge intrusted to him.

Joachim Murat, the new king of Naples, anxious at once to secure the tottering crown on his own head, and to make a peace with the Allies, had been, in 1814, playing a sort of double game between the Congress of Vienna and the Court of Elba. That he would espouse the strongest side was foreseen, and pointed out to Lord Castlereagh by Lord William Bentinck. Murat, after the battle of Leipsic, and the peace of Fontainbleau, negotiated and promised a faithful adherence to the cause of the Allies, and was consequently acknowledged by them; but no sooner had Bonaparte landed, and reached Lyons, than he declared himself the firm supporter of his former patron; and setting his armies in motion, demanded a passage for his troops through the papal dominions. He shortly after attacked the Austrians at Cerina, and obliged them to fall back. The emperor of Austria declared war against him, and the incursions of the Neapolitan army were very soon terminated. Murat saw his impotence, offered excuses; begged for peace of the Allies, and was rejected with merited scorn. A British squadron, under the command of Captain Campbell, of the Tremendous, of seventy-four guns, was ordered by Sir Edward Pellew to the bay of Naples, where the Captain demanded and obtained the immediate surrender of all their ships of war, arsenal, and naval stores, to be held at the disposal of the British government, and Ferdinand, king of Naples. The miserable Neapolitan army, crushed and defeated by the Austrians, disbanded and dispersed, leaving Murat to make the best terms he could with his conquerors. The Allies entered Naples, and spread over the whole kingdom. The Tremendous received Madame Murat and her family on board; and Ferdinand IV. was once more seated on the throne of his ancestors. Sir Edward Pellew, now Lord Exmouth, anchored with his fleet in the bay of Naples, and contributed by his presence to the restoration of tranquillity in that disturbed and corrupt capital. Murat fled from the continent, and took refuge in Corsica, whence he again departed in October, and landed in Calabria, calling on the people to acknowledge him as their king. Imitating the example of Napoleon, he concluded he should like him have reached his capital. The folly of his enterprise seems to deserve the name of insanity. Napoleon was at that time a prisoner at St. Helena, and the whole of the Allies ready to crush any insurrection against the Bourbons, wherever it should appear. The result might have been foreseen by the most inexperienced politician. Murat and his followers were attacked, beaten, and dispersed into the mountains, where their leader and his generals were taken, after a fruitless endeavour to regain the sea-coast and embark in their vessels. A military commission tried them, and they were shot on the 15th of October, just one week after their landing.

In Canada our affairs had taken an unfavourable turn. On Lake Erie, Captain Dobbs, of the navy, had very gallantly boarded two American schooners, and captured them. Two days after this success, the army under Major-general Gordon Drummond, attempted to take Fort Erie by storm; but although our brave soldiers had entered the fort, and would in a few minutes have been masters of it, an explosion nearly destroyed the whole column under Lieutenant-colonel Drummond and Captain Dobbs. The troops on this fell back, and their retreat was covered by the 1st battalion of the royals. The attack on Snake-hill, led by Colonel Fischer, was made at the same time, and was equally unfortunate in its result. The total loss sustained by the British forces in these attacks, amounted to nine hundred officers and men, killed, wounded, and missing. Of the latter there were no less than five hundred and thirty-six, the greater part of whom are supposed to have fallen in the darkness of the night, by the grape and musketry of the enemy.

Gaeta, in the kingdom of Naples, held out in favour of Napoleon, long after the battle of Waterloo. The Austrians by land, and the English by sea, blockaded and bombarded the place with great severity. Captain Fahie, in the Malta, of eighty guns, and Captain Brace, in the Berwick, of seventy-four guns, were chiefly instrumental in its reduction. On the 8th of August, the Governor being informed by Captain Fahie of the surrender of Napoleon to Captain Maitland, thought proper to capitulate. The revolutionary hurricane which for so many years had laid waste the finest parts of the habitable globe, now began to subside, and men to know that their true interests lay in preserving peace with their neighbours. France and England have ever since continued on terms of improving harmony : and the recent reduction of duties on the produce of our ancient rival, will, no doubt, increase their good will towards each other.

Rear-admiral Durham, commanding the Leeward Island station, collected his squadron in the month of August, and, in conjunction with the land forces under Lieutenant-general Sir James Leith, sailed from the Saintes on the 8th, to reduce the island of Guadaloupe. This wretched colony, the continued nursery of rebellion and massacre, had, after the landing of Napoleon in Provence, once more thrown off the government of the Bourbons, and, hoisting the tri-coloured flag, declared in favour of the Usurper. This act of treason the king of France owed to his own generosity. He had allowed Admiral Linois to retain the government of the island, and Adjutant-general Boyer to hold a high official situation under him. These two men, notoriously attached to Bonaparte, no sooner heard of his escape from Elba, than they determined to commit themselves in his cause. Linois is the same officer whom we have noticed at Algeziras; in India; and on his return in 1806, when he was taken in the Marengo, by the squadron under the command of Sir John Warren.

The squadron of Rear-admiral Durham consisted of—

Ships.	Guns.	Commanders.
Venerable	74	Captain Worth
Dasher	18	
Fairy	16	——— Baker
Espiègle	16	
Columbia	16	——— Chads.
Barbadoes	18	——— Fleming
Muros	18	
Chanticlear	10	Lieutenant G. Tupman.
Fox and Niobe, troop-ships.		

The land forces amounted to between five and six thousand men. The landing was effected on the 8th of August, under cover of the Fairy, Columbia, and Barbadoes. The Count de Vaugiraud, the governor of Martinique, detesting the treason of Linois, gave all the assistance in his power to the British enterprise. Two French corvettes and a schooner, commanded by officers of rank, joined the squadron, and were present at the reduction of the island. The British general having defeated Linois, compelled him to capitulate. Himself and his Adjutant-general were sent home to France, to be tried for their crimes. The loss of British troops in this third invasion of the island of Guadaloupe, amounted to about sixteen killed, and fifty wounded. The island was, of course, restored to the crown of France. Some farther particulars of the events in the West Indies having come to hand too late for insertion in this chapter, will be found in the Appendix.

CHAP. V.

1. *Mediterranean.*—State of the Barbary powers—Discussions
with Lord Exmouth—Treachery of the Dey of Algiers—
Murder of the Christians at Bona—Retrospect of the different
attacks made on them by the European monarchs—Attack
on the city of Algiers by the British fleet under the command
of Admiral Lord Exmouth, and the Dutch squadron under
Rear-admiral Van Capellan—Defeat of the Algerines—Re-
lease of all the slaves, and submission of the Dey—Letter of
Lord Exmouth to the Secretary of the Admiralty—Concluding
observations.

2. South American revolution—Affecting the tranquillity of the
West India islands—Insurrection at Barbadoes—Retreat of
the army of occupation from France—Improving state of that
country—Misery of Spain—Its causes—Expedition to South
America, to regain her colonies—Fails—Causes of that failure
—Mutiny of the troops at Cadiz—Portugal similarly situated
with Spain—Death of the king of Sweden—Holland improving in her internal condition—Death and character of his
Majesty King George III.—Accession of his present Majesty
—Motions in parliament respecting the Droits of Admiralty—
Observations of Mr. Brougham and Mr. Canning—Suggestions
on the appropriation of such a fund in future wars—Observations on the evacuation of Parga—Continuation of the
subject—Spanish revolution continued—Naples follows the
example of Spain—The Allied Sovereigns meet at Laybach—
Are determined to repress the attempts of the revolutionists.
West Indies.—Situation of the island of Hayti—Death of Christophe—Boyer gains possession of the whole island—State of
South America—Lord Cochrane joins the insurgents, and
defeats the Spanish squadron—Commanders in the British
navy struck off the list for having joined the insurgents—
Disturbances at Constantinople—and disagreement between
Russia and the Porte—Pirates of the Persian Gulf attacked
and subdued by Captain Collier and Sir William Grant Keir—
State of the kingdom of Naples—the Austrian army enters

·the city, and restores Ferdinand to his former unlimited
authority—Sicily described by Lord William Bentinck in the
House of Commons—Greeks and Turks at war—Attempts
made to induce England to join with the former—Prudence
of the British ministers—*Death of Bonaparte* at St. Helena—
Remarks on the treatment of that prisoner—Difficulties in
which the Rear-admiral and General were placed, as to his
custody—Want of feeling in his followers—Remarkable instance—Inconsistency of those who in this country defended
his character—Copy of his instructions to General De Caen,
proving his enmity to England, and determination to invade
her Indian possessions—Coronation of George IV—His
Majesty sets off for Ireland—Illness and death of the queen—
Fury of the mob at her funeral—Piracies in the West Indies—
Measures adopted for their suppression—Unjust aspersions on
the character of Naval Captains, by a writer in the Annual
Register, answered and refuted—His Majesty King George IV.
embarks on board the Royal George yacht, to visit Scotland
—His last interview with the Earl of St. Vincent—His
Majesty's departure.

THE states of Barbary, which, to the disgrace of
the European powers, had been so long permitted
to carry on their piratical depredations against the
commerce of the Mediterranean, received this year
a severe chastisement from the just vengeance of
Britain, which they had long provoked, presuming
that our forbearance proceeded from fear and im-
·potency. It was not to be endured that England
should tolerate what America had resented and pu-
·nished: and independently of other considerations,
the abolition of Christian slavery among the Bar-
·bary States, was an object well worthy of our
attention. This, and the acknowledgment of the
·flag of the Ionian Islands, became a subject of dis-

cussion between Lord Exmouth, and the Beys of
Tripoli and Tunis. The Dey of Algiers came readily
into every proposal, except that of the abolition of
slavery. The Beys of Tunis and Tripoli agreed
entirely with Lord Exmouth, and promised to act
towards their prisoners of war according to the
usages of civilised nations. The Dey of Algiers
was not so easily convinced of the expediency of
the measure, and requested time to refer to the
Grand Signior, whose subject he was. This request was granted: an Algerine minister embarked
on board the Tagus, frigate, to proceed to Constantinople, for that purpose; and three months
were allowed for the negotiation.

Lord Exmouth in the mean while returned to
England, to receive fresh instructions, and soon
departed again, with such a squadron as could not
fail to command compliance where entreaties had
proved unavailing. In the course of the negotiations, his Lordship stipulated for the independence of Naples and Sardinia, which, under the promise of the payment of the price of the slaves then
in bondage, was agreed to. But the Moors are
never to be trusted, as the tragical event which
followed soon proved.

The coral fishery at Bona is resorted to in the
month of May by the Neapolitan and Corsican
fishermen, for the purpose of carrying on their
occupation. On the 23d of May, the festival of
Ascension, when these poor unsuspecting people

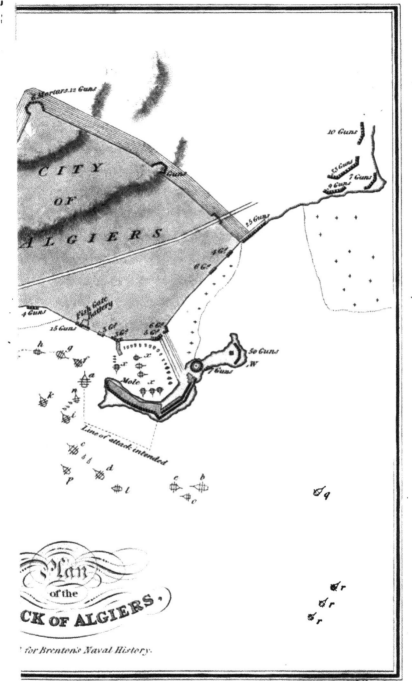

Plan
of the
CK OF ALGIERS.

for Brenton's Naval History.

J.Walker Sculpt.

were going to their most solemn devotions, at one o'clock in the morning, they were surprised by a body of infantry and cavalry, cut in pieces and butchered in the most barbarous manner. Neither the Christians who were in the country nor those in the town, nor those employed in boats, were spared: almost the whole were massacred; and the British flag taken from the Consular office, was torn in pieces and trampled under foot. It is not supposed that these acts were authorised by the government; but the popular mind had no doubt been stimulated by the imprudence, if not the connivance, of the Dey of Algiers; and from that moment negotiation was ended, and it was resolved to attack his capital.

In an expedition of this magnitude, with the officer who performed it still living, it would be an act of presumption to offer any other account of the transactions, than what is contained in the letter of the Commander-in-chief to the Secretary of the Admiralty.

We may observe, however, by way of placing the merit of this action in its proper light, that although the other nations of Europe had often attempted to reduce these savages to reason, none but England succeeded in completely humbling their power.

The Emperor, Charles V.* totally failed, and lost a great part both of his fleet and army. The

* See the elegant history of Dr. Robertson.

Spaniards more recently, in 1601, and the English
in the following year, also failed. The French
fleet under the Admiral Duquesne, bombarded the
city of Algiers, and set it on fire, 1632, and in
1633, repeated the attack. In 1775, the Spaniards
went against Algiers, with a powerful armament,
but retreated with loss. The results of their third
and fourth crusade against these maritime banditti,
in 1783–4, have been related in the early part of
this work.

During the war of the Revolution, we have seen
these people rise in their tone of insolence and
exaction, according to the difficulties in which we
were placed: the firmness of Lords St. Vincent
and Nelson kept them, however, from any acts of
open hostility. In 1816, the measure of their
crimes was full, and the massacre at Bona demanded that vengeance which the navy of England,
in the name of insulted Europe, had the honour of
inflicting.

The accompanying plan, drawn by Mr. Alexander
Lumsdale, master of the Queen Charlotte, on that
occasion, has been most kindly lent to the author,
for the purpose of laying it before the public; and
it is presumed that this drawing, and the elaborate
letter of the noble Viscount, will convey a complete description of the action, and its effects.

The Dutch squadron under Rear-admiral Van
Capellan, joined the English; and we rejoice
to see the flags united for the protection of real
liberty against lawless depredators. The letter

from Lord Exmouth to the Secretary of the Admiralty, is as follows:

"*Queen Charlotte, Algiers Bay, August* 12, 1816.

"SIR,

"IN all the vicissitudes of a long life of public service, no circumstance has ever produced on my mind such impressions of gratitude and joy as the event of yesterday. To have been one of the humble instruments, in the hands of Divine Providence, for bringing to reason a ferocious government, and destroying for ever the insufferable and horrid system of Christian slavery, can never cease to be a source of delight and heartfelt comfort to every individual happy enough to be employed in it. I may, I hope, be permitted, under such impressions, to offer my sincere congratulations to their lordships on the complete success which attended the gallant efforts of his Majesty's fleet in their attack upon Algiers of yesterday; and the happy result produced from it on this day by the signature of peace.

"Thus has a provoked war of two days' existence been attended by a complete victory, and closed by a renewed peace for England and her ally, the king of the Netherlands, on conditions dictated by the firmness and wisdom of his Majesty's government, and commanded by the vigour of their measures.

"My thanks are justly due for the honour and confidence his Majesty's ministers have been pleased to repose in my zeal on this highly important occasion. The means were by them made adequate to my own wishes, and the rapidity of their measures speak for themselves. Not more than one hundred days since, I left Algiers with the British fleet, unsuspicious and ignorant of the atrocities which had been committed at Bona; that fleet on its arrival in England was necessarily disbanded, and another with proportionate resources created and equipped : and although impeded in its progress by calms and adverse winds, has poured the vengeance of an insulted nation, in chastising the cruelties of a ferocious government, with a promptitude beyond example, and highly honourable to the national character, eager to resent oppression or cruelty, whenever practised upon those under their protection.

"Would to God that in the attainment of this object I had not deeply to lament the severe loss of so many gallant officers and men: they have profusely bled in a contest which has been peculiarly marked by proofs of such devoted heroism as would rouse every noble feeling, did I dare indulge in relating them.

"Their lordships will already have been informed, by his Majesty's sloop Jasper, of my proceedings up to the 14th instant, on which day I broke ground from Gibraltar, after a vexatious detention, by a foul wind, of four days.

"The fleet, complete in all its points, with the addition of five gun-boats fitted at Gibraltar, departed in the highest spirits, and with the most favourable prospect of reaching the port of their destination in three days; but an adverse wind destroyed the expectation of an early arrival, which was the more anxiously looked for by myself, in consequence of hearing, the day I sailed from Gibraltar, that a large army had been assembled, and that very considerable additional works were throwing up, not only on both flanks of the city, but also immediately about the entrance of the mole; from this I was apprehensive that my intention of making that point my principal object of attack had been discovered to the Dey by the same means he had heard of the expedition. This intelligence was, on the following night, greatly confirmed by the Prometheus, which I had despatched to Algiers some time before, to endeavour to get away the consul. Captain Dashwood had with difficulty succeeded in bringing away, disguised in midshipman's uniform, his wife and daughter, leaving a boat to bring off their infant child, coming down in a basket with the surgeon, who thought he had composed it, but it unhappily cried in the gateway, and, in consequence, the surgeon, three midshipmen, in all eighteen persons, were seized and confined as slaves in the usual dungeons. The child was sent off the next morning by the Dey, and, as a solitary instance of his humanity, it ought to be recorded by me.

"Captain Dashwood further confirmed, that about forty thousand men had been brought down from the interior, and all the janissaries called in from distant garrisons, and that they were indefatigably employed in their batteries, gun-boats, &c. and every where strengthening the sea-defences.

ſ "The Dey informed Captain Dashwood, he knew perfectly well the armament' was destined for Algiers, and asked him if it was true; he replied, if he had such information, he knew as much as he did, and probably from the same source—the public prints.

" The ships were all in port, and between forty and fifty gun and mortar-boats ready, with several more in forward repair. The Dey had closely confined the consul, and refused, either to give him up, or promise his personal safety : nor would he hear a word respecting the officers and men seized in the boats of the Prometheus.

ſ " From the continuance of adverse winds and calms, the land to the westward of Algiers was not made before the 26th, and the next morning at day-break the fleet was advanced in sight of the city, though not so near as I had intended. As the ships were becalmed, I embraced this opportunity of dispatching a boat under cover of the Severn, with a flag of truce, and the demands I had to make, in the name of his Royal Highness the Prince Regent, on the Dey of Algiers (of which the accompanying are copies), directing the officer to wait two or three hours for the Dey's answer, at which time, if no reply was sent, he was to return to the flag-ship : he was met near the mole by the captain of the port, who, on being told the answer was expected in one hour, replied, that it was impossible: the officer then said he would wait two or three hours; he then observed two hours was quite sufficient.

"The fleet at this time, by the springing up of the sea-breeze, had reached the bay, and were preparing the boats and flotilla for service until near two o'clock; when, observing my officer was returning with the signal flying, that no answer had been received, after a delay of upwards of three hours, I instantly made the signal to know if the ships were all ready, which being answered in the affirmative, the Queen Charlotte bore up, followed up by the fleet, for their appointed sta-tions; the flag, led in in the prescribed order, was anchored in the entrance of the mole, at about fifty yards distance. At this moment not a gun had been fired, and I began to suspect a full com-pliance with the terms which had been so many hours in their hands; at this period of profound silence, a shot was fired at us from the mole, and two at the ships to the northward then following; this was promptly returned by the Queen Char-lotte, who was then lashing to the main-mast of a brig, fast to the shore in the mouth of the mole, and which we had steered for as the guide to our position.

"Thus commenced a fire as animated and well supported as, I believe, was ever witnessed, from a quarter before three until nine, without intermission; and which did not cease altogether until half-past eleven.

" The ships immediately following me were admirably and coolly taking their stations, with a precision even beyond my most sanguine hope; and never did the British flag receive, on any occasion, more zealous and honourable support. To look further on the line than immediately round me was perfectly impossible, but so well grounded was my confidence in the gallant officers I had the honour to command, that my mind was left perfectly free to attend to other objects, and I knew them in their stations only by the destructive effect of their fire upon the walls and batteries to which they were opposed.

" I had about this time the satisfaction of seeing Vice-admiral Van Capellan's flag in the station I had assigned to him, and soon after, at intervals, the remainder of his frigates keeping up a well supported fire on the flanking batteries he had offered to cover us from, as it had not been in my power, for want of room, to bring him in front of the mole.

" About sunset I received a message from Rear-admiral Milne, conveying to me the severe loss the Impregnable was sustaining, having then one hundred and fifty killed and wounded, and requesting I would, if possible, send him a frigate to divert some of the fire he was under.

" The Glasgow, near me, immediately weighed, but the wind had been driven away by the cannonade, and she was obliged to anchor again, having obtained rather a better position than before.

" I had, at this time, sent orders to the explosion-vessel, under the charge of Lieutenant Fleming, and Mr. Parker, by Captain Reade, of the engineers, to bring her into the mole; but the Rear-admiral having thought she would do him essential service if exploded under the battery in his front, I sent orders to this vessel to that effect, which were executed. I desired also the Rear-admiral might be informed, that many of the ships being now in flames, and certain of the destruction of the whole, I considered I had executed the most important part of my instructions, and should make every preparation for withdrawing the ships, and desired he would do so as soon as possible with his division.

" There were awful moments during the conflict which I cannot now attempt to describe, occasioned by firing the ships so near us, and I had long resisted the eager entreaties of several around me, to make the attempt upon the outer frigate, distant about one hundred yards, which at length I gave into, and Major Gossett, by my side, who had been eager to land his corps of miners, pressed me most anxiously for permission to accompany Lieutenant Richards, in this ship's barge. The frigate was instantly boarded, and in ten minutes in a perfect blaze; a gallant young midshipman, in rocket-boat No. 8, although forbidden, was led by his ardent spirit, to follow in support of the barge,

in which he was desperately wounded, his brother
officer killed, and nine of his crew. The barge, by
rowing more rapidly, had suffered less, and lost
but two.

"The enemy's batteries around my division
were about ten o'clock silenced, and in a state of
perfect ruin and dilapidation, and the fire of the
ships was reserved as much as possible, to save
powder, and reply to a few guns now and then
bearing upon us, although a fort on the upper
angle of the city, on which our guns could not be
brought to bear, continued to annoy the ships by
shot and shells during the whole time.

"Providence at this interval gave to my anxious
wishes the usual land wind, common in this bay,
and my expectations were completed. We were
all hands employed warping and towing off, and
by the help of the light air, the whole were under
sail, and came to anchor out of reach of shells,
about two in the morning, after twelve hours' incessant labour.

"The flotilla of mortar, gun, and rocket-boats,
under the direction of their respective artillery
officers, shared, to the full extent of their power,
in the honours of this day, and performed good
service; it was by their fire all the ships in the
port (with the exception of the outer frigate) were
in flames, which extended rapidly over the whole
arsenal, store-houses, and gun-boats, exhibiting a
spectacle of awful grandeur and interest, no pen
can describe.

"The sloops of war which had been appropriated to aid and assist the ships of the line and prepare for their retreat, performed not only that duty well, but embraced every opportunity of firing through the intervals, and were constantly in motion.

" The shells from the bombs were admirably well thrown by the royal marine artillery; and although thrown directly across and over us, not an accident, that I know of, occurred to any ship.

" The whole was conducted in perfect silence, and such a thing as a cheer I never heard in any part of the line ; and that the guns were well worked and directed, will be seen for many years to come, and remembered by these Barbarians for ever.

" The conducting this ship to her station by the Master of the fleet and ship, excited the praise of all.   The former has been my companion in arms for more than twenty years.

" Having thus detailed, although but imperfectly, the progress of this short service, I venture to hope, that the humble and devoted services of myself and the officers and men of every description I have the honour to command, will be received by his Royal Highness the Prince Regent with his accustomed grace.   The approbation of our services by our sovereign, and the good opinion of our country, will, I venture to affirm, be received by us all with the highest satisfaction.

" If I attempted to name to their Lordships the

numerous officers who, in such a conflict, have
been at different periods more conspicuous than
their companions, I should do injustice to many;
and I trust there is no officer in the fleet I have
the honour to command, who will doubt the grateful feelings I shall ever cherish for their unbounded
and unlimited support. Not an officer nor man
confined his exertions within the precise limits of
their own duty; all were eager to attempt services
which I found more difficult to restrain than excite;
and no where was the feeling more conspicuous
than in my own captain, and those officers immediately about my person. My gratitude and thanks
are due to all under my command, as well as to
Vice-admiral Capellan, and the officers of the squadron of his Majesty the King of the Netherlands;
and I trust they will believe that the recollection
of their services will never cease but with my life.
In no instance have I ever seen more energy and
zeal; from the youngest midshipman to the highest rank, all seemed animated by one soul, and of
which I shall with delight bear testimony to their
Lordships, whenever that testimony can be useful.

" I have confided this Dispatch to Rear-admiral
Milne, my second in command, from whom I have
received, during the whole service intrusted to me,
the most cordial and honourable support. He is
perfectly informed of every transaction of the fleet,
from the earliest period of my command, and is
fully competent to give their Lordships satisfaction
on any points which I may have overlooked, or

have not time to state. I trust I have obtained from him his esteem and regard, and I regret I had not sooner been known to him.

" The necessary papers, together with the defects of the ships, and the return of killed and wounded, accompany this dispatch, and I am happy to say Captains Ekins and Coode are doing well, as also the whole of the wounded. By accounts from the shore, I understand, the enemy's loss in killed and wounded is between six and seven thousand men.

" In recommending my officers and fleet to their Lordship's protection and favour,'

　　　　　　" I have the honour to be, &c.

　　　　　　　　　　　　" EXMOUTH."

A general Abstract of the Killed and Wounded in the Squadron under Admiral Lord Exmouth's Command, in the Attack of Algiers, the 27th of August, 1816.

Ships.	Guns.	Killed.	Wounded.	Commanders.
Queen Charlotte	110	8	131	Adm. Lord Exmouth, G.C.B. / Captain J. Brisbane, C. B.
Impregnable··	98	50	160	Rear-admiral Milne / Captain Edw. Brace, C.B
Superb ······	74	8	84	Captain Charles Ekins
Minden·······	74	7	37	Wm. Paterson
Albion ······	74	3	15	John Coode
Leander ·····	50	17	118.	Edward Cheetham, C.B.
Severn·······	44	3	34	Hon. T. W. Aylmer
Glasgow ·····	44	10	37	Hon. A. Maitland
Granicus ····	36	16	42	W. F. Wise
Hebrus ······	36	4	15	Ed. Palmer, C.B.
Heron ·······	16	—	—	George Bentham
Mutine ·······	18	—	—	James Mould
Prometheus ··	16	—	—	W. B. Dashwood
Cordelia ·····	10	—	—	W. Sargent

Ships.	Guns.	Killed.	Wounded.	Commanders.
Britomart ···	19	—	—	R. Riddell
Belzebub ····	bomb	—	—	Wm. Kempthorne
Infernal ······	do.	2	17	Hon. G. J. Perceval
Hecla ·······	do.	—	—	W. Popham
Fury ········	do.	—	—	C. R. Moorson
	Total··· 128		690	

Dutch Squadron.

Ships.	Killed.	Wounded.	Commanders.
Melampus ·····	3	15	{ Vice-adm. Baron Van Capellan { Captain De Muir
Frederica ····	—	5	Captain Vander Straten
Dageraad······	—	4	Captain Polders
Diana ········	6	22	Captain Zervogel
Amstel ········	4	6	Captain Vander Hart
Eendracht ·····	—	—	Captain Wardenburgh
Total ····	13	52	
British squadron	128	690	
	141	742	Grand Total, 883.

Flotilla.

    5 gun-boats
  10 mortar-boats, launches
    8 rocket-boats, flats
  32 gun-boats, barges, and yawls
     ——
  55

The whole commanded by Captain F. T. Mitchell, assisted by Lieutenant John Davies, of the Queen Charlotte, and Lieutenant Thomas Revans, flag-lieutenant to Rear-admiral Milne.

Memorandum of the Destruction in the Mole of Algiers, in the Attack of the 27th of August, 1816.

4 large frigates, of 44 guns.
5 large corvettes, from 34 to 30 guns.
All the gun and mortar-boats, except seven; 30 destroyed.
Several merchant-ships and schooners.
A great number of small vessels of various descriptions.

All the pontoons, lighters, &c.

Store-houses and arsenal, with all the timber and various marine articles, destroyed in part.

A great many gun-carriages, mortar-beds, casks, and ship stores of all descriptions.

" H. B. M. Ship Queen Charlotte, Algiers Bay,
August 28, 1816.

" Sir,

" For your atrocities at Bona on defenceless Christians, and your unbecoming disregard to the demands I made yesterday, in the name of the Prince Regent of England, the fleet under my orders has given you a signal chastisement, by the total destruction of your navy, storehouses, and arsenal, with half your batteries.

" As England does not war for the destruction of cities, I am unwilling to visit your personal cruelties upon the inoffensive inhabitants of the country, and I therefore offer you the same terms of peace which I conveyed to you yesterday in my sovereign's name : without the acceptance of these terms you can have no peace with England.

" If you receive this offer as you ought, you will fire three guns, and I shall consider your not making this signal as a refusal, and shall renew my operations at my own convenience.

" I offer you the above terms, provided neither the British consul, nor the officers and men so wickedly seized by you from the boats of a British ship of war, have met with any cruel treatment, or any of the Christian slaves in your power, and I repeat my demand, that the Consul, and officers and men, may be sent off to me, conformably to ancient treaties.

"I have, &c.

"EXMOUTH."

"To his Highness the Dey of Algiers."

"Queen Charlotte, Algiers Bay, Aug. 30, 1816.

"GENERAL MEMORANDUM.

"The Commander-in-chief is happy to inform the fleet of the final termination of their strenuous exertions, by the signature of peace, confirmed under a salute of twenty-one guns, on the following conditions, dictated by his Royal Highness the Prince Regent of England:—

I. The abolition, for ever, of Christian slavery.

II. The delivery, to my flag, of all slaves in the dominions of the Dey, to whatever nation they may belong, at noon to-morrow.

III. To deliver, also, to my flag, all money received by him for the redemption of slaves since the commencement of this year, at noon, also, to-morrow.

IV. Reparation has been made to the British consul for all losses he may have sustained in consequence of his confinement.

V. The Dey has made a public apology, in presence of his ministers and officers, and begged pardon of the Consul, in terms dictated by the Captain of the Queen Charlotte.

"The Commander-in-chief takes this opportunity of again returning his public thanks to the admirals, captains, officers, seamen, marines, royal marine artillery, royal sappers and miners, and the royal rocket corps, for the noble support he has received from them throughout the whole of this arduous service, and he is pleased to direct, that on Sunday next a public thanksgiving be

offered up to Almighty God for the signal interposition of his Divine Providence, during the conflict which took place on the 27th, between his
Majesty's fleet and the ferocious enemies of mankind.

· " It is requested that this memorandum may be
read to the ships' companies."

" *To the Admirals, Captains, Officers, Seamen,*
Marines, Royal Sappers and Miners, Royal
Marine Artillery, and the Royal Rocket Corps."

" *Queen Charlotte, Algiers Bay*, Sept. 1, 1816.
· " SIR,

" I have the honour to acquaint you for their
Lordships' information, that I have sent Captain
Brisbane, with my duplicate dispatches, as I am
afraid that Admiral Milne, in the Leander, who
has charge of the originals, may experience a long
voyage, the wind having set in to the westward a
few hours after he sailed.

" Captain Brisbane, to whom I feel greatly indebted for his exertions and the able assistance I
have received from him throughout the whole of
this service, will be able to inform their Lordships
upon all points that I may have omitted.

" Admiral Sir Charles Penrose arrived too late
to take his share in the attack upon Algiers, which
I lament, as much on his account as my own; his
services would have been desirable in every respect.

" I have the satisfaction to state, that all the
slaves in the city of Algiers, and immediately in
its vicinity, are embarked; as also three hundred

and fifty-seven thousand dollars for Naples, and twenty-five thousand five hundred for Sardinia. The treaties will be signed to-morrow, and I hope to be able to sail in a day or two.

"The Minden has sailed for Gibraltar to be refitted, and will proceed from thence to her ultimate destination (the East Indies).

"The Albion will be refitted at Gibraltar for the reception of Sir Charles Penrose's flag. The Glasgow I shall be obliged to bring home with me.

            "I have the honour, &c.

                   "EXMOUTH."

" To John Wilson Croker, &c. &c. &c.
         Admiralty."

This was a proud epoch for England,—a climax worthy of her great name, and the cause in which she had fought and bled. The humiliation of these people, so long the pest of European commerce, gained for our navy and country, and the hero who animated our fleet, the unanimous approbation of the world. Europe now, for the first time since the fatal national assembly, was "at unity with itself." Clamours indeed resounded, for the redress of many grievances which had grown out of the war, and many parts of France were supposed to be on the eve of an insurrection in favour of Napoleon; but these discontents were appeased by the wisdom and moderation of Louis XVIII. and the expiring sounds of revolutionary discord were feebly conveyed to England in the "Voice from St. Helena."

On the 7th of November, Rear-admiral Penrose, who was left Commander-in-chief in the Mediterranean, addressed an official letter to the respective British consuls, in which he stated, that after the victory obtained by Lord Exmouth, he had sent dispatches to the government of Tripoli and Tunis, to announce the glorious event, and to recommend to the Bashaw and Bey, to make concessions to the Prince Regent of England, similar to those which had been extorted from the Dey of Algiers: that both these officers had acceded to his proposals, and that not a Christian remained in Barbary against his consent: all had been liberated, and the Rear-admiral had the satisfaction of sending off eighty-three Roman subjects to Civita Vecchia.

South America and the West Indies, after the pacification of Europe, began to feel the flames of civil discord. The landing of Sir Home Popham at Buenos Ayres, and of Miranda at Venezuela, laid the foundation of those scenes, which, after a civil war of fifteen years, are not yet concluded. Bolivar, the South American Washington, took upon him to establish the liberty of his country, and has succeeded; but whether the southern continent of the new world is capable of forming a rational and free government, like the people of the north, is a question on which we have very considerable doubts. The ignorance of the Spaniards in the mother country almost amounts to a proverb: those of the new world are ten times

worse. No sources of information are open to
these people, save what the inquisition or the
priests may think proper to admit. The revolution of the southern hemisphere was, in consequence, marked with more blood, and greater
horrors, in proportion as the people were more
removed from civilization. Their famous declaration was published at Buenos Ayres on the 19th
of July, 1816. By this instrument, Spanish America
was declared to be for ever free and independent
of Ferdinand VII. and his successors. It will not
be expected that this history, already extended
beyond the proposed limits, should enter into the
intricate details of the great western revolution, in
which the navy of England had no participation.

An event-so important, could not fail to produce a corresponding action in the neighbouring
islands: Barbadoes, the seat of the Leeward
Island government, experienced a temporary
revolt among the slaves, during the absence of
Lieutenant-general Sir James Leith on the expedition to Guadaloupe. It is remarkable that this
officer returned to Barbadoes in a French vessel;
but before his arrival tranquillity was restored,
after twenty estates had been laid waste by fire,
and nine hundred slaves killed or wounded, besides many prisoners taken. It must be observed
that the insurrection was not general, though the
effects on the planters were most destructive; and
as the fate of the other islands appeared to depend
on the issue of the conflict at Barbadoes, its pro-

gress was watched with the utmost solicitude, and Jamaica trembled for its existence.

The Nepaul war in the East Indies had in 1815 given activity to all our forces in that part of the world, but here, also, victory crowned the efforts of our soldiers, and the arms of the British empire were triumphant in every quarter of the globe.

The year 1817 was not marked by any naval event worthy of commemoration.

In the year 1818, the army of occupation was withdrawn from the French territory, by the unanimous decision of the allied powers. France, returning to a state of internal tranquillity, began to lose her military mania, which had been cruelly and unjustly nourished by her former governments. In proportion as the soldiers accustomed to serve under the Republican and Napoleon systems died away, the clamour of war subsided; peace, commerce, confidence, and a revival of agriculture, began to operate, and to restore the house of Bourbon to the good opinion of the people. The bloody lesson taught by the revolution has not been lost either upon the king or his subjects; and the relative duties of the one to the other are better understood, and more generally practised. France, an enlightened nation, we may hope one day to see united with Britain in the cause of public freedom, from whatever quarter it may be assailed. We wish we could add as much in favour of Spain; but the rulers of the peninsula being sunk into the most unconquerable ignorance and bigotry, the case of their country is hopeless, without a miracle. Spain, which once lent its assistance to the British colonies of North America to throw off the yoke of the parent state, has now, by the same natural re-action, lost her own. It is true she has her islands both in the East and West Indies, but her continental dominions in the new world, are torn from her for ever.

Charles IV. the abdicated monarch, ended his useless life at Rome on the 20th of January, 1819, in the seventy-first year of his age. Our readers are too well acquainted with the character and talents of his son and successor, to form very sanguine hopes of the melioration of the country under his sway. Divided by factions, the kingdom was infested with robbers; industry, public spirit, learning, and the arts, are lost, because the laws are too weak to support them. The expedition which had assembled in the harbour of Cadiz, for the chimerical purpose of regaining the revolted colonies in South America, had been so long detained for want of money and other causes, that a mutiny broke out among the troops. Spain having no ships of her own to send out, borrowed some from Russia; but when they arrived at Cadiz, they were discovered to be unfit for the purpose of navigation; the soldiers and sailors refused to embark in them; and a general mutiny put an end to the expedition. Elio, the governor of Valencia, in his endeavours to stifle the popular feeling of the south, committed crimes shocking to humanity, and for which he soon after atoned with his life. Ferdinand was the phantom of a king, ruling a desolate country, armed with the attributes of vengeance, but never exercising the prerogative of mercy.

Portugal, ostensibly in a better condition than Spain, is in reality much the same. The provinces which she possessed on the Rio Janeiro and at Pernambuco, have come to a friendly separation, and are governed by the same family.

The King of Sweden died on the 5th of February, and the race of Gustavus was succeeded by Charles John, the fortunate general of Bonaparte.

Holland, though still feeble and emaciated from the persecutions and conscriptions of the French, is regaining strength. United with Belgium, and put in possession of the colonies which had. been wrested from her by England, and restored by an act of gratuitous generosity, she begins to revive; and though she can never be a great maritime power, she may, under the guarantee of Russia and Prussia, be always opulent, respectable, and happy.

In the year 1819, we have nothing to remark, except discoveries, of which we shall speak hereafter.

The year 1820 was memorable for Great Britain. On the 29th of January, his Majesty, King George III. expired at Windsor, in the eighty-second year of his age, and the sixtieth of his reign.

The character of this great monarch and upright man, is displayed in the state of prosperity in which the wisdom of his councils left the country, and the effect which the example of his private virtues produced on society. The firmness of his mind saved the state under the trying vicissitudes of the American rebellion, of the revolutionary and treasonable meetings of 1793, 4, and 5, of the mutiny in 1797, and the Irish insurrection in the following year; and finally, his undaunted and inflexible courage supported the empire in all the perils of a long and bloody war, until it pleased the Almighty to deprive him at once of his sight and his reason. It is not the province of the naval historian to give the character and eulogium of a departed monarch, but as George III. loved his navy, as he was intimately acquainted with every part of our profession, we dwell on his revered memory with peculiar regard and affection. When presented at his levee, His Majesty always conversed with his officers in the most gracious and condescending manner. He knew the force, and generally the qualities, of most of the ships of the line, and many of the frigates. He varied his remarks according to the rank and station of the person whom he addressed: he inquired where he had served, what ship he had commanded, where he had been wounded; and even made himself acquainted with the state of the country, both commercial and political, in which the officer had last

served. None retired from his presence dissatis-
fied : all were charmed and flattered by his notice
and affability.

The empire of the seas having been firmly established during his eventful and auspicious reign;
his son and successor, King George IV. had less of
naval than military conflict. The great sea-fights
recorded in the foregoing history having laid open
the coasts, and almost the harbours, of our enemy,
the navy had little more to do than to land the
army, to co-operate with the troops when near the
sea-shore, or to transport them from one place to
another, according to the calls of the service.
Hence the facility with which the vast supplies
of men and *materiel* were forwarded to the seat of
war. George IV. pursuing the policy of his royal
father, strangled the hydra of revolution, and fixed
the tottering monarchies of Europe on a firmer
basis than they had ever known before.

The application of the Droits of Admiralty became again the subject of debate in parliament; and
as their amount arose chiefly from the exertions of
the navy, during the wars of the revolution, we
think it just that the navy should be informed how
they were disposed of.

On the 2d of May, Mr. Brougham made his
motion respecting this accumulated fund, contending that the honour and dignity of the crown, the
judges, and the speaker of the house of commons,
ought not to depend on such a source; that the
Crown should have the control of these droits, was

a dangerous privilege—it might be induced to go
to war for the sole purpose of obtaining them. He
instanced the conduct of Charles II. who undertook
a war against the Dutch, only for the purpose of
seizing the Smyrna fleet. He referred to much
later times: he mentioned the Dutch prizes (taken
by Commodore Essington), and the seizure of the
Spanish treasure. Whether he meant to refer precisely to the action off Cape St. Vincent, when the
four Spanish frigates were attacked by Captain
(now Sir Graham) Moore, we know not; if he did
he was not correct in stating that "£2,200,000 were
acquired by attacking unarmed, defenceless men,
who knew no reason for such a proceeding, except
that they had dollars on board their ships." By
referring to our account of this action, our readers
will see it in a very different point of view: the
ships were neither unarmed nor defenceless ; and
the reasons assigned for their detention were not
only justifiable but unanswerable. Mr. Brougham
designated this and similar proceedings as foul blots
on the honour of the country, and recommended
the house to wipe away the vile relics of feudal
barbarism.

Mr. Canning answered him with great warmth,
declaring that himself and his colleagues would
reject with disdain any boon which was offered as
an inducement to barter away the honour of the
royal prerogative. He candidly admitted that the
Droits of Admiralty in the late reign amounted to
about £9,700,000, out of which he said there had

been paid to captors, and for various law expenses, £5,372,000 : that something more than £4,000,000 remained to be accounted for—that £2,600,000 had been appropriated to the public service; and that two several sums had been given—one in aid of the civil list, the other to the 4½ per cent. fund: the first of these contributions was £1,300,000; the second £40,000. There still remained £380,000 to be accounted for, and that sum, the honourable gentleman said, had been paid partly in donations, to the different branches of the royal family, and partly in entertainments to foreign sovereigns. After a very long debate, the motion of Mr. Brougham was lost, by a majority of 273 against 145.

As an officer commanding some of his Majesty's ships which had effected many of the captures called Droits of Admiralty, the author is bound to declare, that in every instance, whether Danish, Dutch, or American vessels, the proportion allotted to the captor was an ample remuneration; and he has no doubt that the same feeling prevails generally throughout the navy. That the disposal of the fund has been satisfactorily accounted for, we believe will be admitted; but he still retains the opinion that from such a fund a stream might flow, to increase the annual income of the seamen, or their families, while employed in the service of their country. Emolument arising to the crews of his Majesty's ships in the shape of prize-money, too often found its way into the pockets of the most corrupt and abandoned people at our sea-ports, and it may be doubted whether more than one seaman in a hundred is benefitted by riches so acquired : we do therefore, most earnestly trust and hope, that in a future war, some legislative enactment to remedy this evil will be carried into effect. The detention of vessels which form the fund called Droits of Admiralty, is generally caused by an anticipation of war with the power to which they belong; custom and reason have given a large proportion to the captors, beyond this, a part should go to the general fund. We have no right to say that we cannot raise men without impressment, until we have tried every means by which they might be induced to give their voluntary services: this, it is conceived, would hold out one very powerful stimulus to the lower classes; medals, some exemption from corporal punishment, leave of absence, and limited service, would do the rest.

The cession of Parga to the Turks was brought before the house of commons on the 29th of June. Lord John Russel, who opened the debate, declared that it was a case of as notorious treachery as had ever occurred; for although the Parguinotes were not named in the treaty of 1815, yet being included in that of 1800, they had a right to demand that their property and religion should not be sacrificed to the Turks : that both were, is unhappily too true, and the compensation held out to them for depriving them of their homes and their lands, was totally inadequate. For the deeply-interesting particulars of this transaction, we are indebted to the Edinburgh Review, No. LXIV., to which the reader is referred.   We flatter ourselves that the justice of our country was uncontaminated by its interference in this melancholy transfer; but we cannot help sympathising with the unhappy people who, depending on us for support, were suddenly left with the option of Turkish cruelty at home, or (with their wives and children) to become helpless wanderers in a foreign land.

We never have been, and fear we never shall be, friendly to our colonial system, more particularly as it relates to the government of the Ionian islands and other insular possessions in the Mediterranean. The violation of the quarantine laws at Malta, and the imposition of duties, had, four years ago, reduced that island to the lowest state of commercial distress; much remains yet to be done before these, and other valuable British possessions, can be considered to partake fairly in the benefits of our constitution, we confine ourselves to general terms, unwilling to make an invidious distinction, or excite discontent; some of our colonies and islands are locally and politically better situated than others; but the danger of all is, that their commerce may be smothered by overwhelming duties, and their internal tranquillity endangered by false and meddling sensibility.

All the efforts of Spain to regain her colonies in the New World were blasted, and rendered abortive, in so singular and decided a manner, as to

justify the presumption of the immediate interference of Providence. After the mutiny of the
troops had been suppressed by the Conde de
Abisbal, fresh levies were made, and a new army
again appeared at Cadiz, but the fever, or plague,
destroyed and dispersed it; and in the month
of December, when it had re-assembled to the
amount of sixteen thousand men, another mutiny,
more alarming and better organised than that
of the preceding summer, very nearly overturned
the Spanish monarchy. This great movement
was chiefly planned and executed by the Colonels
Riego and Quiroga. On the 1st of January, 1820,
these officers proclaimed the Constitution of 1812,
as adopted by the Cortes. Corunna, Vigo, Ferrol,
and Pontevedra, where military were stationed;
followed the example. Abisbal himself joined the
cause of the Constitution; and Ferdinand was
forced to submit to the will of a military mob, because he had refused to ratify the promises which
he had made on his restoration to freedom. Portugal partook in the internal commotion of Spain,
and the whole peninsula was in arms for an object
which very few among them understood. A nation
sunk in ignorance, bigotry, and superstition, cannot, by the mere motion of its will, rise at once
into the enjoyment of freedom and rational liberty.
Spain and Italy, having once surrendered their
liberties, could never regain them. History affords
no instance of the resuscitation of kingdoms, without undergoing the evil of foreign conquest—the

ordeal of fire and sword. The causes of the deca-
dency of Spain we have already attempted to account for: her colonies have avenged themselves
on the parent state: the fable of Midas has been
realised by an influx of the precious metals, and
the desire of avarice has been glutted to its own
destruction: true wealth is only to be found on
the surface, not in the bowels, of the earth. England, should she ever possess the mines of Mexico,
which Heaven forbid! will, at no distant period,
be lulled in the lap of luxury, and when senseless
from repletion, and sunk in sloth, will lose the
power and the means of thinking and acting for
herself; she will then experience the fate of other
nations, and her fall will be rapid and terrible, in
proportion to the eminence on which she now
stands.

Naples, governed by the weakest of monarchs,
could not but look with interest on the political arrangements and apparently enviable constitutions
of her neighbours; nor were the Carbonari long
in proclaiming their sentiments: Ferdinand of
Naples was desired peremptorily to adopt the
constitution of Spain. Such was the new ferment
which threatened the peace of Europe. Unlike the
revolution of France, it seemed to have a more rational, peaceful, and legitimate object: here was no
wish to overturn altars and thrones, to murder the
rich and pillage their houses, or to carry arms into
the neighbouring countries, and spread doctrines
destructive of human happiness. The powers of

Europe, however, which had so recently put down
the spirit of wild reform, could not see with perfect
composure the prospect of a renewal of all their labours and dangers. Free constitutions in the south
of Europe might have been imitated in the north:
Austria, too, held the Milanese and the Venetian
states in subjection; Prussia was a military government; Russia an absolute monarchy. These considerations induced the kings composing the Holy
Alliance to choke the stream which, by running
through the neighbouring lands, might increase to
an unconquerable torrent. A conference of crowned
heads and their representatives, was held at Laybach; Ferdinand of Naples was desired to attend;
Lord Stewart, the British ambassador, was there
also, but it is believed gave no encouragement to
hope that England would join in the attempt to
subvert the spirit of continental liberty founded on
honest principles. The result of these delibera-
tions was, that Spain, Portugal, and Naples, should
return to the ancient order of things, and this decree was finally executed.

The island of Hayti, in the West Indies, had
not, after twenty-nine years of blood and conflagration, obtained a government which could protect its people from wrong, and ensure their do-
mestic happiness. Christophe, a cruel and merci-
less tyrant, had succeeded to the government: by
murders he had obtained his power, and by the
same means hoped to keep it. The negroes, left
to themselves, would soon put to silence all the

Utopian theories of our false philanthropists. St. Domingo has proved the truth of this proposition. The Blacks will always govern themselves according to the power of the strongest, by the force of the one acting on the fears of the other party. On the 5th of October, a conspiracy having been formed, the troops of the tyrant revolted, and Christophe, expecting the same treatment which he had shewn to others, prevented the designs of his enemies by a voluntary death.

Boyer, the mulatto chief, who had long been the rival of Christophe, no sooner heard of his decease, than he entered his territories with an army of twenty thousand men, and after a very trifling resistance, took the city of Cape François, the seat of the old government. He was received with joy by all, since none had the power of opposing him, and a new dynasty sprang up in St. Domingo, where civil wars and famine had diminished the population to about one-sixth of what it was in 1792. From the best information we have been able to obtain, the island had, in 1822, little more than eighty thousand people: at the commencement of the unhappy revolution, Mr. Bryant Edwards estimated the number at half a million.

The independence of Hayti, however wretched the people might be with such a change, was an alarming epoch for the inhabitants of Jamaica, and coupled with the mistaken zeal of the emancipators in this country, depreciated their property to a ruinous extent. If the legislature of this country does not give support to the Colonial system, by lowering the duties, and discouraging the wholesale purchase of freedom, our West India property will suffer still further diminution.

War, with all its accompanying horrors, seemed to have taken a western course, and after having for a long succession of years afflicted the old world, it crossed the Atlantic, and ravaged the new. South America, from Buenos Ayres to Maracaibo, felt the scourge: Chili and Peru were drenched in the blood of their people. Lord Cochrane, who had been displaced from the list of British naval officers, offered his services to the Chilian government: he was gladly received, and having equipped a small squadron, defeated that of Spain, and declared the provinces which still held their allegiance in a state of blockade. This district contained the whole coast of Peru, from the 2d to the 21st degree of south latitude. A British squadron was kept constantly in the Southern Pacific Ocean, to watch the movements of the hostile navies, and protect British commerce. Commodore Bowles was succeeded by Sir Thomas Hardy, and both these officers having a very difficult task to perform, obtained the objects for which they were sent, without compromising the interests of their country. Five or six British naval officers having entered the Chilian service: contrary to the king's proclamation, and in direct disobedience to the orders of the Admiralty, were struck off the list of the navy. They were all commanders.

In the year 1820, the city of Constantinople, and the whole Turkish government, exhibited the most alarming symptoms of internal commotion and weakness of counsel. Ali Pacha, of Albania, a daring leader of rebellion, defied the armies and the authority of the Sultan, and though defeated and compelled to retreat, still held out with an obstinacy peculiar to that race of people. He shut himself up in the fortress of Janina, where the Turks blockaded him, but were obliged at the end of the year to raise the siege, and Ali again took the field with another army. Serious discussions commenced about the same time between Russia and the Porte, on the old subject of Moldavia and Wallachia. Great disorders ensued in Constantinople; the Russian ambassador, Count Strogonoff, was insulted by the mob and the Janissaries: some of the latter were strangled, and a due apology being offered was accepted; but the seeds of animosity were not perfectly removed.

The pirates of the Persian Gulf having forgotten the chastisement inflicted on them by Captain Wainwright, began again, after a lapse of nine years, to follow their former practices. The government of Bombay fitted out an expedition to destroy them; and Major-general Sir William Grant Keir was intrusted with the command of the troops. Captain Francis Augustus Collier, of his Majesty's ship the Liverpool, conducted the naval part, followed by two sloops of war, some Bombay marine and transports.

Rear-admiral Sir Richard King, who was Commander-in-chief in the East Indies at that period, had given such orders to Captain Collier as had completely met the whole exigencies of the case. The most perfect harmony prevailed, as it ever should, between the army, navy, and civil service. Four thousand nine hundred and twenty-eight tons of transport shipping were employed on the expedition, containing a body of three thousand troops. The King of Persia, it would seem, viewed the operations of our army with some jealousy, and discouraged the co-operation of his forces. The Prince of Schiraz, however, received from his Persian Majesty such instructions as left him the power to assist the English with water and provisions, if not to co-operate actively in their favour. Ras al Kyma, the principal resort and head-quarters of these freebooters, was again taken by our troops, the fortifications destroyed, and all their vessels burnt or sunk. The Lords Commissioners of the Admiralty, as well as the Government of India, expressed themselves highly satisfied with the conduct of Captain Collier, and the Commanders Loch and Walpole, of the Eden and Curlew, sloops of war. It is remarkable that our navy, at peace with the powers of Europe, should have been employed about the same time in the East and West Indies, in repressing piracies, and in both countries with equal success.

The political movements of the Holy Alliance at Laybach, with reference to the revolutions in Spain, Portugal, and Naples, were watched with the most unceasing vigilance by the people of England, both in and out of parliament, and it is probable that on no subject did the whole country, from the king to the lowest of his subjects, ever feel more perfectly unanimous. We had not fought against liberty : for twenty-two years we wished all the nations of the earth the same freedom which we ourselves enjoyed ; and we hailed the dawn of their emancipation without taking any active part in the cause. Our squadron, it is true, cruised in the bay of Naples, and the Vengeur, a British ship of the line, conveyed Ferdinand to Leghorn, on his way to Laybach, to answer the summons of the Allied Monarchs ; but here our co-operation ended, and the British government declared its decided neutrality, unless Austria and Prussia sought to aggrandize themselves at the expense of the disturbed countries. The Austrian army found no obstruction on its way to Naples, which city it entered early in the year, and re-established the royal authority.

Much and very animated discussion ensued on these important subjects, in parliament, where his Majesty's ministers completely exonerated themselves, and carried with them the voice of the country.

On the 19th of January, Lord William Bentinck

whom we have frequently had occasion to mention
in honourable terms for his conduct in Sicily, and
on the coast of Calabria, made a very important
motion in the House of Commons, respecting the
affairs of Sicily. His Lordship, in a short but clear
and able speech, presented a masterly sketch of the
political state of that island, and of the want of
faith which the king of Naples had evinced towards
his people.

In 1805, said his Lordship, the royal family
quitted Naples, and retired to Sicily, where they
had the protection of the British army. Murat had
possession of Naples, and meditated the invasion
of Sicily, from whose government Sir John Stewart
could only obtain one regiment of cavalry for its
defence; and when Murat's invasion did take place,
it was repelled by British valour, aided not so
much by the Sicilian government as by the voluntary efforts of the people. Six years elapsed in
much the same spirit, when it was determined to
place matters on a better footing. The Neapolitan
advisers were removed, and Sicilian ministers placed
in their stead. Unfortunately the king made his
appearance at that moment, and it was feared that
by pursuing the former measures, the country
would be ruined by the annihilation of the new
constitution. Under these circumstances the he-
reditary prince was appointed to a commanding
situation: the new code was formed and every
thing went on well. In the course of nine months

seven thousand men were detached to Spain, and shortly after, more than double that number were available. The Neapolitan army, which before that period had been perfectly useless, soon became worthy of assisting in the common cause.

In 1812, the three houses had unanimously agreed on the basis of a new form of constitution. On that occasion the Barons of Sicily presented one of the most glorious spectacles that the world ever beheld, or history ever recorded. They surrendered their own feudal rights, and determined to adopt, as far as possible, the form of the British constitution: the three chambers were reduced to two: the lords spiritual and temporal formed one, and the commons the other. The parliament met in the years 1813, 14, and 15. In 1814 the British troops evacuated the island: the king resumed the reins of government, and renewed his oath to observe inviolably the form of the constitution which had been established. In 1815, his Majesty returned to Naples; but before his departure, the British minister gave in a document, stating, that from a total change of circumstances, British influence was about to cease in the island, and that if the government of Sicily required alteration, this country could have no objection to it, provided such alteration were made conformably to the existing laws, and with the free consent of the nation; concluding with the express statement that England could not allow any violent or arbitrary change in the existing constitution.

Instructions had been sent out in 1815, than which nothing could have been drawn up better calculated to promote the welfare of Sicily; but what efforts, said Lord William, were made, to give effect to these instructions? none whatever: they were received with joy in Sicily, but were immediately followed by a decree of the king, which united Sicily and Naples. This act of union, so far from supporting the Sicilian constitution, destroyed it altogether: it destroyed the rights and privileges of the people, and made Sicily a Neapolitan province. Such is the history of this interesting island, taken from the lips of a man of honour, and a soldier of character, who knew more of Sicily than many of his contemporaries. His motion founded on the above statement was lost, in a very thin house. The British government did not feel itself pledged to support the new constitution of Sicily, however analogous to our own: it was moreover stated by Lord Castlereagh, that the transactions having taken place six years before, he did not see the necessity of our referring to it at so late a period.

The naval establishment at St. Helena, for the safe custody of Bonaparte, had long, and we think unjustly, been complained of, as an intolerable expense to the country. Economy is no doubt desirable in a state; but there is a point where the existence of this virtue ends in extravagance, and such Great Britain will no doubt find it, should she reduce her naval forces in peace to so low an ebb as to destroy their elasticity, and prevent their rising when the emergencies of war call for their services.   The custody of Bonaparte, it was triumphantly stated by the advocates for economy and reform, cost us £400,000 per annum: true; but this money, "though cast upon the waters," was not thrown away.   An active squadron between the Cape of Good Hope and St. Helena, gave employment to between two and three thousand officers and men; rendered them expert in their profession; and being all volunteers, they were available to any service that might have occurred.   The flag of a Rear-admiral was flying on the station, in a ship of the line, and a strong squadron of frigates and sloops of war, kept a constant watch round the island, and held frequent communication with the Cape of Good Hope and with England.   The burthen, however, of supporting this expense was effectually removed from us by an unexpected event.   Napoleon, from long inactivity, and a want of that stimulus to action which had been the employment of his early life, added to a deep sense of the privation of liberty under which he laboured, had contracted a disease which he seems to have had no wish to conquer, and which, on the 5th of May, terminated his earthly career.   As the enemy of this meteor of the human race, we have ever held him up as a bold, bad man.   The sufferings which he inflicted on mankind were dreadful, and when it is remem-

bered that his object was the gratification of private ambition, we cannot easily forgive him, nor
can we think these evils counterbalanced by any
benefit derived to his country; of his detention at
St. Helena we are not prepared to speak: we have
read all that has been written on the subject, and
have met with such contradictory evidence, from
men of honour, that we shall forbear to enter
deeply into the question. That he was well treated
by Sir George Cockburn, Sir Pulteny Malcolm,
Admiral Plampin, and Admiral Lambert, is proved.
Of the military part of his guardianship we can say
nothing.   The safety of Europe required that he
should be debarred from holding any communication with his friends, and the order was complied
with to the letter, but, in its utmost extent, what
was it compared to the sufferings of the unhappy
English treacherously captured by him in the time
of peace, and sent to Verdun; that coercion was
needlessly resorted to we deny, knowing as we do
from the very best authority, that it was quite impossible to be sufficiently guarded against the spirit
of intrigue and rapacity which pervaded the residence at Longwood.   No supplies could be sufficient for such a table: no Argus could guard the
avenues to secret intelligence.   The situation both
of the Governor and the Admiral was one of
extreme anxiety; and perhaps no man who did
his duty could have obtained the approbation of
Napoleon Bonaparte. The pretended tears and

affectation of grief so pompously displayed by
many of his attendants, should be looked at with
caution : facts were communicated to the author
by a captain of a frigate on the station, which
would go far to convince us that little was felt
by his followers, whatever might have been said on
the subject of the death of Napoleon.

Preparations we believe were made for leaving
him previous to his decease by some who affected
the most unbounded attachment to his person.
Ill-humour and discontent were visible in the
countenances of many; and it is supposed that
the death of Napoleon was an event which they
secretly rejoiced at, as the only means of ending
their exile and captivity.

Considering the great part he had played in Europe, it was wonderful how little sensation was
felt at his sudden exit. In England, the economist
looked only to the saving of money by the paying
off the ships and recall of the troops; in France,
the Ultras had long ceased to fear, and the Repub-
licans to hope, any thing from him. His departure was therefore regarded with indifference by
both parties.

As soon as the news of his death reached
England, orders were given to recall the squadron
from the St. Helena and Cape stations. At the
latter the dock-yard had been supplied with stores
for the use of the shipping. The Commissioner
was recalled, and the establishment reduced to a
store-keeper, and a master-attendant.

Conversant as the author of these pages has been for many years with politics, and with the various opinions of changing men, he has never been able to discover how the friends of England and of liberty, could be friendly to the public character of Bonaparte. That kindness shewn to an individual may have softened the sentence which public duty would pronounce, we may admit; but that Bonaparte, after all his public acts, should have found admirers among the patriots of this happy land, is an enigma which can only be solved by supposing that patriotism means no more than opposition to "the powers that be."

Those who could ever doubt the unalterable hostility of Bonaparte to Great Britain, may be convinced by reading his instructions to the Governor-general of the French possessions in India; and what were his real views from the moment the peace of Europe had given him leisure to consider the importance of our colonies and settlements in that part of the world. In the month of February, 1803, before his Majesty's message to both houses of parliament, we find the following digest of instructions, which must have taken some time to compose and to arrange:—

Paris, February, 1803.

Independently of the instructions which the Minister will give to the Captain-general of the French settlements in India, and to the Admiral, both of them will have instructions of a superior order, which will be signed by the Chief Consul.

———— The Captain-general will arrive in a country where our enemies command and oppress all the people of those vast regions.

He should therefore endeavour to give them no cause of alarm—no subject for quarrelling; and to *dissimulate* as much as possible.

He must adhere to these indispensable arrangements for the security and the supplies of our establishments, and with the relations which he will have with the people or the princes who bear with the greatest impatience the yoke of England, he must shew no partiality;—give them no disquiet: they are the tyrants of the Indies, restless and jealous; he must act towards them with *mildness, dissimulation,* and *candour!* (simplicité.)

Six months after his arrival in India, he will send home an officer (the highest in his confidence), with his despatches, to make known in detail all he has learnt of the strength, disposition, spirit, and situation of the different people of India, as well as the force and situation of the British establishments; he will make known his views, and the hopes he might have of support, in *the event of a war,* to maintain himself in the Peninsula; the number and quality of the troops; the arms and provisions of which he would stand in need, to sustain the war during many campaigns in the centre of India; he should pay the greatest attention to the *phrases* of his memoir, because they will all be weighed, and may decide in unforeseen circumstances on the steps and the policy of government. Every six months an officer is to be sent home in the same manner.

To sustain the war in India for many campaigns, he must reason on the hypothesis that we shall not be masters of the seas, and cannot expect any considerable succours.

——————It is not easy to conceive how we can have a war with England, without bringing Holland into it along with us. One of the first cares of the Captain-general should be, to assure himself of the situation of the establishments of the Dutch, Portuguese, and Spaniards, and of the resources which they might contain.

The mission of the Captain-general is, in the first instance, a mission of observation, political and military, with a small body of forces, and the occupation of the factories for our commerce; but the first Consul, well instructed by the Captain-general, and by the punctual execution of these instructions, may perhaps place it in his *power to acquire a great glory, which prolongs the memory of men beyond the duration of ages.—Precis Militaires, vol.* xi. *p.* 189.

Such was the instruction furnished to General De Caen, the governor of the Isle of France, by Napoleon, at the moment that he professed himself the friend of England, and a lover of peace. We have frequently given extracts from the invaluable collection of papers united under the title of "Precis des Evènemens Militaires." We much fear the French government will not permit many more to be given to the world; they have only come down to 1805, and in their present state, with the maps and plates which accompany them, are to the historian treasures of incalculable value.

The extract here given would alone have justified the caution of the gallant Admiral Rainier in refusing to deliver up the fort of Pondicherry. The secrets of Bonaparte were sometimes betrayed in his lifetime; but since his death the disclosures of the Count De Dumas and the Duke of Otranto have destroyed and annihilated all that remained of his character, and have fully exonerated the British government for having pursued such a man to his dissolution.

Parliament was prorogued this year at an unusually early period. The coronation of the king, which was fixed to take place on the 19th of July, occupied the attention of every branch of the legislature, as well as the nation at large. The event was differently viewed by many. The determination of the ministers to exclude the queen from that honour, caused some alarm for the public peace: her Majesty's friends were known to be numerous, and, with some exceptions, consisted of that party who had ever been inimical to the government. On the morning of the 19th, Queen Caroline presented herself at the door of the Abbey, but was refused admittance. Then was the eventful moment which it was supposed would prove the strength of her cause; but, except a few voices, all were in favour of the king, and the *single coronation* of his Majesty: the guards were steady, the people loyal, and sedition was put to silence. The great ceremony was conducted with becoming solemnity: his Majesty was received with cheers and congratulations; and the queen retired, mortified and disappointed, to her residence at Brandenburgh House.

Whether her Majesty's mind had been wrought up to feverish excitement by the exertion she had undergone during the preceding days, or whether a disease was produced by exposure to the night air, in returning from the theatre, is not certain; perhaps both causes combined to establish a disorder which terminated in death on the evening of the 7th of August. At the funeral procession, which took place on Tuesday the 14th, the last efforts of despair and rebellion were united, to throw the country into confusion: the mob attacked the guards, who escorted the body on its way through Kensington, blocked up the road, and finally succeeded in compelling the procession to pass through Hyde Park and the city, contrary to the intentions of government. The scene in

Hyde Park and Park Lane, was disgraceful beyond
description; the life guards were attacked with
stones and filth, but behaved with the utmost
composure, nor did they fire a shot until their
lives were in imminent danger: two of the mob
were killed at Cumberland Gate. Tumult and
disorder continued till the hearse reached Brent-
wood, in Essex. The Glasgow, a large frigate,
commanded by Captain (now Sir B. C.) Doyle, received the royal remains at Harwich, with the
usual ceremonies, and conveyed them to the river
Elbe, whence the corpse was removed to Bruns-
wick, and interred in the family vault, agreeably
to the last will of the deceased queen.

While these scenes were passing in London and
on the coast, the King was at Holy-head in his
yacht, on his way to Ireland. Expresses were
sent off, to announce to his Majesty the alarming
illness of the queen; the voyage was suspended;
and the royal squadron awaited the event with all
due respect.

At length the news was conveyed to his Majesty,
who immediately retired to his apartment, commanding the colours of the squadron to be lowered
half-mast, and every solemnity to be observed.
To pursue the voyage, however repugnant to his
Majesty's feelings at the time, was absolutely necessary, and the King landed at Howth on the
12th of August. Privacy was impossible; the
whole population of the kingdom of Ireland flew
to welcome their monarch; and his Majesty, after

having been present at the most fervent demonstrations of loyalty and affection, returned to his capital on the 16th of September. On the 24th, though very late in the year, the King set off to visit his electoral dominions. His Majesty landed at Calais, and proceeded to Brussels; thence to Hanover, where he was received, as in France, with respect and admiration, as the monarch of a free and happy people. After having listened to the addresses and the representations of his subjects in Hanover, and given them proofs of his attachment, his Majesty returned to England, where, during his absence, sedition and treason had been vainly endeavouring to procure for him an unwelcome reception.

The year 1821 is also memorable in history for the efforts made by the Greeks to throw off the Turkish yoke, and, as if England had not had enough of war, there were many who advocated our espousing the cause of liberty in the Morea. A petition was presented to parliament by Sir James Macintosh, from the inhabitants of Lees, in the parish of Ashton-under-Line, praying the house of commons to interfere in behalf of the Greeks: there were even men, in other respects of sound sense and judgment, who proposed driving the Turks out of Europe. The folly of such a crusade was justly exposed by Lord Castlereagh. The Turks in Europe, he said, amounted to about five millions of souls, and he did not conceive it a very easy matter to carry the sentence of transportation,

which had been pronounced against them, into
execution : as far as negotiation could go the
government had gone, but the noble lord said,
that neither the government nor the country were
so wild as to take up arms with a view to the more
impartial administration of justice in Turkey. The
same subject was brought before the Lords by
Earl Grosvenor, with similar success. It was contended, that the British government had evinced
its partiality to the Porte, by allowing a Turkish
frigate to be refitted in the dock-yard of Deptford,
and to be navigated home by British sailors. The
Earl of Liverpool replied to this charge with great
perspicuity. The frigate, his Lordship said, had
arrived in this country previously to any acts of
hostility between the Greeks and Turks : she had
come in the character of a merchant-ship, partly
laden with antiquities for the British Museum :
under these circumstances the government could
not but permit her to be refitted, and to be navigated back as far as Malta only, by British sailors.
In other respects, said the Earl, the impartiality
of the British government was proved, by its
positive refusal to supply this vessel with arms, or
to permit the Pacha to purchase two frigates in
this country, which he was most desirous of doing.
Detesting the horrible cruelty of the murder of
the Sciote hostages, his Lordship contended that
the British government was excluded from interference, by the universally admitted rule, that one
government could not interfere in the internal re-

gulations of another, except in cases where its own security was menaced. The motion of Earl Grosvenor was lost without a division.

Turkey, when no longer in imminent danger of the power of Russia, with whose vengeance she had been threatened in the preceding year, increased her cruelty and injustice towards the oppressed Greeks. The object of Earl Grosvenor's motion was, to hold no communication with such a government; and, if we could not interfere to save the unhappy Greeks, at least to be perfectly impartial. This last object of his Lordship was, we believe, fully attained, without the interference of the legislature.

The commerce of the West Indies, particularly the trade which passed through the gulf of Florida, had been this year much annoyed by pirates—a nest of banditti of all nations and colours, infesting the wild shores of the western side of Cuba, inaccessible to ships of war, from the shoals and reefs which interrupt navigation. These wretches, many of them Spaniards of Cuba, many Englishmen and Americans, committed the most atrocious murders on the crews and passengers of the vessels they had taken. The Spanish government, which still claimed the allegiance of Cuba, was too weak or too indolent to remedy the evil, and the pirates "sailing under the flag of Spain, or taking refuge within the neutrality of her shores," were spoken of as "difficulties which could not be easily overcome." Where the difficulty exists of

seizing a pirate on any coast, or under any flag, we
are at a loss to discover: we are quite sure that no
British officer seeing a pirate, and having proof of
his being one, would have hesitated one moment in
securing both vessel and crew, wherever he might
find them, leaving the question of flag and neutrality to be settled by his government. On the
subject of these depredations, Mr. Canning presented a petition from Liverpool, to which he
begged to add some facts which had come to his
knowledge. On the 13th of December, 1821, a
British ship (whose name he did not give), when
within five miles of Cape St. Antonio, had been
boarded by a pirate, who demanded of the
steward, whether there was any specie on board?
The answer being in the negative, the man was instantly stabbed by the pirates: they then endeavoured to extort confession from the captain, and
compelled his own crew to haul him up by the
neck, to the yard-arm, where he entreated his men
to fasten weights to his feet, that his misery might
be more speedily terminated: this was, of course,
not allowed, and when taken down and lying
almost insensible on the deck, the wretch who had
stabbed the steward, blew out the brains of the
captain. The pirates appeared to be all either
Spaniards or Portuguese.

Mr. Canning mentioned other similar transactions, and observed, that the petitioners had first
applied to the Admiralty, "which had represented
the matter to the court of Spain;" but the peti-

tioners felt that a time would arrive, if it had not already arrived, when the mother country would be unable to redress the grievances committed under the flag of their colonies, and when it would therefore be necessary for this government to adopt some course for the protection of the trade of the empire.

Sir George Cockburn, on the part of the Admiralty, said, that proper steps had been taken to repress the depredations of these pirates. The gallant Admiral stated, that they lay in wait for vessels off Cape St. Antonio; that they made their attacks sometimes in schooners, at other times in open boats, according to circumstances, and the state of the weather. While our ships of war were near the coast, they did not come out; but as soon as winds or current had drifted them off, they came out and attacked the merchant-vessels.

The Marquis of Londonderry said, if the facts complained of were cases of undisguised piracy, there would be no difficulty in dealing with them; but the peculiarity was, that these vessels had commissions. Artigas, one of the chiefs of the Spanish insurgents, had issued many, which had been sold to cover piracies; in consequence of which, orders were given to seize all vessels sailing under commissions, from governments in whose ports they were not fitted out. The local governments of South America had shewn every disposition to keep their cruisers within bounds, and, considering the difficulties of the case, they had made great efforts to do justice: but when vessels sailing under such commissions were seized, it became difficult to prove they had committed acts of hostility. His Lordship enumerated three distinct acts of piracy committed in the gulf of Florida, on British merchant-vessels. They had been properly represented to the court of Madrid, and the Spanish minister had promised that search should be made for the criminals, and punishment inflicted if they were found.

In the mean time the evil went on, until the sense of the country was expressed in so strong and decided a manner, as to induce the government no longer to depend on the leaden councils of Madrid, but to seize with a strong hand the robbers in their dens, and execute that vengeance which was sought in vain from the Spanish authorities.

"Notwithstanding the negotiations with Spain, and the exertions of our navy," says a writer in the Annual Register (Baldwin and Craddock's edition), for the year 1822, "the outrage of the pirates continued throughout the year, and towards the end of it, an opinion prevailed very generally, that the measures which the Admiralty had taken to suppress the evil were extremely inadequate. One great topic of complaint was, that the captains of our frigates on the West India station, allured by the profits which they have in the freight of bullion, were more assiduous in transporting gold and silver from the contiguous parts of South America, than in protecting the trade."

We cannot tell whether we are most shocked at the ignorance and contradiction, or at the cruelty and absurdity, of a charge like this, from a writer who certainly must be allowed to possess the power of discrimination in no very limited degree. "The exertions of our navy" immediately precede the inadequate measures of the Admiralty; and "the captains of frigates," who can only act in obedience to the orders they receive, are accused of neglecting a duty they were not ordered to execute, and of doing that which could only have been done under the directions which they must have received from their Commander-in-chief. Could a charge like this be for one moment entertained against our honourable profession, it should be carried to the fountain head; an imputation like this would suppose the Lords of the Admiralty to participate in the profits or to connive at the crime: the first is absurd and impossible; and for the second, we know full well that could negligence or corruption have been even suspected, against the Commander-in-chief, or the captains and commanders on the Jamaica station, a speedy investigation of their conduct before a court-martial would have amply vindicated the honour of the British flag: we therefore repel this charge as false and malignant. If blame was imputable, it was to those persons, who, having too successfully advocated retrenchment, left the government without sufficient means to protect the trade. The nature of the West India climate is peculiarly adapted for the commission of piracy, and to such acts it has been exposed since the earliest periods of colonization. In many instances the evil might have been prevented, by the captains of merchant-vessels using more precaution in permitting boats to approach the ship: boarding-nettings and close quarters, with a proper supply of small arms and ammunition, would either have kept off the robbers, or cleared the decks of them when they came on board. Ships of war cannot be ordered to attend every merchant-vessel that sails through the gulf stream: convoys were appointed, and every human precaution taken; still the utmost vigilance might be eluded, where the points of attack are so much more numerous than the means of defence. On the whole, we might as reasonably blame the sitting magistrate for a murder in his district, as an admiral or captain for the capture, under these circumstances, of a British merchant-vessel by an enemy or pirate.

When the Lords Commissioners of the Admiralty found that no effective redress was to be expected from the court of Spain, an additional number of fast-sailing sloops of war were sent out, and the young and gallant officers commanding them acted with so much vigour, that in a very short time these pirates were exterminated. North America partook also of this honour: her trade was as much exposed as our own, and numerous instances occurred where the freebooters of the coast of Cuba expiated their crimes on a gibbet erected at the mouth of Port Royal Harbour, Jamaica.

On the 10th of August, 1822, his most gracious Majesty having long entertained a desire to visit the northern part of his kingdom, embarked on board of his yacht, the Royal George, commanded by the Honourable Captain Charles Paget, lying off the Royal Hospital, Greenwich. It was on this occasion that he took leave of his oldest naval friend and faithful counsellor, the late Earl of St. Vincent. The venerable Peer, then in the 88th year of his age, and in the costume in which he is represented in the first volume of this work, went on board the yacht to receive his Majesty. The king, with that kindness of manner, and gentlemanly demeanour, for which he is justly celebrated, took the veteran by the arm and led him to a seat on the quarter-deck, where his Majesty placed himself beside him, and they conversed for some time in presence of the most crowded and numerous circle of spectators which had perhaps ever met together so near the metropolis: the acclamations at this gratifying scene were heard far distant on the banks of the Thames, and the pensioners of Greenwich Hospital were the appropriate witnesses of this tribute of respect from the greatest of monarchs to one of the most celebrated of his admirals. On the year of his coronation, his Majesty had presented the Earl with a baton of Admiral of the fleet: it was conveyed to his seat at Rochetts by a special messenger, with a very gracious letter dictated by his Majesty, and written by Sir Benjamin Bloomfield. It was in consequence of having received this signal mark of favour from his sovereign, that the gallant Admiral resolved to make the exertion of returning thanks in person on the element where it was acquired. On taking leave, his Majesty presented his arm to his aged friend, who leaned on it, and the King of Great Britain was seen descending the side of his yacht to assist the Earl of St. Vincent into the boat. After this affecting attention the yacht slipped her moorings, and being taken in tow by a steam-boat, was conveyed with rapidity down the river, amidst the applauses and congratulations of a grateful and loyal people.

APPENDIX.

APPENDIX.

Particulars relating to the rebellion in Guadaloupe, and the treachery of Admiral Linois to Louis XVIII—Situation of Rear-admiral Durham and Lieutenant-general Leith, as to orders from home.

Voyages of Discovery—Alceste and Lyra, on the coast of Corea—Captain Hall's account of the Loo Choo Islands—the Alceste returns to the Bocca Tigre—Insolence of the Chinese, and determined conduct of Captain Maxwell—Action between the Alceste and the forts at Chumpee—Strange conduct of the government of Canton—Lord Amherst re-embarks to return to England—Loss of the Alceste in the Straits of Gaspar—Heroic exertions of the captain and crew—Lord Amherst is landed at Java, and sends assistance—Generous conduct of Captain Maxwell contrasted with that of the Captain of La Meduse—Capture of the pirate Proa, by Lieutenant Hay—Voyage of Captain Tuckey to the Congo, or Zaire—Digression on Captain Flinders' detention at the Isle of France—Vindication of General De Caen—Death of Captain Tuckey and his officers—Voyages of Ross and Parry.

Miscellaneous—Gallant action between the Brevdrageren and Danish brigs—Capture of two Danish gun-vessels in the river Elbe by Lieutenant Devon—Letter of Admiral Young—Anecdotes of Captain Ed. W. Hoare and of Captain Edmund Lyons in the East Indies—of Captain Harris, in the Sir Francis Drake—of Captain Maunsell, in the Procris—Observations on the action off Lissa, between Sir William Hoste and the French squadron—Perilous situation of one of the prizes, and wonderful presence of mind of the young British officers—Capture of the American sloop of war, Frolic, by the Orpheus—the Imperieuse at Salerno—Battle of Barossa—Observations on the loss of the St. George and Defence—Weak and frivolous policy of the Spanish government towards its colonies—Commodore Cockburn is sent out Ambassador extraordinary to treat with them, but fails—Instructions

THE expectation of the re-landing of Napoleon
from Elba, had reached and infested the French
colonies in the West Indies; and some degree of
indecision seemed to prevail in the councils of our
government, which entertained an apprehension of
the renewal of the war, or of the necessity that
might present itself, of concluding a peace a second
time with Bonaparte.

Rear-admiral Durham, who commanded the
British squadron, was in habits of intimacy with
the Count de Vaugiraud, governor of the island
of Martinique, and with Admiral Linois, the governor of Guadaloupe: the former was as decidedly
loyal and attached to his king, as the latter was to
the fortunes of Napoleon. In this state of things,
Rear-admiral Durham received a private letter in
the spring of 1815, from Lord Melville, written immediately on the return of Bonaparte to Paris, most
explicitly directing him, whatever flag might be
seen to fly on the French islands, or whatever course
the French Governor might pursue against us, to
abstain from all offensive measures against them

This letter was brought by a king's schooner, com-, manded by a lieutenant, who was the bearer of no other dispatches!

It is not a little remarkable, that Lieutenant-general Sir James Leith, who was then commander of the forces in the Leeward Islands, alleged that he had received, about the same time, orders from Lord Bathurst of a contrary nature, in which, as he asserted, he was enjoined to attack the French: it is difficult to conceive that Lord Bathurst could have meant that his orders should have gone to such an extent, nor is it probable that two ministers sitting in the same cabinet, should have given at the same moment such opposite instructions.

When the intelligence of the landing of Bonaparte reached the French islands, insurrections were hourly expected to take place in his favour, and hostile to the interests of the king. The Count de Vaugiraud applied to the Rear-admiral and Lieutenant-general, for some British troops to assist in keeping down the rising spirit of insubordination that had extended from Guadaloupe to Martinique. Some troops were instantly embarked at Barbadoes, on board the ships of war and transports, which conveyed them to Gros Islet bay, in St. Lucia, immediately opposite to Fort Royal. The promptitude of this measure seemed to have a paralyzing effect on the Count, who, after having claimed their assistance, began to hesitate whether

he should admit them: he opened a kind of negotiation on the subject with the Rear-admiral, but
the latter brought the question to a speedy conclusion, by informing the Governor, that unless
the men were permitted to land, he must immediately send them back to Barbadoes. This message
produced decision in the mind of the Count; the
necessary permission was sent; and the Rear-
admiral having run over in the night, landed at
daylight one thousand five hundred troops on the
island of Martinique. This force, being accompanied by Sir James Leith, was found fully equal
to preserve the tranquillity of the island.

The same assistance which had been extended
to Martinique, was craved at Guadaloupe, but not
with equal zeal and earnestness. The Rear-admiral
some time after fell in with a French national
schooner, bearing the tri-coloured flag. She had
been dispatched from Rochefort, by Decrées, the
minister of the marine, to give information to the
colonies, and her commander acknowledged to the
Rear-admiral, that he bore the-commission of
Napoleon, had landed his dispatches at Guadaloupe, and was then on his way to Martinique.

Notwithstanding this confession, and contrary
to the earnest entreaties of Sir James Leith, the
Rear-admiral felt it his duty still to adhere to the
letter of Lord Melville, and declined either de-
taining the vessel, or taking any active part in the
invasion of the island of Guadaloupe, although he

consented to carry thither a body of troops, to assist Admiral Linois in supporting his authority as the governor appointed by Louis XVIII.

For this purpose he proceeded with a body of troops to Basse-terre Roads, but at the dawn of day perceived the tri-coloured flag flying on the forts. Suspecting the course which had been pursued by Linois, yet affecting to disbelieve that he would have acted a part so unbecoming, the Rear-admiral sent Lieutenant (afterwards Captain) Wemys to him, with a kind message, assuring his Excellency that he might rely on every support from the British forces, and as the Rear-admiral saw the flag of Napoleon flying, he was quite sure that the person of his Excellency must be under restraint; he therefore offered the cabin of the Venerable for himself and family, to convey them to a place of safety.

Captain Wemys delivered this message to the Governor, in presence of a large assembly of the inhabitants. Monsieur Linois replied, that having adopted the cockade of Napoleon, which he pointed to in his hat, he was determined to stand or fall by it! This answer being delivered to the Rear-admiral, he returned to Barbadoes, where he shortly after received orders from home to proceed and attack the French islands, which had thrown off the authority of their king.

On the return of the squadron to Barbadoes, a correspondence took place between the Commanders-in-chief, upon the subject of a hostile

attack upon Guadaloupe; Sir James Leith urging
and the Rear-admiral declining it, assigning as his
reason the directions he had received from the
first Lord of the Admiralty, and the responsibility
that would rest upon him, or any officer so situated,
if he should of his own authority presume to ori-
ginate hostile operations between the two greatest
nations on the earth. The Admiral's reasons were
afterwards fully approved of by his superiors at
home. On the arrival of instructions from the
Admiralty, the Rear-admiral proceeded with the
land and sea-forces to the attack of the island, and
the event was such as we have related at p. 227
of this volume.

A singular incident being recalled to mind on
this occasion, caused a renewal of friendship between Rear-admiral Durham and the Count de
Vaugiraud. In 1795, the Rear-admiral, then
Captain of the Anson, was ordered on the memorable expedition to Quiberon Bay, and the
island of Noirmoutier: the Count de Vaugiraud
undertook to be the pilot, and gave a more favourable opinion of his courage than of his seamanship, by running the Anson on shore under a battery. This circumstance, after a lapse of twenty
years, occasioned much mirth between them.

It is both the duty and interest of civilized
nations to extend their discoveries, and carry the
arts, the improvements, and the comforts of life
into those regions where the naked savage, wan-
dering in the woods, or along the sea-shore in

search of precarious subsistence, hesitates not to make even man his prey. The spirit of inquiry, the love of learning, and the superior education, which distinguish the naval officers of the nineteenth century, had enabled them not only to execute the orders of their government with zeal and ability; but in many instances, where orders have not been given, they have voluntarily exposed themselves to responsibility, with the laudable view of extending the boundaries of science, and meliorating the condition of their fellow-creatures.

Such, it may fairly be presumed, were the objects of Captain (now Sir Murray) Maxwell, and Captain Basil Hall, who, commanding his Majesty's frigate, the Alceste, and sloop of war, the Lyra, took advantage of an interval when their services were not otherwise required.

His Majesty's government having, in 1816, determined to send an embassy to China, Lord Amherst sailed in the Alceste on the 9th of February of that year, accompanied by the Lyra. On the 11th of August his Lordship landed at the mouth of the Pei-ho river, in the Yellow Sea, and while he was employed on the duties assigned to him, Captain Maxwell proceeded to survey the adjacent coast and neighbouring islands, which had not been accurately laid down by geographers, nor described by circumnavigators. The history of the discoveries made in this short excursion, has been given to the public by Captain Basil Hall, in a very able and interesting quarto volume, with maps and draw ings, éxecuted in a very superior style, and pub-lished by Murray in 1818.

The first object which attracted their notice was a cluster of islands, which Captain Maxwell named Sir James Hall's Group, in honour of the father of his young friend and companion, the commander of thé Lyra. These islands are situated on the coast of Corea, in long. 124° 46′ E. and lat. 37° 50′ N. The description given by Captain Hall, of the manners and customs of these newly-discovered people, for such they were to us, is sufficiently interesting, but the natives did not seem anxious that the ships should prolong their stay; they refused every offer of barter or exchange, and though they possessed bullocks and poultry, declined parting with them for dollars, or any other consideration. This was most probably the effect of the rigid orders of their government, which appeared to have interdicted, under the severest penalties, any communication with strangers. They did not understand the Chinese language, which was spoken to them by an interpreter. The British vessels weighed the same evening, in pursuit of other discoveries.

The next visit was to another group of islands, one of which they examined and named it after Dr. Hutton the geologist. This island lay also close to the coast of Corea. It was not laid down by geographers, and a space of two hundred miles in extent along the coast, thickly strewed with countless numbers of unknown islands is not noticed in the charts, and many large islands were not laid down within sixty miles of their proper places. It is singular, that without offering any offence to the visitors, the natives invariably expressed a wish for their speedy departure. Having made as accurate a chart of the coast of Corea and the Archipelagos, as the shortness of their visit would allow, the frigate and brig sailed on the 1st of September; and on the 15th, after encountering and overcoming the imminent danger of shipwreck, the Lyra and Alceste approached and came to an anchor at the now celebrated Loo Choo Islands.

In considering the incidents related by Captain Hall, we are amazed at the combination of highly improved science, gentlemanly deportment, and suavity of manners, possessed by the British officers, which enabled them not only to acquire the friendship and esteem of the happy natives of Loo Choo, but to present their country with a topographical, geological, and natural history, together with such an account of the manners and customs of the people, as will render their names deserving of a high place in the literary annals of their country. The voyage to the great Loo Choo Island will be read with pleasure by future generations, and we will venture to predict, that the amiable and endearing deportment of Loo Chooans will excite the admiration of the most enlightened reader. The drawings are well executed, and convey an admirable idea of the scenery of the country, and the costume of the people. The description of Port Melville, in the great Loo Choo Island, is animated and beautiful, and we feel a sensation of regret at laying down the book, as if parting from an agreeable companion and friend. The narrow escape of the Lyra from shipwreck, as related at page 148, will be felt by all seamen, particularly the *brig sailor*, those vessels being particularly liable to run wild when in stays, and to make the most alarming stern boards, when there is little space for such excursions. The history of this voyage is rendered doubly interesting to the philosopher and the philanthropist, from the harmony that invariably subsisted between the parties: although ignorant of each other's language, no disagreement nor unpleasant feeling ensued. The interchange of civilities and presents, the conciliating manners, the noble generosity of both parties, vying with each other, the fairy scenes of the country, and the striking difference between these happy islanders and the jealous and sometimes inexorable Chinese, cannot fail to inspire a British reader with an ardent desire not only to peruse the voyage of Captain Hall, but to become more intimately acquainted with a people who seem to realize the innocence of the golden age.

We have made these few remarks on the work of Captain Hall, strictly in conformity with our general plan to notice all the circumnavigators of the period in which we have written, or at least such of them as bore his Majesty's commission. To have said less on the subject would have been improper—to have said more would have been unjust to Captain Hall, as many would have felt themselves satisfied with a larger extract, and left his book unheeded. We cannot conclude this article without recommending in the strongest manner the work of this gallant officer on South America: it is, in our humble judgment, as much superior in interest to Johnson's 'Tour to the Hebrides,' as South America is in extent to those little islands. We now pursue the history of the embassy to China, the remaining particulars of which have been related by Mr. John M'Leod, surgeon of the Alceste. This book we are also bound to speak of in terms of approbation: it is a modest unaffected narrative, full of incident; and the reader who lays out his money in the purchase of it, will be amply repaid for the expense.

We shall pass over the parts of M'Leod's book, until we come to the 13th of August, when the Alceste was off the Sha-loo-poo-tien Islands, coasting along the western shore of the gulf of Lea-tong, till then unexplored by any British ship. On the 14th, in lat. 39° 29' N. and long. 120° 6' E. "the great wall of China opened to view (to use the words of Mr. M'Leod), rising from the sea. This immense barrier passed over the first, or lowest hill, and mounting the second, was seen stretching to the right (in our point of view) obliquely towards the summit; then on the third, and still higher land, enclosed to the left, making an

angle with the last range, and ultimately ascend-
ing the highest and most distant mountain it was
there lost." The great wall of China has, we
know, been often spoken of and described before;
but seen from the quarter-deck of a British frigate,
it seemed to demand our attention: we, however,
proceed to that part of the voyage, where the frigate having received Lord Amherst on board,
prepared to return to England. Before this event
was accomplished, the British officers had many
insults to receive, some difficulties to overcome,
and some honour to acquire.

On the 2d of November, as soon as the Alceste
had anchored off the island of Lintin, the mandarins
came on board and informed Captain Maxwell
that the British Ambassador had been dismissed
from the court of Pekin in disgrace: the Viceroy,
it appears, was aware that the object of the
embassy was directed in a great measure against
the extortions and the oppression which our commerce laboured under, from the fraudulent practices
of his subordinate officers. The General Hewit,
an Indiaman, which had brought out the valuable
presents from the King of England to the Emperor
of China was not permitted to load a cargo of teas,
under the absurd pretence that the space on board
of her would be entirely occupied with the same
presents, which having been indignantly rejected,
were to be conveyed back in her to England. The
Alceste was refused permission to proceed higher
up the river for the purpose of procuring refresh-

ments, and it was insolently added, that a British merchant-ship must be held by the Chinese as a security for the good behaviour of the crew of the Alceste. Captain Maxwell desired them very quietly " not to repeat this part of their conversation, unless they wished to be thrown overboard," observing, that he would wait a reasonable time for a pass to proceed up the river, first, because his ship required repairs, and secondly, because the Lion, in 1791, with Lord M'Cartney on board, had been admitted to a place of security; and as Captain Maxwell knew that the Emperor had expressed his pleasure that the Alceste should be received in the same manner, he was determined to have his right, and if a pass was not sent down in forty-eight hours, he should consider that leave was given.

The period expired, and no answer was received. The pilot who had been procured to conduct the ship up the river secretly absconded, observing before his departure, that it was dangerous to have any communication with the ship. The situation of Captain Maxwell was at this time one of the most difficult and important that could be conceived: the British Ambassador was in the power of these insolent and unbending people; the British frigate was kept by them in an open and exposed roadsted, in the winter season; the flag was insulted, and the common offices of hospitality denied to him; tame submission, he knew would only increase their presumption—open violence would have endangered the life of Lord Amherst.

On the 12th of November, Captain Maxwell came to a determination to weigh and run up the river, which he did, as high as Mr. Mayne, the master of the Alceste, could carry him, anchoring off Lankleet flat for the night, and the next day, with the flood-tide, reached as high as the Bocca Tigre, or Tiger's Mouth (so the principal branch of the river of Canton is called). Dr. M'Leod says, it is about as wide as the Thames at London, but the banks are high, and were at that time guarded by fortifications of immense strength, mounting one hundred and ten pieces of cannon, of different calibers, including the island of Wangtong, the whole within half gun-shot of each other, and garrisoned by one thousand two hundred men.

As the Alceste gallantly and silently advanced, with every thing prepared for a fight of no trivial importance, the Chinese war-junks, to the number of seventeen or eighteen, formed a line off Chumpee. These poor representatives of 'battle ships' carry from four to eight guns, with a complement from sixty to eighty men. It was five o'clock in the evening when an interpreter came on board from the mandarins, and desired that Captain Maxwell would anchor his ship on pain of being sunk. The Captain calmly observed, that he would first pass the batteries and then hang him (the messenger) at the yard-arm, for daring to bring so insolent a message to a British ship of war: his boat was then cut adrift, and himself handed down below to a place of security. The junks now began to fire blank cartridges, which the Alceste returned with three guns unshotted, affecting to consider it as a salute.

On the following day the frigate weighed and passed the junks. These got under weigh, and when the Alceste had advanced as far as Chumpee, they, and the forts, began to fire on her with shot. Light and baffling airs at this moment compelled the Alceste to come to anchor; but determined to convince them that he was not intimidated, the Captain fired one gun shotted at the Admiral. This gun he very honourably and considerately fired with his own hand, that in the event of the Chinese government demanding, as was their custom, the man that fired, *he* might place himself in the situation of responsibility, instead of letting the weight of their revenge fall on an innocent person, as had been done on a former occasion.

The scene that now ensued, considering with whom the British frigate had to contend, was one of unusual interest. Whether the shot from the Alceste silenced the junks and the forts, or whether they ceased firing from her having anchored, is uncertain. She lay quietly and unannoyed till eight o'clock at night, when the wind permitting her to lay the course, she weighed, and ran still higher up the river: the junks observing this, beat their gongs, fired guns, and threw up skyrockets to give the alarm. "The batteries were instantly illuminated (says the Doctor) with lanterns as large as balloons," offering a fine mark for the great guns of the Alceste, which, as she passed along, was exposed to a heavy but ill-directed fire from both sides of the river. This she returned in a cool and deliberate manner, as fast as her guns could be brought to bear, with a light breeze majestically keeping on her steady and undeviating course. Coming at last within half pistol-shot of the angle of the heaviest battery, and just before they could get their guns to bear on the ship, the Alceste gave them a broadside from her long-eighteens, and her thirty-two pound carronades, which was heard to produce a very considerable dilapidation on the batteries. The lights disappeared as if by magic; the fort was silenced on one side, while the fire from the other, directed at the ship, missed its aim, and did execution on its opposite neighbour. After an hour's contest in this narrow channel, and for the first time that any European vessel had dared to direct a shot against the shore, the Alceste was permitted to ascend the river, and take up her anchorage, without having a man hurt, only two shot in her hull, and her rigging a little damaged. The confined space in which this action was fought, the high banks of the river, the calm surface of the water, the brilliancy of the fire, and the rapidity of its effect, produced a scene amounting to something sublime. The poor astonished Chinaman who had been sent below under a threat of execution, as soon as the frigate had passed the batteries, came trembling on deck, and falling prostrate, kissed the feet of the Captain and begged for mercy, considering very justly, that the execution of himself was a matter of very little importance, compared to the decisive step taken by Captain Maxwell. Tiger Island was passed in silence; not a gun was fired from thence; and the Alceste at daylight was at an anchor in a good berth, with the British colours flying, surrounded, though at a very respectful distance, by "the grand fleet of China." The number of natives who lost their lives on this occasion was carefully concealed, though it was presumed that many suffered. Whether the transaction was communicated to the Emperor, or not, is uncertain: no farther insult was offered to the British flag. The news at first excited considerable alarm among the merchants at Canton, but their fears were relieved by the arrival of several tea-junks alongside the General Hewit, with permission for her to load her cargo immediately. It must be evident from these facts, that the Chinese are by no means indifferent to the profits of their trade with England; and it was subsequently proved, when our factory took their departure and struck the British flag, that the Chinese authorities became alarmed, and, entreating them to return, granted all their demands. We cannot, therefore, sufficiently execrate the cowardice of those captains, who gave up, on two occasions, innocent men to be murdered in cold blood by these people, because they had accidentally been the cause of the death of two of the natives.

The remonstrance of Captain Maxwell to the government of Canton, on the gross insult offered to our flag, produced nothing more than the usual subterfuges of falsehood and evasion: they said it was all a mistake; that the pass had been delayed or not received by the Mandarins at the forts, and that these had therefore acted according to orders; but their Gazette letter, in the course of a few days, made it a Chinese puzzle, by stating it to have been a "Chinchinning," or salute between the two flags! It was long after dark when the affair took place, and British ships never salute after sunset. Forty-seven men were reported to have been killed, and several others wounded, but the truth could never be ascertained, as a public edict forbade any man to talk on the subject: this the Chinese call "making face." The seasonable chastisement inflicted by Captain Maxwell, whether considered as a salute or an attack, answered every purpose of a decided victory, and the Viceroy, when the frigate advanced to Whampoa, congratulated the Captain on his safe arrival, after having vainly used every means in his power to obstruct his passage.

The interview between Lord Amherst and the Viceroy having terminated in mutual distrust and coldness, his Excellency re-embarked, and proceeding down the river to Whampoa, was saluted by the Chinese junks in the most respectful manner. The same ceremony was repeated when the Alceste, having his Lordship on board, passed the batteries of Chumpee.

The Alceste sailed from Macao on the 9th of January, 1817, on her homeward voyage. The remarks made by Mr. M'Leod, on the Spanish settlements of Manilla and the Philippine Islands, are amusing and instructive. On the 9th of February, the Alceste weighed, and unfortunately parted company with her consort the Lyra, which was sent with dispatches to India. Passing through the Straits of Gaspar, and near the island of Pulo Leat, with the lead going on each side, and a vigilant look-out from the mast-head, the ship at half-past seven in the morning of the 18th, "struck on a sunken reef of rocks, with a horrid crash, and remained immovable." From that moment it became evident that she was lost: the pumps were useless; she filled to the orlop-deck, and nothing remained to be done but to hoist out the boats and save the people, with as much provision as could be procured. The Ambassador and suite were landed on the nearest part of the island, then about three miles and a half distant, while Captain Maxwell, with his officers and crew, remained on board to secure such supplies from the wreck as were necessary for their subsistence.

If Captain Maxwell was unfortunate in losing his ship, he acquired great honour by the fortitude,

judgment, and good conduct displayed in the preservation of the lives of those intrusted to his care.
The first consideration was to save the Ambassador, with his suite, and as many of his books
and papers as had been rescued from the waves.
It was judged that a boat, with the assistance of
the current, would reach Batavia in three days;
and as it was impossible for all the crew to be
conveyed at one time in the ship's boats, it was
thought advisable to send away a small part, with
the hope of receiving more speedy and effectual
assistance. Having performed this indispensable
part of his duty, Captain Maxwell remained with
his crew, to provide for their safety, and to share
their misfortunes.

Lord Amherst was placed in the barge and attended by the cutter. The boats were commanded
by Lieutenant Hoppner. Mr. Ellis, the secretary,
with some other officers of the ship, and a strong
guard of marines, accompanied his Lordship: they
had a very slender stock of provisions, and were
particularly ill supplied with water, so much so
that the people were nearly exhausted with thirst
and fatigue, when approaching the island of Java,
but at a considerable distance from the land, they
accidentally discovered a stream of fresh water,
running out between the two head-lands which
form the bay of Batavia. Mr. M'Leod, in speak-
ing of this circumstance, which so providentially
relieved the thirst of the sufferers in the boat,

mentions the same discovery off the Rhone, as already referred to in the fourth volume of this work. He adds with great justice and propriety, that streams of fresh water are in like manner to be found in the neighbourhood of all great rivers. This very natural effect, produced by the most obvious causes, has never been sufficiently attended to by navigators: ships being short of fresh water, might frequently get into a stream when they could not approach the land. Care should always be had to take it up from the surface, and at a short distance from the ship's side, to avoid the effects of the copper, or the dirt which might be thrown overboard.

The honourable and seaman-like conduct of Captain Maxwell has been forcibly contrasted with that of the captain of the Meduse, placed under similar circumstances. It has ever been contrary to our plan to cast reflections even on our enemies, unless some great proposition is to be established, or some useful lesson inculcated, likely to be conducive to the future benefit of the navy, and, consequently, to the empire. The example set by Captain Maxwell is precisely that which should be followed by every British officer under similar circumstances. It was that conduct which, pursued by the immortal Riou, saved the crew of the Guardian, and it is that conduct which, we trust, will ever be pursued by the rising generation. The captain (unless an example is wanted to induce

the men to quit the wreck) should be the last man
on board, and he should preserve the discipline of
his ship in the same manner as if she were at
Spithead : by exposing his own person to greater
risk and privation than that of his men, he will
animate and cheer them to the performance of
their labour, and be the means of preserving them
from destruction.   The want of attending to this
duty in the captain of the Meduse, produced a
scene of horror from which we turn away with
pain and disgust: the crew of the Meduse were
sacrificed, not to the want of courage, but to the
want of conduct in their officers : not a man need
to have been lost, had they been kept on board
the ship, and their efforts combined for the general
good.   Had the ship been commanded by Riou,
Rowley, or Maxwell, the dreadful picture of the
raft had never existed.   Had these three officers
sought their own safety, the fate of the crews of
the Guardian, the Laurel, and the Alceste, would
have been nearly the same as that of La Meduse.*
The history of the exertions, the sufferings, and
the persevering ingenuity of the captain and crew
of the Alceste, are recommended to the young
naval reader, as well worthy of his serious attention.   Few are at a loss to know how to act in
presence of an enemy, that kind of courage is so common as to be almost negative; the want of it sub-

* A French frigate, lost on the coast of Guinea, in the year
1817.

jects the offender to shame or death : in cases of shipwreck, presence of mind, firmness, and a ready adoption of such resources as may be at hand, shew the value of an officer, and often produce the most beneficial results. The history of the wreck of the Alceste, and the defence of Pulo Leat is the reality of De Foe's fable of Robinson Crusoe: the preparation to receive the savages, husbanding the stores, digging wells, and raising fortifications, under the most trying privations, fill us with admiration, and shew the true character of British seamen in a very noble point of view, and one in which, through the course of this work, we have not had so good an opportunity of contemplating it. The burning of the Alceste by the Malays, on Saturday, the 22d of February, is an incident which seems to bring the history to a climax, and deserves to be recorded.

" Two of the largest proas (says Mr. M'Leod) were now at work on the ship, but on observing their comrades abandon the wreck, and the advance of our boats, they made sail away; having previously set fire to the ship, which they did so effectually, that the flames burst from every port, and she was soon enveloped in a cloud of smoke : the boats were unable to board her, and therefore returned.

" The ship continued burning during the whole of the night, and the flames, which could be seen through the openings of the trees, shed a melancholy glare around, and excited the most mournful ideas." But this conflagration which the men had seen with so much despondency, turned out to be an interposition of Providence in their favour. The crew had been assembled on Sunday morning to Divine service, while the boats were sent in hopes of obtaining some articles of provision liberated from the hold of the ship by the burning of the decks and topsides. They returned just as the morning service was completed, and the officer announced that they had procured some flour, a few cases of wine, and a cask of beer: of this last article the captain ordered a pint to be issued to each man. The decree was answered with three hearty cheers: the poor fellows perhaps meant to express as much gratitude to Heaven as could be conveyed by any words of their own; and it was good-naturedly observed by the chaplain, that those who might be fastidious would please to recollect that they had never seen a congregation suffering the agony of thirst dismissed from the church-door in England with such a donation. The contention between the barge and a Malay proa, and the desperate conduct of the savages, are also very remarkable. On Wednesday, the 26th, at daylight, two of the pirate boats, with each a canoe a-stern, were discovered close in with the cove where the boats were moored. Lieutenant Hay, who had the guard that night, and of course slept in the boats, immediately dashed at them with the barge, cutter, and gig: the savages cut their canoes adrift and made all sail; they rather distanced the cutter and gig, but the barge gained on them. On closing, the Malays evinced every sign of defiance, placing themselves in the most threatening attitudes, and firing their swivels at the barge: this was returned by Mr. Hay, with the only musket in the boat, and as they closed nearer, the Malays commenced throwing their javelins and darts; several fell into the barge, but without doing any injury. Soon after they were grappled by our brave fellows. Three of the savages had been shot, a fourth was knocked down with the butt end of the musket, five threw themselves into the sea and were drowned; and two were taken prisoners, one of whom was desperately wounded. After having won the boat by this gallant enterprise, it was mortifying to lose her; but she sunk as soon as she was taken. So desperate are the savages who infest these seas, that a wounded prisoner who was shot through the body, on being removed into the barge to save him, as his own boat was sinking, grasped a cutlass which lay within his reach, and would have done some mischief with it, had it not been forcibly wrenched from his hand: he died in a few minutes after. The consort of the proa escaped. The canoes were brought on shore, containing several articles of plunder from the ship: the proas appeared to be the two which set her on fire. The prisoners, one elderly, the other young, seemed to have no hope, of being permitted to live, and sullenly awaited their fate; but on the wounds of the younger one being dressed, the hands of the elder one untied, and food offered to them, with other marks of kindness, they became more cheerful, and were particularly gratified on seeing the bodies of their dead companions, which had been brought on shore, decently interred. Those who stupidly contend against the good effects of moral instruction and Christian education among the lower orders, would perhaps deny the superiority of Captain Maxwell and his gallant associates over the uncultivated barbarians whom they subdued and relieved. It would be impossible to do justice to the conduct of this forlorn band of heroes, without entering more deeply into the contents of the volume than our limits will admit. We may be allowed to say, that the narrative is one of the most interesting that ever came from the pen of a sailor.

Lord Amherst having, by the care and assiduity of Captain Maxwell, been enabled to reach Batavia, with Lieutenant Cooke, Mr. Ellis, the secretary to the embassy, and Mr. Hoppner, these last two gentlemen, agreeably to a promise they had made at parting, returned to the assistance of their shipmates, in the Ternate, one of the Company's cruisers, and pushed back to the island with the utmost diligence. Nothing, except the supply of provisions, could have been more providential than the arrival of this vessel, at the very time when famine threatened the garrison of the island (which in compliment to their leader they had named Fort Maxwell), and where upwards of fifty piratical proas had assembled to blockade, and threatened every hour to attack, them. The appearance of the Ternate, on the morning of the 3d of March, induced the barbarians to depart; and on the 7th, Captain Maxwell, having embarked the whole of his crew, quitted the island, and was received on board the Company's vessel, commanded by Captain Davidson.

During the latter part of the reign of his Majesty King George III., the insatiable thirst for knowledge kept pace with the glory of our arms by sea and land; and it is justly observed, by the editor of a work which claims our attention, that that period will be referred to by future historians as one not less distinguished by the brilliant exploits of our countrymen in arms, than by the steady and progressive march of the sciences and the arts. The same writer is, however, greatly mistaken in the lines immediately following, where he says (Preface to Captain Tuckey's Expedition to the River Zaire, p. 1), that these pursuits experienced little interruption from the war, "except in one memorable instance, where a French general brutally seized the person and papers of a British naval officer, on his return from a voyage of discovery, and with unparalleled meanness, injustice, and inhumanity, detained the former nearly seven years in captivity, and purloined a part of the latter."

It may naturally be concluded that the author of a naval history would lean to the side of a British seaman, and particularly when he happened to be a British officer; but justice even to an enemy is, and ever will be, a paramount consideration with him. The name of General De Caen, we know, has been branded with infamy for the conduct which he thought proper to pursue towards Captain Flinders, who, in the Investigator, was detained at the Isle of France on his return from a voyage of discovery to the coast of New Holland. Few of our readers are acquainted with the cause of the dispute between these officers: the facts are here given as they have been recently stated to the author by a gentleman of veracity who was present, and who was himself the bearer of Captain Flinders's papers to England. It appears that Captain Flinders, when lying with his vessel at Port Louis, in the Isle of France, had been reported by some Frenchmen to have taken soundings in the harbour: this report, whether true or false we have not the means of knowing, was the cause of all the misfortunes which attended Captain Flinders. Summoned to appear before the General, his Excellency in a violent rage told him he was convinced that he (the Captain) was not the man he represented himself to be: this very naturally irritated the honourable mind of Captain Flinders, who till that day had been in habits of intimacy with the General. Madame de Caen, an amiable and excellent woman, used her endeavours to restore harmony: she entreated Captain Flinders to think no more of the harsh words of the Governor, who after all meant nothing; that he was irritable, and the pressure of business had hurried him to expressions which she was sure his sober judgment would condemn. "Come," said the kind-hearted lady, "come and dine with us to-day, and all will be forgotten." Captain Flinders had, however, been too deeply wounded in feeling and character, to pass it over in this manner. In whatever light the act might be viewed, he was conscious that he had not forfeited his claim to be treated like a gentleman, and that he was unlawfully detained. Being a British naval officer, furnished with a commission which had ever been respected among civilized nations, he therefore replied to the overtures of Madame de Caen, that he could never think of sitting at the General's table until the offensive words were recalled. This being refused, Captain Flinders was placed under surveillance, while an account of the transaction was sent home to Napoleon. General De Caen would, we have reason to believe, have liberated Captain Flinders soon after, but having referred the matter to his court, he was forced to await the result, and the subsequent detention was in consequence of orders from the French government, and not depending on the will of the General. We have thought this explanation necessary, not only in justice to the General but to Captain Flinders, to whom science is so much indebted.

The benevolent solicitude of Madame De Caen must not be overlooked : this amiable lady made it her study to lighten the chains of the English captives, and cheer the dull hours of hopeless separation from their friends. Without having the honour of being personally known to her, the author of these volumes, is happy in an opportunity of testifying his sense of the obligations which the English prisoners at the Isle of France owed to the Christian virtues of Madame de Caen; in some future wars, this humble tribute may be the means of affording consolation and relief to other prisoners, not from the selfish hope of remuneration, but from the certainty of the facts being known and approved of by the wise and the good.

We have been informed that the papers taken from Captain Flinders, were only such as related to the Isle of France.

From this digression we return to the subject on which we set out, namely, the voyage of Captain J. K. Tuckey, of the royal navy, to explore the river Zaire, in 1816.

The object of this expedition was to ascertain whether the river Congo, or Zaire, might be the outlet of the Niger, running into the Southern Atlantic, in the sixth degree of south latitude. Such appears to have been the conviction of the celebrated Mungo Park to the end of his life, or to the latest accounts which were ever obtained from him. In his letters to Lord Camden, to Sir Joseph Banks, and to Mrs. Park, from the banks of the Niger, he expressed a confident hope of reaching England by the way of the West Indies, by arriving at a distant part of the western coast of Africa, conducted thither by the stream of the Niger joining the Congo.

Captain Tuckey, who volunteered his services to explore this inland navigation, was an officer of rare merit. He had been first lieutenant of the Coromandel of fifty-four guns, when captured by the French in 1805; his conduct on that occasion was so highly commended by his captain, that it led to his promotion, after a cruel and inhuman detention of nine years in France, during which he was made to suffer all the miseries that the tyrant of Europe could inflict. Of this subject we now speak for the last time: we have, we trust, fairly proved that all the sufferings of prisoners both in France and England were the work of Napoleon; this proposition, let Mons. Dupin and his apologists in this country say what they will, is undeniable.

The Congo, to which Captain Tuckey was appointed in the latter end of 1815, was a vessel constructed by Sir Robert Seppings, for the express purpose of navigating the African rivers; she drew little water, was calculated to stow a quantity of provisions, and to afford large accommodation to her establishment of officers, and men of science embarked on board of her. Captain Tuckey, having received his orders from the lords commissioners of the admiralty, sailed from

Deptford, on the 16th of February, 1816. On the 5th of July, we find him at the mouth of the river Congo, where from eighteen fathoms water he obtained no bottom at the next cast with one hundred and fifty fathom of line. He was then, as he says, in the deep water channel of that great river.

The difficulties of navigating this river were increased by the bad sailing of the Dorothy transport, on board of which Captain Tuckey had embarked: finding, when off Shark Point, that he was losing time in his endeavour to move her up against the stream, he hoisted out all the boats, and rigged his double canoes which had been prepared for him in England with platforms; in these he placed all the stores necessary for his immediate use, and, leaving the unwieldy vessel to follow when the wind permitted, he proceeded to join the Congo, which, under the command of Lieutenant Hawkey, had got ten miles a-head of them.

The result of this most unfortunate voyage threw very little light on the question for which it was undertaken, but ended in the death of Captain Tuckey, Lieutenant Hawkey, and almost every person engaged in it; such has, with very few exceptions, been the fate of every traveller who has ventured into that inhospitable quarter of the globe.

The voyages of Captains J. Ross and Edward W. Parry, to discover a north-west passage to China, have been so elaborately detailed to the public, that we need do little more than mention them. The desirable object of ascertaining whether an opening or channel exists between Asia and America, has occupied the attention of the learned and the enterprising for the last two hundred years. The solution of this question would, however, be more curious than useful, that, and the exploring of the interior of Africa, are almost the only objects left for geographical speculation: should the persevering efforts of Captain Parry succeed in finding a passage from the Atlantic to the Pacific ocean, through Behring's Straits, it is not likely the attempt will ever be repeated, particularly if the modern project of cutting through the isthmus of Panama should offer a passage to China in a milder parallel of latitude. Captain Ross, having reached far into Lancaster Sound, conceived that he saw the land joining to the westward, and forming a deep bay: the season being advanced, and hopeless of finding any outlet, he returned to England. Captain Parry, who accompanied Captain Ross, drew a different conclusion, and was in the following year appointed to the command of an expedition fitted for the purpose of pursuing the same track, and exploring the extremity of the Sound, through which he penetrated, making the discovery of the Prince Regent's inlet, and the North Georgian islands. This intrepid navigator, having reached the 114th degree of west longitude, passed ten long months in the harbour of Winter Island, where for eighty-four days he never saw the sun; he had now penetrated six hundred geographical miles further than any of his predecessors, and obtained the reward bestowed by Act of Parliament, of five thousand pounds, to be distributed as prize-money between the officers and men, for having passed the 110th degree of west longitude in that parallel of latitude.. Captain Parry is now absent on his third expedition to the Polar regions; whatever success he may meet with, his character as a navigator will stand unrivalled for science and perseverance.

ANECDOTES OF NAVAL OFFICERS,

OMITTED IN THE FOREGOING HISTORY.

In consequence of information that an enemy's privateer had made many captures up the Elbe, Lieutenant T. B. Devon, of the Brevdrageren, proceeded up that river on the night of the 28th of March, 1813, with his own gig, and the Blazer's six-oared cutter, in search of her. At daylight two galliots were discovered at anchor, and on the supposition that they were merchantmen, the gig advanced considerably a-head of the cutter to examine them ;. nor was it discovered until within hail, that they were two Danish gun-vessels. To retreat, or even wait for the support of the other boats, was alike impracticable; nor was there time for hesitation, as the enemy, on hailing, immediately commenced firing. The gig boarded the nearest (the Commodore) under the smoke of the second discharge, which most providentially passed over the boat, though close to the muzzles of the guns; at the same moment an explosion of some cartridges on the enemy's deck threw them into utter confusion;

and to these circumstances must be attributed the unexpected success of a small gig with eight men and a youth, the lieutenant's brother, carrying a formidable Danish gun-vessel, mounting two long eighteen pounders, and three twelve pound carronades, with a complement of twenty-six men, and commanded by a lieutenant, fully prepared, and in open daylight. The cutter soon arriving up, the prisoners were effectually secured under hatches; in the mean time the enemy's other gun-boat, panic-struck, had made sail for a fort, from which the distance was not more than four miles.

The guns of the captured vessel were re-loaded and put in fighting order, cable cut, and sail made in chase, and she was soon perceived to gain fast on the enemy; but being so very near his own port, from which the whole proceeding might be distinctly seen, no time was to be lost. Mr. Dunbar, the master of the Blazer, was dispatched in the cutter to intercept and board, if necessary: seeing her former consort ranging up, and ready to pour in a broadside, and retreat being effectually cut off, this vessel struck her colours without further resistance. They proved to be the national gun-vessels Du Jonge Troutman and Du Liebe, of equal force, commanded by Lieutenants Lutkin and De Witt, of the Danish navy.

Admiral Sir William Young, at that time commander-in-chief in the North Seas, addressed the following letter to Lieutenant Devon, on the occasion just related; and it, we think, does honour equally to the chief and the officer to whom it was addressed:—

Deal, April 4th, 1813.

SIR,

I have had the pleasure, this morning, of sending Lieutenant Bankes to convey to you and to those who were with you, the expression of the Admiralty's approbation of your conduct in the capture of the Danish gun-boats, which does indeed well deserve to be approved of. I am afraid that gun-boats make but bad prizes, but whatever they may produce, I have desired my agent to distribute my share of it among the crews of the two boats by which they were taken, and heartily wish it were much more than I fear it will be.

I am, Sir,
Your humble servant,
WILLIAM YOUNG.

To Lieutenant Thomas Barker Devon.

On the evening of the 31st of July, 1811, the Algerine cutter of ten guns and sixty men, Lieutenant Blow, and Brevdrageren gun-brig of twelve guns and forty-seven men, Lieutenant Devon, being in company, off Long Sound, on the coast of Norway, fell in with a Danish squadron, consisting of three brigs of the largest class, the Langland (or Lowland) of twenty guns and one hundred and seventy-five men, and Logan and Keil, of nearly the same force. Our two vessels were necessitated to approach the enemy to pick up their boats, which had been previously sent away to cut out some vessels in shore. Having, with difficulty, effected this object, a retreat was com-

menced, in which great exertions were necessary
by sweeping, &c. At daylight in the morning of
the 1st of August, the enemy's squadron were
somewhat scattered, the nearest of them being
four miles distant, and separated about half that
distance from her consorts. An attempt was made
to bring this vessel to action, which it soon appeared impossible to effect, as the Dane instantly
bore up to concentrate his force.

The retreat was again commenced, and the
pursuit renewed by the enemy with redoubled
exertions. At eleven A. M. the enemy's largest
brig, which appeared to be the Commodore, was
still about two miles in advance of the others,
when a simultaneous attack on this vessel was resolved on, in the hope of carrying her by boarding
before she could receive any effectual support.
This bold attempt was frustrated by the prompt
exertions of the enemy's second astern, and the
Algerine hauling out of action, which she did with
ease, being well manned and swift on her sweeps.
The Brevdrageren was at this time in close action
with the largest brig, and the second astern had
already commenced with his foremost guns on the
starboard quarter. This hopeless contest was continued some time, but it was apparent that the
Brevdrageren, however gallantly defended, must
have soon fallen a sacrifice to such an overwhelming superiority of force, when, at one P. M. a cats-
paw (light air) sprang up on the starboard quarter:
prompt advantage was taken of this favourable cir-

cumstance, the firing was ordered to cease, the sails instantly trimmed, and with every hand at the sweeps, a considerable distance was obtained from the enemy. This was facilitated by their having previously clewed up all their sails, and being too intent on firing, which he continued by sweeping the bow round, and keeping the broadside to bear. Indeed the enemy seemed scarcely to have been aware of this sudden manœuvre, and when at length he sheeted home and trimmed sails, the breeze entirely failed; the Brevdrageren had however attained a distance of long shot. The exertions on both sides continued until sun-set, the enemy keeping up a teazing fire, but unable to bring the Brevdrageren to action: at nine P. M. the chase was given up, the enemy being as completely exhausted as the small crew of the Brevdrageren; both sides had stood upwards of thirty hours at the sweeps, with the additional fatigue of more than an hour's close action: by daylight of the 2d, the enemy were distant about five or six miles, and did not resume the chase.

In this action, the Brevdrageren had fortunately only one killed and three wounded, but sustained much damage in the hull, sails, masts, and rigging, with several shots between wind and water; but, the weather being fine, she reached Heligoland in safety, and was from thence sent to Sheerness to be docked and repaired.—The Algerine had one man killed. A very serious investigation would have taken place on the conduct of the Lieutenant of the Algerine, but before any complaint could reach the Admiralty he was dismissed from the command of his vessel, for another breach of discipline.

Captain Edward Wallis Hoare, of the Minden, of seventy-four guns, had landed a small body of seamen and marines at Point St. Nicholas, in the island of Java, for the purpose of procuring supplies for the squadron in 1811. This party was attack- by a very superior force of the enemy, who approached within a few yards of them. After contending for a quarter of an hour the enemy fled. During the action, Captain Hoare joined his men with a reinforcement, making about two hundred in all. A second time assailed, the English reserved their fire until the enemy came within fifteen paces, when a very spirited contest was quickly decided; the French running in every direction, and leaving forty-four of their men killed, among whom were many officers, and taking away with them a great number wounded. Our loss was ten men killed and twenty-three wounded. The force of the enemy consisted of more than five hundred European and native troops.

Lieutenant (now Captain) Edmund Lyons, of the Minden, with the launch and cutter of that ship, carrying no more than thirty-four seamen and marines, stormed the Dutch fort of Marrack, on the coast of Java, mounting fifty-four guns, and having a garrison of one hundred and eighty soldiers. This desperate service was undertaken contrary to the orders of Captain Hoare, who was obliged to call on Lieutenant Lyons to account for his conduct. We find a disciplined body of men, prepared with walls, cannon, and every species of offensive weapon, defeated and dispossessed of a strong fort by one sixth part of the number. Mr. Lyons, in his modest defence, says, "Being convinced the enemy did not expect an attack, and that they had no suspicion of a British army being in Java, we thought the surprise of Marrack might draw their forces towards that quarter, and operate as a favourable diversion for our troops." Having made his arrangements during the day, he placed his boats at sunset behind a point which concealed them from the enemy's sentinels: at half-past twelve at night, he rowed in to the attack, and was received with a volley of musketry. Seeing there was no hope of surprising them, he boldly ran his two boats on the beach in a heavy surf, under the embrasures of the lower tier of guns, placed his scaling ladders, mounted the walls, killed three men in the very act of applying matches to their guns, and in an instant was master of the lower battery. Without giving the enemy time to recover, he re-formed his men, placed the ladders again to the upper fort, reached the summit, and found the Dutch drawn up to receive him. They stood the first volley from the English, but on Lyons calling out that he had four hundred men with him and would give no quarter, the enemy fled: at one o'clock, a third battery and two gun-boats opened their fire on this adventurous officer and his little party; but they returned it with some of the guns they had just taken, while his men were busily employed in spiking and disabling the others. By dawn of day, having nearly completed the destruction of the whole, he retreated to his boats, and found his launch had beat so high up on the beach with the force of the surf as to leave no hope of getting her afloat; he was therefore compelled to embark all his party in a six-oared cutter. At sun-rise, the enemy, from their walls, beheld the small force, by which, during the night, they had been invaded, and disgracefully beaten, return to their ship.

Captain Harris, in the Sir Francis Drake, off Rembang, in the month of May, 1811, fell in with nine sail of felucca rigged gun-boats and five proas, armed in the same manner: five of these vessels he captured by his own guns. Shoal water prevented his ship approaching the others, but dispatching his boats, under the command of Lieutenant Bradley, the whole were taken before eight o'clock in the morning, without the loss of an Englishman. Numbers of the enemy jumped overboard and were drowned; others were killed in boarding; many were upset in their small boats, with which they attempted to gain the shore; nor could the British officers and men, with every endeavour, succeed in saving many of these victims to their own base fears. These boats were all quite new: they were eighty feet long, seventeen wide, pulled sixty oars, and were fitted to carry an eight inch howitzer abaft, and twenty-four pound carronade forward; only one of them had her guns in, the others were either thrown overboard in the chase, or had not been put on board. Captain Harris was under the necessity of burning the whole of them except one, which he reserved for a dispatch boat: it is remarkable, that these vessels were all under French colours, commanded by French officers, and crews partly of that nation, and partly natives; the numbers on board of each were generally from twenty to thirty men, not having their full complements.

Captain Robert Maunsell, in the Procris sloop of war, in the same month, defeated a similar force at the mouth of Indromay river, where six gunboats, having under their convoy forty or fifty sail of proas, had come to an anchor. The sloop not having water enough to approach them, Captain Maunsell took his boat and two flat-boats, with an officer and a party of twenty-two men each, from the 14th and 89th regiments. Five of the gunboats he boarded and carried; the sixth blew up before the assailants reached her. The crews, after throwing their spears into the boats of the Procris, jumped overboard and swam away; the convoy escaped up the river. These boats carried one brass thirty-two pound carronade forward, and one eighteen pounder aft. Their complement of men, sixty each. The British had eleven men wounded; the loss of the enemy was never known.

Macassar, the capital of the island of Celebes, was occupied by a detachment of troops from Madras, under the command of Captain Phillips, and conducted over by Captain Crawford, in the Hussar frigate. Captain Crawford also concluded a treaty of peace with the rajah of Bonni, the most powerful prince on the island of Celebes. Captain Thurston, of the Hesper sloop of war, announced the surrender of Coupang, in the island of Timor.

SIR WILLIAM HOSTE'S ACTION OFF LISSA.

As soon as the action was concluded, and the ships and prizes rendered in some measure sea-worthy, Captain Hoste proceeded to Lissa, with his squadron, whence he addressed a letter to the captain of the Flora, lying at Lessina, and peremptorily demanded the surrender of his ship, as having struck to the Amphion, to prevent being sunk: an answer was returned by the Captain of the Danae, but neither signed, dated, nor even addressed, in official form. This document stated, that the Captain of the Flora having been wounded, he (the Captain of the Danae) had taken upon himself, as the senior officer, to answer the letter; he affirmed that "the colours of the Flora were not struck, but shot away." This impertinent letter was returned to the writer for date and signature, and Captain Hoste observed, that he should not ask *him* whether the Flora had struck, but would appeal to the captain of that ship, and if he was too ill to answer, to the succeeding officer: " but," continued the British captain, "I again assert, and ever shall maintain, that, by the laws of war, his ship belongs to my sovereign, and his sword to me." This reasoning had no effect on the French officer, who being secure in his port declined coming out. The facts are correctly stated by Sir William Hoste, and the claim was properly made, but it was not to be supposed that the ship would be given up, we have no instance of the kind, though many of their having been claimed.

Of the crew of the Favourite, two hundred only remained alive unhurt, after the destruction of their ship. These took refuge at Lissa, where they were summoned to surrender by Messrs. Lew and Kingston, two midshipmen of the Active (who had been left there in charge of prizes), with several men belonging to privateers. The French officer acceded to the terms, and the whole of them laid down their arms and became prisoners of war. The spirited conduct of these young men is admirably contrasted with the dastardly behaviour of a Sicilian privateer, a brig of fourteen guns, called La Victoire: her captain (Clemento Farma) while lying in the port of Lissa, and previously to the action of the frigates, struck his colours to a small one-gun Venetian schooner. This was witnessed by every officer and man in the British squadron. The noble youths, Lew and Kingston, instantly boarded her, hoisted the colours, beat off the schooner, and prevented her destroying the vessels in the bay. Another act of heroism was

performed by the Lieutenants Dickenson of the
Cerberus, and Hay of the Active. These officers,
soon after boarding the Corona, found her on fire
in the maintop, and the whole of the rigging and
sails on that mast being instantly in a flame, and
in the disabled state of the squadron, without the
possibility of any assistance being afforded to
them, Captain Hoste considered the ship as lost;
but, left to their own resources, these young officers cut away the mast, extinguished the flames,
and saved the ship and the lives of those on board,
particularly of the unfortunate wounded men.

In the gulf of Florida, Captain Hugh Pigot,
took the American sloop of war Frolic, of twenty-
two guns (twenty thirty-two pound carronades
and two long eighteen pounders) with one hundred
and seventy-one men. This vessel struck to the
Orpheus, of thirty-two guns, without a shadow of
resistance. She was upwards of five hundred tons
burthen, and the Americans might please themselves by calling her a sloop of war. She was in
effective force superior to our twenty-eight gun
frigates. So great was the panic, under which the
officers and crew appeared to labour, that they
threw all the lee guns overboard, and continued
throwing over their shot and small arms until the
boats of the Orpheus got on board.

In the month of October, 1814, Captain the Hon.
Henry Duncan, in the Imperieuse, of forty-four
guns, attacked three French gun-boats, each car-

rying an eighteen pounder, and moored under a strong fort, near the town of Positana, in the gulf of Salerno. One of the gun-boats was immediately sunk by the fire of the frigate, which had silenced the fort, but the enemy not being driven out, Captain Duncan ordered Mr. Eaton Trevers, his first Lieutenant, and Lieutenant Pipon of the Royal Marines, to land and storm it, which they did under a heavy fire of musketry, and against treble their numbers. The enemy fled, leaving thirty prisoners and fifty stand of arms: the guns, which were twenty-four pounders, were spiked by our men and thrown over the cliff.

BATTLE OF BAROSSA.

In this brilliant affair, the enemy had eight thousand men engaged, of whom they lost three thousand in killed, wounded, and prisoners. General Ruffin was taken and sent to England. Our loss amounted to twelve hundred in killed and wounded. The Spanish general and his army had no share in the action. The service of the navy, on this occasion, would have been far more useful, had the Rear-admiral been apprised, as he ought to have been, in due time, of the approach of Sir Thomas Graham, from Algeziras, towards the French lines, but the officer charged with the despatches thought proper to give chase to a suspicious vessel, and by so doing nearly blasted the efforts of the combined movement.

This is a case so nearly parallel to that of Lord

William Fitz Roy, who, under circumstances nearly similar, has been censured for not having pursued an enemy's frigate; that we cannot refrain from referring to it, in order to point out the pernicious consequences which might arise from officers preferring their own before their country's honour. The defeat of the enemy would have been much more decisive, had the dispatches been delivered as they should have been.

It was not till 11 o'clock on the 5th of March, that Sir Richard Keats received intelligence, by telegraph, of the approach of Sir Thomas Graham, with the army from the southward; he immediately made the signal for the Implacable and Standard to weigh, and the flotilla to move up. At this moment, the dastardly pilots declined taking charge of the ships, and while the squadron was preparing for action, the battle of Barossa was decided.

LOSS OF THE ST. GEORGE AND DEFENCE.

From both these ships, about eighteen men only were saved: they reached the shore in the last stage of human suffering: the fate of the Defence was exactly similar to that of the St. George : the body of the gallant and self-devoted Captain Atkins, was picked up by the Danes, ere life was perfectly extinct; but all the kindness of the hospitable people failed in restoring animation, and he was buried with military honours, by order of the Danish government. While we applaud the heroic determination of Captain Atkins to save his admiral, or perish in the attempt, what shall we say for the memory of Captain Pater, who chose what he considered a line of duty equally imperative? Is an officer, seeing a ship inevitably lost, to run his own along-side of her, without the most distant prospect of saving one person on board? On this question, we decline offering an opinion; but leave it to the judgment of those who may unfortunately be so situated: certain it is that no blame was attached to Captain Pater; his view of the case was, " that if by staying near his admiral he could have afforded him any relief, he never would have quitted him ;" conceiving that to be impossible, he supposed his next duty was to preserve his own ship, and the gallant crew, The loss of these ships was the subject of conversation in the house of commons : in consequence of a question from Mr. Whitbread, Mr. Yorke, the first lord of the admiralty, gave a short account of the facts, and evinced so much feeling on the occasion, that it drew forth a very elegant compliment from Mr. Whitbread, who ob-served, that the whole calamity was the effect of misfortune alone; and that it was a consolation to reflect, that no blame could be imputed to any one.

We calculate the number of lives lost in all these wrecks, including the Saldanha, at about two thousand, exclusive of the seamen drowned in the numerous merchantmen which foundered in the same winter, and which, taken altogether, will amount to five thousand men, and very far exceeds the number of slain in all the general actions since the commencement of the war.

SPAIN.

How invariably does the injustice of men recoil upon their own heads. What exertions did not Spain make? what men, and what treasure did she not expend in the cause of North America? When those colonies threw off the easy yoke of England, little did the short-sighted rulers of Spain imagine they were fostering a nation, whose example would soon be followed by the neighbouring countries from which she derived her wealth.

The junta of Seville, which exercised the provisional government in the name of their absent king, offered that freedom to the South Americans, which they no longer had it in their power to withhold. From the first landing of Sir Home Popham on the banks of the Rio de La Plata, the inhabitants of the great southern continent had gazed on the dawning of liberty, until dazzled by its full effulgence in 1811; but this light, without instruction, without the gradual experience and improvement of the human mind, only served to make "darkness visible." Liberty awoke from the slumber of ages; but so loaded with the fetters of bigotry and despotism, that her first acts were those of a maniac: like the revolutionists in France, the South Americans laid their country in blood, and with returning reason regretted the havoc they had made.

Had the British government acted by the common and narrow law of retaliation, she would have fomented the dissensions between Spain and her colonies, and even among the colonists themselves, as the means of advancing her own interests; but the policy of Great Britain was more enlightened, she sought her interest in the straight forward road of honesty, and the happiness of the human race: had gold or conquest been her object, she might have bribed avarice and ambition, till (if it were possible) the wide range of those passions were gratified.

His majesty, King George IV. then Prince Regent, having made a treaty of alliance, offensive and defensive with Spain, could no longer act but as her real friend : such were not only the sentiments of the royal bosom, but also those of the nation at large.

Sir Henry Wellesley, the British ambassador, at Cadiz, and Rear-admiral Sir Richard Keats, perfectly acquainted with the benefit which England and Spain might derive from mutual assistance, and foreseeing that the loss of the Spanish colonies might deprive the parent state of her only resources for carrying on the war, proposed, to the executive government at Cadiz, to send a proper person to England, with instructions for explaining their views to the minister. Captain Cockburn was selected for this service, having been at Vera Cruz, and become acquainted with the wishes of the colonists ; he had also acquired the favour of the Spaniards, by the attempt he had made to rescue their king from the prison of Valançay : resigning the command of the Implacable, he proceeded to England in the Druid frigate, arrived on the 5th of May, 1811, and communicated his instructions to his majesty's ministers, who determined to send out an embassy of mediation, in the name of the Prince Regent, between Spain and the revolted colonies of South America. Captain Cockburn was chosen as one of the commissioners; and ordered, in the month of November, to hoist a broad pendant on board the Grampus, of fifty guns, with the rank of Commodore: his colleagues were, Thomas Sydenham, Esq. and J. P. Morier, Esq.: these gentlemen were nominated his majesty's commissioners of mediation, with the diplomatic rank of envoys extraordinary, and ministers plenipotentiary.

It was not till the 2d of April, 1812, that the commissioners received their final instructions, on the receipt of which, they sailed in the Grampus from Spithead, and arrived at Cadiz on the 21st. But here their difficulties began; and by the narrow-minded prejudices and sordid views of the Spanish executive government, and the majority of the Cortez then assembled at Cadiz, their labours were rendered abortive.

These ignorant and selfish people, instead of openly acknowledging and confirming the independence of the colonists, as their predecessors had done, insisted on confining the mediation to particular parts of Spanish America: this was so contrary to the views of the commissioners, that reference was had to England; and, after repeated delays, the commissioners finding they could make

no impression on the junta, and being resolved not
to proceed to America with limited powers, put
an end to the conferences as they were authorised
to do, and returned home.   Such was the state of
things between Old and New Spain, in 1811-12;
when the Honourable Vice-admiral, Michael De
Courcy, held the command on the South American
station, with a small squadron, for the protection
of the British trade.   The harbour of Rio Janeiro
was his head-quarters; and we had our envoy
with the Portuguese government: their provinces
continuing in a tranquil state, while those of Spain,
in the south, west, and north, were in the highest
ferment of civil discord.

In the month of June, 1811, the states of Venezuela declared their independence.

In the West Indies, we have nothing of a maritime nature to commemorate in 1812.   At
Jamaica, the Commander-in-chief, Vice-admiral
Bartholomew Samuel Rowley, died of the yellow
fever: he was a zealous and gallant officer, highly
respected in his profession.

The instructions given to Rear-admiral, Sir Samuel Hood, on his sailing for India, are deserving
of our attention, as they lead to the true interests
of our eastern empire, always keeping in view the
best means for preserving our maritime superiority.

The Rear-admiral, in addition to the private
communication from the first lord of the admiralty, the Right Honourable Charles Yorke, was
officially directed by the Board, to pay particular

attention to the settlements of the Dutch, in the eastern seas; and, in case of their falling into our hands, to use every endeavour to conciliate the esteem and good-will both of the settlers and the natives.

The Captains of His Majesty's ships were to be very particular in their inquiries, as to what supplies those islands might be able to afford to the squadron, and also what articles of commerce are raised in the islands, and what the natives would require in exchange for them.

To the Philippine islands, he was to look with great circumspection, as the port wherein the greatest annoyance might arise to our China trade, by affording shelter to the enemy: a line of conduct is here marked out, fraught with prudence, justice, and moderation; how infinitely have we improved in this line of political economy since the year 1782.

The Admiral was to keep a frigate and sloop in the Persian Gulf, to watch the movements of the enemy; and occasionally to open a communication with the Red Sea.

Provisions were to be procured in India, in preference to their importation from England or Ireland: viz. beef, pork, biscuit, rice, calevances, tea, sugar, cocoa, and spirits; and great attention was to be paid to contracts, in order to see justice done to the public.

Hospitals were to be inspected with care, and the utmost attention paid to the patients.

Naval stores were to be procured in India; such as cordage, canvass, and spars, all of which are abundantly produced in the peninsula of India, and the island of Ceylon. The great advantages of this discovery are, the vast saving to the mother-country, and insurance of good articles; our cordage and canvass generally being found decayed from the length of the voyage.

India abounds with a variety of vegetable productions, yielding fibres that are suitable for the manufacture of cordage: the strongest, and, for some purposes, the best, is that which is obtained from the cocoa-nut, and known usually by the name of Coir: next to this is the rope manufactured from the fibres of the aloe, which has been found superior to the best English wheel-ropes made in our dock-yards; but no certain dependance can be placed on any considerable supply of either of these articles; that which is most in use throughout India, is the produce of a plant called Sunne, the quality of which differs materially, according to the soil and situation in which it grows, and perhaps also, according to the process of steeping and preparing the fibre. From experiments made in Chatham dock-yard, the hemp of Bengal, was found to be of so inferior a quality, as to be wholly unfit for naval purposes, while the fibres of the same plant, produced on the western side of the peninsula, where it is usually known by the name of Concan or Salcotte-hemp, has been found much superior to the best Riga hemp. The real hemp is also a native plant of India : the fibres of all these articles, and of some others, are manufactured by the natives, into cordage, with considerable skill. English rope-makers were, in consequence of this discovery, sent out to Bombay and Madras; and the resident commissioners had orders to confine their purchases to clean Salcette, or Concan hemp; by which means it was hoped, that for small cordage, at least, the squadron in India, might be entirely independent of England; and, finally, for cables, shrouds, and halsers. The introduction of iron cables in the navy, has added still more to the resources of our Indian squadron.

Bengal canvass was found, on experiment, equal to English; and our ships were supplied with it on equitable terms, by contract. Timber in India, for the purposes of ship-building, had been discovered some years before to possess superior qualities ; and as far back as 1802, we find the Admiralty employed in the consideration of constructing ships of the line at Bombay, and sending home in them the component parts of a ship of equal size. The Admiralty, in 1811, directed the Commander-in-chief to make inquiry into the quantity of wood, either for masts, yards, or building, particularly of teak, and other forest trees, growing on the Malabar coast, which are found to be superior to those of Pegu, and the countries on the eastern side of India.

The country of Travancore, is represented as abounding with poon timber, applicable to the purposes of masts and yards, for ships of the largest dimension : and Sir Edward Pellew, stated to the Admiralty, that while he held that command, he purchased, through the assistance of Mr. Baber, the Collector of Malabar, fifty-two of the largest spars, for the sum of six thousand rupees, which sum he had been compelled to pay for two only, on former occasions. The island of Ceylon is also reported to abound with good timber: and inquiry was directed to be made in the neighbourhood of Point de Galle and Trincomalee.

The Admiralty directed the attention of the Commander-in-chief to the regular relief of the ships and crews that had been the longest in the country; by which salutary precaution an act of justice was done to that class of men, on whom our existence, as an empire, chiefly depends. There is an instance of a ship's company who, after eleven years' servitude in India, were sent home, and immediately drafted into another ship and sent out again, without having their foot on shore in their native land: this was a cruel case, and one which did infinite injury to the naval service : it happened in the administration of Lord Barham.

The Admiral was next directed to inspect all the naval ports of India, and to make himself well acquainted with their local advantages and defects. The principal stations of this description are Calcutta, Prince of Wales's Island or Pulo Penang, Bombay, Madras, and Trincomalee.

Calcutta, in consequence of the shifting of the sands in the Ganges, the rapidity of the tides, the hazard of approaching the sand heads during the S.W. monsoon, and the extreme unhealthiness of the shores of the river, was never to be resorted to but in cases of absolute necessity.

The docks at Bombay will receive our largest ships employed on that station, where it is to be observed that 1st and 2d rates are never sent. Prince of Wales's Island, as a naval port, is only of value to the China trade; it has an excellent harbour, and is a beautiful and flourishing colony. Trincomalee is our best naval port on the east side of the peninsula of India; it is a noble harbour, and the only good one in the island of Ceylon, or on the east side of the bay of Bengal; but unfortunately it is liable to dreadful diseases in the months of July, August, and September: these were unknown in former years. Madras is an open roadsted, with a perpetual surf beating on the shore and rendering the communication at all times difficult, frequently dangerous, and sometimes impossible. Bombay on the west side of the peninsula is a fine harbour, having a great rise of tide, by which the docks are rendered particularly efficacious. The Minden, of seventy-four guns, was built here, and in 1810 the Admiralty directed that the Cornwallis, of seventy-four guns, should be laid down on the same slip, and be built after the model of the Ajax; and at the same time timber for the construction of another seventy-four was directed to be converted, put on board the Cornwallis, and sent home in her.

The naval establishment of Madras was directed by Mr. Yorke to be removed to Trincomalee, where docks were intended to be constructed, and the Commander-in-chief ordered to report on the expediency thereof.

Such were the instructions given to our admirals in India. Let us hope they will never be lost sight of.

LIMITS OF NAVAL STATIONS.

Much litigation and disagreement between the flag-officers of his majesty's fleet having arisen during the late and former wars, in consequence of the limits of the different stations not having been properly defined, the present Board of Admiralty have, by a recent regulation, so marked the limits of each command, that future dispute is almost placed beyond the reach of possibility. The following will be found a correct copy of their lordships' orders on this subject :

Chatham, &c.

Chatham, Sheerness, and the Buoy of the Nore ; in the river Medway, and northward, as far as the sixty-fourth degree of north latitude; westward, as far as the fourth degree of west longitude; southward to Dungeness, on the coast of England ; and eastward, to within a league of the opposite continent, from the before-mentioned degree of north latitude, to Cape D'Alprée, to the westward of Boulogne.

Portsmouth.

Spithead and Portsmouth harbour; and on a station bounded on the east by a line drawn from Dungeness to Cape D'Alprée, to the westward of Boulogne, and on the west, by the Start Point.

Plymouth.

Bounded on the east by the meridian of the Start; on the south, by the forty-eighth degree of north latitude; and on the west, by the tenth degree of west longitude, between that latitude and the latitude of the Land's End; and northward, from thence, by a line drawn from the point where the eighth degree of west longitude intersects the latitude of the Land's End; midway through St. George's Channel, including the Isle of Man, and four leagues on the western side of that island, as far north as the mid-channel of the Solway Frith.

Cork, &c.

Bounded on the north, by the sixty-fourth degree of north latitude, and the fourth degree of west longitude; on the west, by the fifteenth degree of west longitude; on the south, by the latitude of the Land's End; and on the east, by a line drawn from the point at which that latitude is intersected by the eighth degree of west longitude; midway through St. George's Channel, and the north channel, but not including the Isle of Man, and four leagues from the western coast thereof, until the said line shall intersect the latitude of sixty-four.

Mediterranean.

In the Mediterranean, and without the Straits of Gibraltar, as far westward as the meridian of Cape St. Vincent.

North America.

Bounded on the north, by the fifty-fifth degree of north latitude; on the east, by the fortieth degree of west longitude; on the west, by the coast of America, including the river St. Lawrence, to Quebec; and on the south, by the thirtieth degree of north longitude.

West Indies.

Within a line drawn from the eastern coast of North America, at the thirtieth degree of north latitude, along that parallel to the seventy-fourth degree of west longitude; thence, diagonally, to the intersection of the seventy-second degree of west longitude, with the tropic of Cancer; then along the tropic, to the fiftieth degree of west longitude, and along that degree of longitude, till it meets the continent of South America; and bounded by the continent of America, on the west and south.

South America.

On the eastern coast of South America, and on the Pacific Ocean; on the eastern side of the said continent, from the equator to the antarctic circle, and as far east, as the fiftieth degree of west longitude; and on the western side, from the antarctic circle, along the whole extent of the western coast of America; and as far west as the hundred-and-seventieth degree of west longitude.

Africa.

To the southward of the latitude of Madeira, and to the eastward of the meridian of St. Anthony, one of the Cape de Verd Islands; and as far to the southward as the Commodore's orders may render it necessary for him to proceed.

Cape of Good Hope

And the seas adjacent, as far to the northward as the equinoctial line, and as far westward as the fifteenth degree of west longitude; southward, to the antarctic circle; and eastward, to the sixtieth degree of east longitude.

East Indies.

On the west, to the northward of the equator, by the coasts of Africa and Asia; and the southward of the equator, by the sixtieth degree of east longitude.

On the south, by the equator, from the coast of Africa to the sixtieth degree of east longitude; and by the antarctic circle, from the sixtieth degree of east longitude, to the hundred-and-seventieth degree of west longitude.

On the east, by the hundred-and-seventieth degree of west longitude.

On the north, by the coast of Asia.

STEAM-VESSELS.

At present there are but three steam-vessels employed by the government for the naval service, and these for the purpose of towing ships out of harbours or rivers. The Comet, of two hundred and thirty-eight tons' measurement, and having two engines of forty horses' power each, is stationed at Deptford, and employed chiefly in towing ships

out of the rivers Thames and Medway. The station
of the Meteor is at Plymouth, she measures two
hundred and ninety-six tons, and has two engines
of fifty horses' power each. The engines for the
two aforementioned vessels were made by Messrs.
Bolton and Watt. The Lightning, similar in construction and size to the Meteor, is stationed at
Portsmouth, she has also two engines, each of
fifty horses' power, which were constructed by
Mr. Maudsley. This vessel has been lately employed before Algiers, for the purpose of towing
the bombs and mortar-vessels into their stations.

In still water, the rate at which the Comet
moves may be reckoned at eight knots, or nautical
miles an hour, the rate of the Meteor and Lightning
at nine. When the Comet is towing large frigates,
and the Lightning and Meteor ships of the line,
their average rate, in still water, may be estimated
at five miles an hour.

The advantages which have arisen from steam-
vessels employed in internal commerce both in
this country and in America, by the expeditious
and certain conveyance of passengers and light
goods, are too well known and appreciated to be
insisted on in this place; but, from the few years
which have elapsed since these engines have been
used for propelling vessels, it may be fairly concluded, that steam navigation is still in its infancy.

In turning our view to the probable consequences which may arise from the application of
such vessels to the purposes of war, we can reason

only from what is now in use, without adverting to any supposable advantages which may be hereafter derived from improvements in the adaptation of these engines to ships—in a greater force being obtained with less consumption of fuel—by alterations in the propelling apparatus—or in the application of the motive power.

The capability of steam engine vessels to act in a troubled sea, is no longer to be questioned, as the constant voyages which are made in them between this country and ports on the continent of Europe, as well as from England to Ireland, in all weathers and at all seasons of the year, without any serious accident having happened, have put this point beyond a doubt. The great space which the machinery occupies, and the large consumption of coals, prevent vessels of this description from being employed on long voyages. It is true that the Savannah, an American ship, crossed the Atlantic, but on her arrival at Liverpool it was ascertained that the steam-engines with which she was fitted had been used for fifty-four hours only, on account of the want of fuel.

These vessels appear but little adapted for attack in war, from the exposed situation of their paddle wheels, of the machinery which puts them in action, and of the boilers, as one shot well directed would derange or destroy the whole of the power. But it appears probable that they may be used with great effect in towing a ship of war in or out of action, as the vessel towing may be protected or placed out of danger by the ship towed; or these vessels may be used against fleets of merchants' ships that may be becalmed.

The attention of the naval powers on the continent of Europe is directed to the consideration of this novel but powerful method of propelling ships. Not only have their best engineers visited this country for the purpose of ascertaining the progress made in steam navigation, but the French government sent M. Marestier to America to ascertain what had been done there, and his able report recently made to the institute, fully justifies the propriety of the selection.

With better machinery than is made in any other country, and with coals far better adapted to the purpose of steam engines, it appears probable that we shall not be rivalled in our exertions in this species of navigation. Let us not, however, slumber in security, but be constantly alive to improve this science, which may at no distant period change the face of naval warfare.

The introduction of steam-vessels for the purpose of taking ships in and out of harbour is traced as far back as the year 1734, when Jonathan Hulls invented a vessel of this description, having one fly-wheel over the stern instead of one on each side as now used.—See a reprint of this invention in the Mechanics' Magazine. We sincerely wish the editor of this work would confine himself to "mechanism" only; he would then have the hearty support of a respectable body of the community.

Copy of the commission given to the Earl of St. Vincent, appointing him an Admiral of the Fleet.

By the Commissioners for executing the office of Lord High Admiral of the United Kingdom of Great Britain and Ireland, and all his Majesty's Plantations.

To the Right. Hon. John, Earl of St. Vincent, G.C.B. Admiral of the Red.

By virtue of the power and authority to us given, we do hereby constitute you an Admiral of the fleet, hereby willing and requiring you to take upon you the charge and command of his Majesty's said fleet as Admiral and Commander-in-chief accordingly, and authorising and requiring you, whenever you shall receive our order to hoist your flag, to wear the Union at the main-topmast-head on board such ship of his Majesty's said fleet where you shall happen at any time to be, hereby willing and requiring all " *captains,*" *commanders,* and *other officers* and companies of the said fleet, to obey you as their Admiral and Commander-in-chief, and you likewise to observe and execute, all such orders and instructions as you shall, from time to time, receive from us, the Lord High Admiral of the United Kingdom of Great Britain and Ireland, or the Commissioners for executing the office of Lord High Admiral of Great Britain and Ireland, &c. for the time being. And we do hereby authorise you, whenever you shall receive our order to hoist your flag as aforesaid, in case of any neglect, disability, or other default, or defect, of any of the said officers, or seamen, to displace them and appoint and constitute others in their stead, until our pleasure shall be made known, and for so doing this shall be your warrant.

Given under our hands and the seal of the office of Admiralty, this 19th day of July, 1821, in the second year of His Majesty's reign.

MELVILLE.
G. COCKBURN.
H. HOTHAM.

By command of their Lordships,

J. W. CROKER.

In consequence of this commission, there were then two admirals of the fleet; His Royal Highness the Duke of Clarence being the senior.

Admiralty Office, 19th August, 1815.

The following are to be observed as the Regulations for Midshipmen on the Peace Establishment :—

1. The captains of the respective ships will enter the usual number of "Mates," "Midshipmen," and "First Class Boys" of their own selection, whenever there may be vacancies in the *complement*, observing, however, that no person is to be rated as Mate of a line-of-battle ship, or 5th rate, who shall not have passed the usual examination for Lieutenant, and that previously to the first entry into the service of any young gentleman, the approbation of the Lords Commissioners of the Admiralty shall be obtained on a statement by the captain of his age, family, and education.

2. A certain number of supernumerary Mates and Midshipmen will be appointed by their Lordships, and are to be borne by their order only.

3. No Captain shall discharge or disrate any Mate or Midshipman, or First Class Boy, without an order from their Lordships, on a home station; or, if the ship be on a foreign station, without the order of the Commander-in-chief, who is to report the case and the cause of the discharge or disrating, for their Lordships' information.

4. The Captains are to report the names of all Mates, Midshipmen, and Boys of the first class, as they join the ship, and are carefully to report all deaths, invalidings, discharges, or other changes.

5. The Captains are to be very particular in attending to the instructions relative to the ratings of the several classes, and to take care that on no account whatsoever are any young gentlemen kept on board the ships under any other ratings than " mate," " midshipman," or " first class boy."

By command of their Lordships,
J. W. CROKER.

Copy of Treasury Minute of the 9th of April, 1813.

READ letter from the Secretary to the Admiralty of the 9th ult. transmitting and recommending memorials from Admiral Sir J. DUCKWORTH and Vice Admiral SAWYER, praying the full benefit of American ships captured by him; together with an opinion of the King's Advocate upon his claim. Read a further letter from the Secretary to the Admiralty of the 27th ult. referring to the above, and to a prior letter from the Admiralty of the 3d of March, and calling the early and favourable attention of this Board to this subject. Read, also, a letter from Admiral SAWYER of the 26th ult. requesting the serious attention of government to his memorial, and stating that ill consequences may be expected to arise from any further delay in the distribution of the American prizes.

Read, also, a letter from the Secretary of the Admiralty of the 7th instant, referring again to his former letters, and transmitting a copy of a memorial from Admiral Sir JOHN BORLASE WARREN, praying a grant of the proceeds of captures made in the West Indies, prior to the 13th of October last, which have been condemned as droits to the crown.

My Lords having taken into their consideration the peculiar circumstances attending the commencement of hostilities with America, and the very meritorious conduct of the captors on the American stations, and particularly the considerable sacrifices which they made of their own immediate interests for the public service, by destroying a number of vessels which they might have sent into port, in order to avoid the necessity of weakening their own crews, and thereby disabling themselves from acting so efficiently against the enemy, are of opinion that those special grounds will warrant them in recommending to his Royal Highness the PRINCE REGENT, in addition to the proportion usually granted to captors of droits to the crown, to make a further grant to the captors of vessels on American stations, as a compensation to them for the loss which they will sustain in consequence of the vessels so destroyed as aforesaid, of nine-tenths of the reserved proceeds of all vessels and cargoes taken by them at sea, and condemned as droits of the crown in the Vice Admiralty Courts of *Newfoundland, Halifax,* and *Bermuda.*

Transmit copy of the minute to Mr. CROKER, for the information of the Lords of the Admiralty.

. The following answer to an application for head-money is given without any comment.

Treasury Chambers, Feb. 20, 1815.

SIR,

HAVING laid before the Lords Commissioners of his Majesty's Treasury, your memorial of the 13th ult. requesting to be paid head-money on four American privateers destroyed by the *Spartan* and *Maidstone*, I am commanded by their lordships to acquaint you that as it appears that the captures in question were made previous to the date of the order in council authorising reprisals against America, they cannot comply with your request.

I am, Sir,
Your obedient servant,
R. LUSHINGTON.

Capt. Brenton, No. 4, *Park-lane.*

In 1822, Russia, by an imperial ukase, claimed the exclusive right of navigating the Pacific Ocean to the northward of the 51° of north latitude from America to Asia. The subject was mentioned in the house of commons on the 5th of July, by Sir James Macintosh, who asked the Marquis of Londonderry whether this claim was acceded to by Great Britain, to which the minister replied that it was *not*, and that a protest had been sent to the Russian Ambassador, and an amicable explanation entered into; in the meantime the rights of British subjects to navigate those seas were to remain undisturbed.

In the Naval Chronicle of 1811, vol. 2. p. 234, is a letter from Mr. Fulton to Count Marbois, proposing to destroy the whole British fleet by means of torpedoes. This man first proposed his plans to Mr. Pitt and Lord Keith; they were tried at Boulogne and failed. He next invented the famous stone-ships, which he was to have conducted himself to the harbour of Boulogne, but by some means never could find a favourable opportunity of doing so: he was, however, well paid for what he performed. After this he was no more seen in England; and we hear of him in America, receiving money from that government, for perfecting his inventions there, while at the same time he is in correspondence in 1809 with the Count de Marbois, to impart his secret to Napoleon, to rid his imperial majesty at once of all his enemies, to smooth the way to universal empire, and the conquest of England. On completing this last, though not least object, the modest projector only demands two millions sterling, to be paid to himself, his heirs, or assigns. Admiral —— (who once held the command in the Downs) asked a projector of this description, and we believe the same person, where he expected to go when he died? The man hesitated: "Why to Hell to be sure," said the honest veteran.

SUPPLIES VOTED BY PARLIAMENT FOR THE N

FROM THE

YEAR 1805 TO 1825, BOTH INCLUSIVE.

Year	No. of Seamen and Marines.	Wages.	Victuals.	s.	Ordnance.	Wear and Tear.	
		£.	£.	s.	£.	£.	£.
1805	120,000 / 30,000 Marines	2,886,000	2,964,000	0	390,000	4,680,000	10,920,
1806	120,000 / 29,000 Marines	2,886,000	2,964,000	0	390,000	4,680,000	10,920,
1807	130,000 / 31,400 Marines	3,126,500	3,211,000	0	422,500	5,070,000	11,830,
1808	130,000 / 30,000 Marines	3,126,500	4,985,500	0	591,500	3,048,000	11,752,
1809	130,000 / 31,400 Marines	3,126,500	4,985,500	0	591,500	3,295,500	11,999,
1810	145,000 / 31,400 Marines	3,345,875	4,453,312	10	659,750	3,295,500	11,754,4
1811	145,000	3,345,875	4,453,312	10	659,750	3,675,750	12,134,6
1812	145,000*	3,345,875	4,453,312	10	659,750	3,675,750	12,134,6
1813	140,000	3,230,500	4,299,750	0	637,000	3,549,000	11,716,2
1814	140,000 for 7 months / 90,000 for 6 months	2,698,000	,819,000	0	532,000	3,268,000	10,317,
1815	70,000 for 3 months / 30,000 for 10 months	1,970,250	2,788,875	0	388,500	2,386,500	7,534,1
1816	33,000	761,475	1,077,862	10	150,150	922,350	2,911,8
1817	19,000	469,300	506,350	0	49,400	531,050	1,556,1
1818	20,000	611,000	520,000	0	91,000	559,000	1,781,
1819	20,000	565,500	520,000	0	91,000	533,000	1,709,
1820	23,000	650,325	612,950	0	104,650	612,950	1,980,8
1821	22,000	622,050	557,700	0	100,100	586,300	1,866,1
1822	21,000	593,775	532,350	0	95,550	559,650	1,781,3
1823	25,000	763,750	455,600	0	81,250	243,750	1,543,7
1824	29,000	885,950	584,350	0	94,250	282,750	1,847,
1825	29,000	923,650	603,200	0	94,250	328,450	1,941,

* From this period Marines are not distinguished

The following ABSTRACTS of the Fleets of Great Britain and of the other Powers of Europe, taken at two distinct Periods of the War, will convey the best idea of the relative Force of each, and the Nature of the Contest which the British Navy had to sustain.

Number of Line of Battle Ships and Frigates, belonging to Foreign Powers, from Minutes of Intelligence received at the Admiralty.—July 2nd, 1810.

	French.		Spanish.		Dutch.		Russian.		Danish.		Swedish.		Portuguese.		Turkish.		Of which are ready for Sea.		Fitting for Sea.		Total.		Ships of the Line not included in the foregoing Columns.	
	Line.	Frigates.	Line.	Frigates.	Line.	Frigates.	Line.	Frigates.	Line.	Frigates.	Line.	Frigates.	Line.	Frigates.	Line.	Frigates.	Line.	Frigates.	Line.	Frigates.	Line.	Frigates.	Ordinary and unserviceable.	Building.
Total in 1810 - - - -	27	33	25	3	10	9	18	11	1	-	13	-	10	10	14	5	83	51	14	13	117	71	27	33
And in 1812, as follow	59	51	11	9	-	-	19	11	1	2	11	6	10	10	14	5	57	47	15	18	125	94	36	35

FLAG OFFICERS	Ships of the Line. Total.	50 Gun Ships	Frigates	Sloops	Bombs, Fire-ships, &c.	Gun Brigs, &c.	Hired Armed Ships	Hired Cutters	Stationary Ships
Vice-adm. Sir J. Saum[arez]	21	-	8	13	1	7	-	3	1
Rear-adm. Reynolds									
Rear-adm. Dixon	-	-	-	3	-	3	-	-	-
Rear-adm. Sir E. Nagle	-	-	1	6	-	6	1	1	1
Vice-adm. Douglas	-	-	-	1	-	3	3	2	1
Vice-adm. Sir E. Pellew	11	-	4	11	-	12	-	9	—
Vice-adm. Stanhope	-	-	-	3	-	4	-	-	1
Vice-adm. Campbell	1	-	1	22	-	7	-	3	2
Admiral Sir R. Curtis	3	-	4	10	-	7	-	3	1
Admiral Sir R. Calder	-	-	-	9	-	3	3	1	—
Rear-adm. D'Auvergne	-	-	2	2	-	6	-	3	1
Vice-adm. Whitshed	-	-	7	4	-	2	-	1	1
	1	-	3	—	-	—	-	—	—
	2								
Admiral Lord Gambier	3	-	6	1	-	3	-	2	—
Rear-adm. Sotheby									
Rear-adm. Stopford	-	-	6	1	-	2	-	—	—
	2	-	2	1	-	2	-	1	—
Vice-adm. Berkeley	5	-	3	5	-	5	-	—	—
	15	—	—	—	—	—	—	—	—
Admiral Sir C. Cotton	3	—	—	—	—	—	—	—	—
	1	—	—	—	—	—	—	—	—
Rear-adm. Martin	2	—	†	†	†	—	—	—	—
Rear-adm. Pickmore	1	—	—	—	—	—	—	—	—
Rear-adm. Sir S. Hood	10	—	—	—	—	—	—	—	—
	1	—	—	—	—	—	—	—	—
Vice-adm. Sir J.T.Du[ckworth]	1	1	3	5	-	3	—	—	—
Vice-adm. Sir J. B. W[arren]	1	-	7	11	-	10	-	-	1
Vice-adm. Rowley	1	-	8	16	-	5	—	-	—
Vice-adm. Sir A. Cochrane	6	-	8	29	-	16	-	-	1
Commodore Columbine	-	-	1	-	-	—	-	-	—
Rear-adm. De Courcy	2	-	2	2	-	2	—	-	—
Vice-adm. Bertie	1	1	7	3	-	2	-	-	—
Rear-adm. Drury	3	1	19	6	-	2	-	-	1
	2	1	3	—	—	—	—	—	—
	-	-	1	1	—	—	—	—	—
	-	-	-	6	—	—	—	—	—
	-	-	1	2	—	1	—	—	—
	-	-	2	-	-	—	—	—	—
	-	-	-	1	—	—	—	—	—
	-	-	1	—	—	—	—	—	—
	-	-	-	1	—	—	—	—	—
	-	-	3	1	-	1	-	1	—
	-	-	1	—	—	—	—	—	—
	2	-	1	7	-	4	-	2	6
	-	-	7	6	-	1	—	—	—
	3	-	5	4	-	2	—	—	—
Total		4	153	225	1	130	7	32	19

Ships in Ordinary, [...]
fours, 7 sixty-fours [...]
and 22 gun-brigs, [...]
Prison Shi[ps] [...]

Sloops	Bombs, Fireships, &c.	Gun Brigs, &c.	Hired Armed Ships	Hired Cutters	Troop Ships	Stationary Ships	STATIONS	1st Rates	2d Rates	80 Guns	74 Guns	64 Guns	50 Guns	44 to 36
4	-	1	—	—	—	—	Channel	1	1	-	11	-	-	5
7	-	4	—	—	—	—								
8	-	3	2	-	-	1	North America . .	-	-	-	-	1	1	3
4	-	2	-	2	-	1	Jamaica	-	-	-	-	-	1	2
2	-	9	-	7	—	—	Leeward Islands .	-	-	-	-	-	1	2
9	-	15	-	5	-	1	East Indies . . .	-	-	-	1	-	-	4
6	-	5	-	3	-	1	Cape of Good Hope	-	-	-	1	-	1	1
7	-	3	2	-	-	1	Mediterranean . .	-	-	-	1	-	-	2
3	-	7	-	2	-	1	Newfoundland . .	-	-	-	-	-	-	2
6	-	2	2	1	-	1								
1	-	1	-	2	—	—								
2	-	2	—	—	—	—								
2	-	1	-	1	—	—								
—	—	—	—	—	—	—								
—	—	—	—	—	—	—								
4	-	4	-	-	2	—								
1	9	8	-	-	-	2								
2	-	1	—	—	—	—								
9	-	6	-	-	-	1								
9	-	3	-	-	-	1								
3	-	8	-	-	2	1								
1	-	3	—	—	—	—								
-	-	1	—	—	—	—								
3	—	—	—	—	—	—								
5	-	-	-	-	-	2								
-	-	3	-	1	1	—								
2	-	5	-	-	4	6								
1	-	-	-	-	2	—								
7	2	5	-	-	2	—								
8	**11**	**105**	**6**	**24**	**14**	**21**								
-	—	—	—	—	—	-								
3	—	—	—	—	—	—								
4	—	—	—	—	—	—								
0	-	5	—	—	—	—								
-	-	7	—	—	—	—								
r	-	12	—	—	—	—								

Ships in Ordinary, 2 first-rates, 7 second-rates, 5 guns, 36 seventy-fours, 16 sixty-fours, 8 fifties, gates, 44 sloops, 9 bombs, fire-ships, &c. and brigs, &c.

Prison Ships, Prison Hospital Ships, &c. 1 first-r cond-rate, 4 eighties, 21 seventy-fours, 16 six 3 fifties, 4 frigates, 5 sloops, and 1 bomb, &c.

We here present a NEW RETURN of the Commerce, and Number of Seamen in the United Kingdom. This includes Ireland, which, in the last Return in Vol. 3, p. 158, was imperfect. By these the Reader will perceive an Increase in the building of Merchant Vessels, and in the Number of Seamen employed to navigate them: this is the true criterion of our wealth and power—the political barometer by which our National Securities should rise or fall.

MERCHANT VESSELS OF GREAT BRITAIN.

An Account of the Number of Vessels, with the Amount of their Tonnage, cleared Inward and Outward at the several Ports of Great Britain, during the years ending 5th January, 1822—23—24.

Shipping entered Inwards in Great Britain from all Parts of the World.

YEARS,	British and Irish.			Foreign Vessels.			Total.		
	Vessels.	Tons.	Men.	Vessels.	Tons.	Men.	Vessels.	Tons.	Men.
Ending 5th January, 1822	18,738	2,263,813	134,699	3,091	366,377	24,400	21,829	2,630,210	159,099
- - - - - 1823	20,212	2,390,238	147,603	3,113	419,694	25,808	23,325	2,809,932	173,410
- - - - - 1824	18,561	2,328,396	147,088	3,806	534,674	31,329	22,367	2,863,070	178,417

Shipping cleared Outwards from Great Britain to all Parts.

	British and Irish.			Foreign.			Total.		
	Vessels.	Tons.	Men.	Vessels.	Tons.	Men.	Vessels.	Tons.	Men.
1822	18,624	2,223,869	136,384	2,446	351,283	20,415	21,070	2,575,152	156,709
1823	19,436	2,286,713	139,487	2,582	408,417	22,817	22,018	2,695,130	162,358
1824	16,756	2,095,013	128,551	3,179	515,774	25,844	19,935	2,610,787	155,395

Vessels engaged in the Irish Trade, are directed to be considered as Coasters after the 10th of October, 1823, per Order in Council, 4th November, 1823. Ireland employs about 38,000 Seamen in this and her Foreign Trade.

NAVIGATION OF THE UNITED KINGDOM.

New Vessels built, with the Amount of their Tonnage, ending 5th January, 1822—23—24.

	1822.		1823.		1824.	
	Vessels.	Tonnage.	Vessels.	Tonnage.	Vessels.	Tonnage.
United Kingdom - - - -	585	58,076	564	50,928	594	63,151
Isles—Guernsey, Jersey, and Man -	12	1,406	7	605	10	637
British Plantations - - -	275	15,365	209	15,611	188	14,679
Total - -	872	74,847	780	67,144	792	78,467

Number of Vessels, with Amount of Tonnage, and Number of Men and Boys usually employed in navigating the same, that belonged to the several Ports of the British Empire, on the 30th Sept. 1821—22—23.

	30th Sept. 1821.			30th Sept. 1822.			30th Sept. 1823.		
	Vessels.	Tons.	Men.	Vessels.	Tons.	Men.	Vessels.	Tons.	Men.
United Kingdom - - - -	21,163	2,329,213	150,424	20,756	2,288,999	147,529	20,578	2,275,995	147,058
Isles—Guernsey, Jersey, and Man -	489	26,639	3,859	482	26,404	3,788	469	26,872	3,680
Plantations - - - -	3,384	204,550	14,896	3,404	203,641	15,016	3,500	203,893	14,736
Total - -	25,036	2,560,202	169,179	24,642	2,519,044	166,333	24,542	2,506,760	165,474

NAVAL ASSOCIATIONS.

The following statement of the charities and institutions founded for the relief of the widows and orphans of officers in the naval service, for officers themselves, and for sick or disabled seamen, is submitted to the public, with a view to forwarding the interests of the objects of our solicitude.   The first is, "The Navy Amicable Society," and at the head of it stands the name of his most gracious majesty King George the IVth; those of the princes of the blood, many of the nobility, and a large proportion of the officers of his Majesty's navy.   Its funds have been disposed of with a liberality proportioned to its means, and much good has been done, though not to the extent which the members could have wished.   None can receive relief unless their relatives were subscribers to the fund, and this, though a prudent regulation, is a source of much pain to the claimants as well as to the board of managers.   There are many officers who cannot afford from their half-pay, even the small contribution which constitutes a member; there are others who, not foreseeing the misfortunes which have overtaken their families, had neglected to provide this support for them; and there are a few who, from carelessness or indifference to the sufferings of their fellow-creatures, have not subscribed at all: the society is, however, daily adding to its numbers, and we hope one day to see, in addition to the illustrious, the noble, and the opulent, that a list of its members will be the official admiralty list of naval officers.

The Devonport Royal Naval Annuity Society is next to be considered. It was first established by Lieut. George Field Somerville of the Royal Navy, on the 11th day of April, 1823, and its success has exceeded the most sanguine expectations of the founder. The following is a list of its chief supporters.

PATRON.

HIS ROYAL HIGHNESS
Prince Wm. Henry, Duke of CLARENCE, K. G. G. C. B. K. T.

VICE-PATRON.

The Right Hon. Robert, Lord Viscount MELVILLE, K. T.

PRESIDENTS.

ADMIRALS.

Right Hon. J. Lord GAMBIER, G. C. B.
Sir J. H. WHITSHED, K. C. B.
Sir J. SAUMAREZ, Bt. G. C. B. Vice-Adm. of Great Britain.
Right Hon. Edw. Visc. EX-MOUTH, G. C. B.
Hon. Sir A. I. COCHRANE, G. C. B.

VICE-ADMIRALS.

Sir H. SAWYER, K. C. B.
Sir R. G. KEATS, G. C. B.
Sir B. HALLOWELL, K. C. B.
Sir W. J. HOPE, K. C. B.
Sir G. COCKBURN, G. C. B.

LIEUTENANT-GENERALS.

Sir H. BELL, K. C. B.
L. DESBOROUGH,
W. TENCH.

REAR-ADMIRALS.

Sir E. CODRINGTON, K. C. B.
Sir J. P. BERESFORD, Bart. K. C. B.
R. D. OLIVER,
Right Hon. J. Lord COLVILLE,
J. COCHET,
Sir R. BARLOW, K. C. B.

CAPTAIN.

Sir T. M. HARDY, Bart. K. C. B.

NUMBER OF MEMBERS AT PRESENT ON THE BOOKS.

1 Admiral of the Fleet,	117 Commanders,	73 Masters,
13 Admirals,	14 Majors,	27 Surgeons,
2 Generals,	412 Lieutenants,	127 Pursers,
74 Captains,	23 Captains, R. M.	3 Chaplains,
7 Colonels,	93 Lieutenants, R. M.	31 Widows,
		Total 1017 Members.

Society's invested Capital £9,000, the 18th day of April, 1825.

Since the establishment of the parent society, branch societies have been formed at Portsmouth, Falmouth, Chatham, Deal, London, and Bath; the advantages held out are too obvious to require much explanation. No annuity office in the world we believe can give better security, or so large an amount on so small a deposit: this proposition is best supported by referring to the rapid increase of the society, and the respectability of its members. For the trifling annual contribution of £2. 10s. paid only for five years, a subscriber may leave a considerable life annuity to a relative.

These two associations are highly honourable to the officers of the Navy and Royal Marines, who after having served their country in war, freely deposit a part of their hard earnings to prevent their families becoming burthensome to the community in time of peace.

That seamen who have long and faithfully served are amply requited will appear from the following statement:

"Every one who has served fourteen years in his Majesty's navy, one-third of which as able seaman, will be entitled to a pension of 10 12 0

Increasing every year, until it amounts to 27 4 0

" In addition to these pensions, he will be allowed 15s. 2½d. for every year that he has served as a petty officer of the first class. If he has served twenty years as a seaman, and seventeen of these as a petty officer of the first class, he will be entitled to a pension of 26 12 0

Increasing in proportion to his servitude, until it amounts to £50, and upwards."

The liberality of the government has gone very great lengths to provide a retreat for seamen in time of peace, or when they are reduced by misfortune. Greenwich Hospital, and the rewards for past services just stated, have relieved the wants of a great many. Still at the conclusion of the war, numbers of brave fellows were seen begging their bread, or dying in the streets with hunger, cold, and disease; these, though not eligible, from the short time they had been in the navy, to the benefits of reward, were nevertheless objects of compassion, and were in consequence protected by the Committee for the Relief of destitute Seamen, as related in the third volume of this work (p. 159). That institution is still in existence, though its funds have been greatly impaired by too large an extension of its bounty; the motives of the committee were however so proper, that we have no reason to regret one step they have taken, and we may honestly claim the farther contributions of the charitable. The Grampus, hospital ship, still lies at her moorings off Greenwich, and we again invite our countrymen and women to visit her; they will see nothing disgusting, even to the most fastidious taste; cleanliness, order, regularity, cheerfulness, and gratitude, are apparent, through every part of the ship.

After having stated the services performed by the British navy, after having, as we humbly hope, proved that under Providence it has saved the Empire and Europe from slavery, we cannot conclude our labours more gratefully than by commending to the national benevolence such as have been the greatest sufferers in the cause of their country.

INDEX.

ABERCROMBIE, Sir Ralph, arrives in the West Indies, ii. 215. Retakes St. Lucia, 216. His public order respecting the navy, 217. Subdues the rebels in St. Vincent and Grenada, 220. Lands in Holland, 406. Defeats the French and Batavians, 409. Takes the island of Trinidad, 428. Attacks Porto Rico, 430. Commands the expedition to Egypt, iii. 62. List of the forces, 63. Effects a landing, 65—70. Attacks the French, but is obliged to retreat, 71. Takes the castle of Aboukir, ib. Attacked by Menou, over whom he gains a complete victory, 71. His death, 72.

Abercrombie, Major-general, sails from Madras, in the Ceylon, iv. 472. Is captured, 473. Retaken, 482. Commands the army in the reduction of the Isle of France, ib.

Aboukir, battle of, between the French and Turks, ii. 464. Attack on the castle of, 465. Landing of the British troops in the bay of, iii. 65—69. Taken, iv. 152.

Abydos and Sestos, situation of the forts of, iv. 144. Description of the artillery employed in, 145. Effects of their fire, 147.

Achilles, captures the Entreprenante, ii. 444.

Achmuty, General, arrives in South America, iv. 190. Attacks Monte Video, 191, which is taken by storm, 193. Success of his division in the assault on Buenos Ayres, 198. Commands the forces destined to reduce the island of Java, 564. Lands near the city of Batavia, 567. Enters the town of Samarang, 571. Entire reduction of the island, 572. Appoints agents for the army, 576. Receives the thanks of parliament, v. 41.

Acre, siege of, ii. 495—499.

Adam, Capt. C. gallantly attacks a French frigate and battery, iii. 177. Assists in the defence of Tarragona, iv. 531—535. Attacks the ports of Ampollo and Perello, v. 89. Co-operates

Algiers, 132, to the King of the Two Sicilies, 135. Retreats
to Gibraltar with the Smyrna fleet in tow, 138. Arrives at
Lisbon, 141. Entrusts Nelson with the evacuation of Elba, ib.
Instructions to Mr. Master, 143. Letter to Francis Drake,
Esq. 148. Reception from the court of Portugal, 150. Rein-
forced by Rear-admiral Parker, ib. Defeats the Spanish
fleet off Cape St. Vincent, 152. Created Earl St. Vincent,
155. Despatches to the Admiralty, 157. Letter to the
Speaker of the House of Commons, 230, to the Lord-mayor
of London, 231. See *St. Vincent*, Earl.

Jervis, Capt. defends the post of Irois, ii. 431.

Johnstone, Commodore, places Captain Sutton under arrest, i.
77, who obtains a verdict against him, 78.

Jolliffe, Lieut. H. his narrow escape from a French soldier in
Egypt, iii. 69.

Jones, Captain, conveys the last division of the British from Holland after their retreat, i. 186.

Jones, Lieutenant T. recaptures the Urania, v. 9.

Jones, Gale, cause of his committal to Newgate, iv. 410.

Joseph II. emperor of Germany, his plans for the improvement
of Ostend and Trieste, i. 22. 24. Invades Holland, ib. 25.
Demands the free navigation of the Scheldt, 26. Failure of
his projects, 29. Joins the Russians in a war with Turkey, 113.
Replies to the note of the Turkish minister, 120. His
death, 143.

Josephine, Empress, is divorced by Bonaparte, iv. 415.

Jourdain, General, defeated by the Archduke Charles, ii. 89.
Compels him to retreat, 90. Defeated at Vittoria by Wellington, v. 78.

Joyce, Capt. conducts the Zephyr fire-ship, against the French
squadron in Basque Roads, iv. 284. His dangerous situation,
ib. Is promoted to the rank of post-captain, 287.

Jumelle, French general, taken prisoner, iv. 571.

June, battle of the first of, i. 274. Observations on, 278. 300.
306, 307.

Junon, French frigate, escapes from Guadaloupe, iv. 374. Attacked by the Superieure and Horatio, ib. Surrenders to
the Latona, 376. Recaptured by four frigates, after a gallant
defence, 391. Is burnt, ib.

Junot, General, retires to Lisbon, iv. 252. Defeated at Vimiera,
256. Evacuates Portugal by the convention of Cintra, ib.

Jurien, Captain, attempts to procure the exchange of Captain Brenton, iii. 229.

K

Kamenski, General, attempts the relief of Dantzic, iv. 95. Is defeated, 96.

Kangaroo, gallantly engages La Loire, ii. 368.

Keating, Colonel, storms the batteries of St. Paul's in the isle of Bourbon, iv. 397. Co-operates in the reduction of the island, 459, 460.

Keats, Captain, (afterward Admiral Sir R. G.) attacks a Spanish three-decker, iii. 40. Captures the San Antonio, 41. Demands satisfaction of the Dey of Algiers, 408. Hoists the flag of Sir J. Duckworth, 520. Pursues the Rochefort squadron, 521, which he engages off St. Domingo, 524. Joins the Channel fleet, 530. Detached off Belleisle, iv. 28. Chases four French frigates, 31. Detached by Admiral Gambier to secure the passage of the Great Belt, iv. 102. Reaches Gottenburg, 219. Assists the Spaniards under Romana in regaining their liberty, 221. Generously restores the Danish prizes, 222. Commands the flotilla in the Scheldt, 318. Reduces the islands of Schonen and Duiveland, 319. His letter to Sir Richard Strachan, 320. To the Earl of Rosslyn, 322. Advances up the Scheldt, 323. Sails for Cadiz, 442, where he assumes the command of the squadron, 443. 527. Sends a Spanish squadron to Mahon and the Havannah, 445. Resigns the command at Cadiz, and proceeds to the Mediterranean, 530.

Keenah, Captain, storms the fort of Belgica, iv. 489.

Keene, Major-general, commands the troops who land in the Bayou Catalan, v. 192. Repulses the Americans, 193.

Keir, Sir W. G. chastises the pirates in the Persian Gulf, v. 265, 266.

Keith, Lord, pursues the French and Spanish fleets, ii. 379. 475. Summons Cadiz, 514. Assumes the command in the Mediterranean, iii. 10. Blockades Genoa, 13. Proceeds to Gibraltar, 25. Rejects the treaty of El Arisch, 55. His letter to General Kleber, ib. and to M. Poussielgue, 57. Collects the forces destined for Egypt, in the harbour of Valette, 59. Proceeds to Marmorice, ib. Sails thence to Egypt, 60. List of ships under his command, 61. Anchors in Aboukir-bay,

L

P

U

V

Yorke, Sir Joseph, cruises off Belleisle, iv. 22. Commands a squadron in Basque Roads, 426, and stops the enemy's coasting trade, ib. Arrives in the Tagus with reinforcements for Lord Wellington, 522.

Yorke, Captain J. S. takes the Alliance, a Dutch frigate, i. 191.

Young, Admiral, presides on the trial of Sir Home Popham, iv. 82. Commands the North Sea fleet, v. 12. 81. His letter to Lieut. T. B. Devon, 326.

Young, Captain William, superintends the landing of the troops in Egypt. iii. 66.

Younghusband, Captain, engages the Egyptienne, iii. 414.

Z

Zaire. See *Congo.*

Zante, island of, taken by the Turks and Russians, ii. 469. Reduced by the British, iv. 355.

Zara, reduction of the port and castle of, v. 106.

Zayas, Spanish General, conducts an expedition against the French blockading Badajoz, iv. 529.

END OF VOL. V

Printed by J. F. Dove, St. John's Square.

ERRATA.

Vol. iv. p. 352. l. 1. *for* Bayntun, *read* Hervey.

—— p. 352. l. 13. *for* off Cette, *read* in the habour of Cette.

—— p. 450. l. 5. *for* Malta, *read* Minorca.

Lightning Source UK Ltd.
Milton Keynes UK
UKHW02f1833210818
327592UK00013B/640/P